Benjamín Vicuña Mackenna, James W Duffy

Francisco Moyen

Or, the inquisition as it was in South America

Benjamín Vicuña Mackenna, James W Duffy

Francisco Moyen
Or, the inquisition as it was in South America

ISBN/EAN: 9783337318857

Printed in Europe, USA, Canada, Australia, Japan

Cover: Foto ©ninafisch / pixelio.de

More available books at **www.hansebooks.com**

FRANCISCO MOYEN:

OR

THE INQUISITION

AS IT WAS IN

SOUTH AMERICA.

BY

B. VICUÑA MACKENNA.

Translated from the Spanish with the Author's Permission,

BY

JAMES W. DUFFY, M.D.

MEMBER OF THE ROYAL COLLEGE OF SURGEONS,
AND OF THE UNIVERSITY OF CHILE, ETC.

LONDON:
HENRY SOTHERAN & CO., 136, STRAND.
1869.

ALL RIGHTS RESERVED.

TABLE OF CONTENTS.

TRANSLATOR'S PREFACE . . . . *page* 1
BIOGRAPHICAL SKETCH OF THE AUTHOR . . . . *page* 11
DEDICATION . . . . *page* 16
PREFACE . . . . *page* 17

INTRODUCTION.

Enthusiasm of the Prebendary Saavedra for the Inquisition.—His system of comparisons, the *basket* and the *tree*.—God was the first Inquisitor.—The Inquisition was established against the punishment of death imposed by the civil power, and as an asylum for the heretics themselves.—Ingratitude of modern philosophers to the Inquisition.—Unbelievers in witchcraft are deserters from Catholicism.—The Inquisition was not an impediment to science and literature.—Opinions of Mariana and Pulgar of the establishment of the Inquisition.—St. Ignatius and the Inquisition.—The jury in offences by the press a substitute for the Inquisition.—The punishment of death, a *divine right*.—The torture, a *natural right*.—The exhumation of the bodies of heretics perfectly justifiable.—The Sambenito is not a stigma of infamy,—Exoneration of the Inquisition by the Prebendary Saavedra . . . *page* 27

CHAPTER I.

Birth of Francisco Moyen, his life until his arrival at Buenos Ayres in 1748.—His duel with the magistrate of Oruro and his imprisonment.—His journey to Potosi.—Heresies uttered by him on the road.—Storm near the volcano.—Theological discussion in Santiago de Cotagaita.—It is agreed to denounce Moyen.—Arrival at Potosi . . . . *page* 54

CHAPTER II.

Review of the Inquisition, and its state of decadence about the middle of the 18th century . . . . . . *page* 67

CHAPTER III.

The Inquisitorial denunciation.—Opinions of Pascal, Motley, and the Peruvian writer Garcia Calderon.—Warrant of imprisonment issued by the Commissary of the Inquisition in Potosi . . *page* 71

CHAPTER IV.

Laborious and dissipated life of Moyen in Potosi.—His imprisonment.—Effects confiscated.—Theological disputes in his prison.—His horrible situation during the first year of his confinement.—Writes to the Inquisitors at Lima asking them to tell him the cause of his imprisonment, and begging that his fetters may be removed.—Attempts to commit suicide.—Discussion of the historical question, whether the Inquisition was received with joy by the Spaniards.—Official letter from the commissary of Potosi to the Inquisitors at Lima, giving them an account of the heresies of Moyen.—Qualification of these by the Holy Office at Lima.—Moyen is sent to Lima, the journey occupies two years on account of his sickness.—Practical example of hypocrisy in habits produced by the Inquisition.—Opinion of Buckle.—His analysis of the assertion that the Holy Office exalted the character of the Spaniards.—Opinions of Coquerel, Michelet, and Mariano Egaña.—Copy of the work entitled "Triumphs of the Holy Office" in the library of Egaña.—Recent example of the Spanish minister Gonzalez Bravo.—Confinement of Moyen in the secret prisons at Lima.—His registration and premature decrepitude.—His stock of clothes and daily rations . . . . *page* 79

CHAPTER V.

State of the Inquisition in Lima on the arrival of Moyen.—The Inquisition was established in America more for the sake of its gold than against heresy.—Practical examples in Peru.—The poverty of Chile in a great measure its safeguard from the rapacity of the Inquisitors.—The Inquisition in Mexico.—Robberies by the Inquisitors Unda and Calderon in Lima.—Celebrated process to which they give rise.—Confiscation of the jewels belonging to Unda.—The judge visitor Arenaza is also accused of being a thief by his colleagues.—Demoralized state of the Peruvian clergy at that period . . . , ... *page* 99

CHAPTER VI.

The trial of Moyen commences at the end of the third year of his imprisonment.—Admonitions.—Accusation of the fiscal.—The fiscal demands the application of the torture to Moyen.—Infamous inquisitorial fraud with respect to its application.—Discussion whether the Inquisition condemned its criminals to death or not.—Enumeration of the *charitable precautions* employed in the application of the torture.—Abominable hypocrisy in the formulas of the Inquisition.—Enumeration of the heretical propositions of Moyen. I. The fear of God.—II. God and Tempests.—XV. The Pontiffs.—XX. The Ave Maria.—XXVIII.—The Eucharist.—XXIX. The appearance of Jesus Christ on earth.—XXXI. Simony.—XXXII. Astronomy.—XXXIII. Geology.—XXXIV. The Luxury of the Clergy.—XXXVII. The Cross.—XXXIX. Fatality.—XL. The Mule.—A specimen of Moyen's defence by Doctor Valdivieso . . *page* 108

CHAPTER VII.

The discussion of the charges occupied a whole year.—Moyen besides the epilepsy is attacked with gangrene, and the inquisitors permit one of his shackles to be removed in the fourth year of his imprisonment.—Was the Inquisition or the Quakers the author of the penitentiary system?—Description of the hall of torture of the Inquisition of Lima in 1813.—Most usual punishments of the Inquisition.—Actual state of the secret prisons of Lima.—What were the state of the prisons of the Inquisition of Lisbon, Goa, and other places?—Lamentations of Moyen.—He paints upon the wall of his dungeon a representation of madness.—Taste of the inquisitor Amuzquibar for paintings.—Moyen attempts to escape in the fifth year of his imprisonment.—Proceedings for the ratification last two years.—Publication of proofs in the seventh year of the process.—The publication of the audiencias suspended twenty-one months.—The defence is presented about two years later.—Philosophical and American importance of the process of Moyen compared with that of other victims of intolerance.—Definitive sentence of Moyen.—Reflections.—Moyen is sent to Spain after nearly twelve years' imprisonment and perishes off Cape Horn . . *page* 147

CHAPTER VIII.

Review of the Inquisition of Lima, from the condemnation of Moyen until that of the seaman Urdaneja in 1812.—The Englishman Stevenson and the Frenchman Millet, before the Inquisition of Lima, in 1806 and in 1816.—Last days of the Inquisition; its abolition in Chile in 1811.—Ideas of the Inquisition taught in the National Institute of Chile in 1828.—What is our progress? *page* 173

CHAPTER IX.

Discussion concerning a most notable equivocation attributed to the author of this work relating to the income of the Inquisition.—Fresh data concerning the covetousness of the Inquisitors of Lima, and their enormous frauds.—Examination of the error, about the burning of the Chilian *flea*, and of the miner Obando . *page* 184

CHAPTER X.

Conclusion . . . . *page* 195

APPENDIX.

I. Extracts from the Manual of Inquisitors for the use of the Inquisitions of Spain and Portugal . . . *page* 197

II. Description of the *auto de fé*, celebrated in Lima the 23rd of December, 1736 . . . . . . *page* 207

III. Power of the Chapter of Santiago, given to the Inquisitors of Lima to represent it in the application of the torture, and in all other inquisitorial judicial proceedings *page* 217

IV. Official letter from the Chilian Congress of 1811, to the administrative Junta to stop the sending of the inquisitorial quota to Lima, which the Church in Chile paid to the Holy Office . . . . *page* 218

CONTENTS.

V. Representation of the last treasurer of the Inquisition in Chile, Don Judas Tadeo de Reyes, protesting against the anterior resolution . . . . . *page* 218

VI. Minute of the official letter from the Inquisitors of Lima to their treasurer in Santiago, giving him thanks for his endeavours to recover the rent of the Holy Office in Chile
page 224

VII. Official letter from the Holy Office in Lima to General Osorio, soliciting his intervention in the payment of the inquisitorial quota suppressed by the National Government in 1811
page 225

PREFACE BY THE TRANSLATOR.

THE following work first made its appearance before the public a short time since, in a fragmentary form, in a daily paper, the MERCURY of Valparaiso. The reason for its publication is fully explained by the learned author in his preface, where it will be seen, that it was intended as a reply to a most extraordinary production written by a clergyman of Santiago, the capital of Chile, for the express purpose of undeceiving the world in the almost universal but erroneous conceptions formed by the public with regard to the Spanish Inquisition. Generally speaking, most people, at least those who thought any thing at all upon the subject, have hitherto considered that institution to have been one of the greatest curses, which the cruelty and blasphemy of man ever inflicted upon the human race, that it was established expressly to prevent the exercise of God's choicest gift, the use of our reason, to stifle the freedom of thought, to crush and root out from the heart all natural and manly feelings, and thus to reduce mankind to the level of the brute creation. But what will be the astonishment and surprise of all those who have entertained these opinions, to learn that they have been all their life long labouring under a most egregious error, that their education has been the means of perverting the mind, by imbuing it with false impressions and distorting the truth of history, and that the prejudices imbibed in their youth have deceived them and led them astray. For, according to the assertions of the worthy clergyman abovementioned, it will be found, that the Inquisition was established for the purpose of protecting the lives of heretics, to rescue them from the punishment of death, and to afford them an asylum against the ill-treatment of infuriated mobs, to give lessons of moderation and humanity to the people, and point out to kings the path of mercy. It was established by the Catholic Church as a most precious guarantee of human life, and no sooner did it begin to exercise its benevolent functions, than its great advantages were immediately perceived, for in those countries where it was admitted and acknowledged as a national institution, the sciences began to flourish, universities to be founded, and printing introduced, it encouraged the study of the classics, favoured poetry and the fine arts, and produced an unusual activity for scientific investigations! Let not the English reader start at beholding these astounding assertions, nor look upon them as the ravings of a maniac! The clergyman who has had the hardihood to send them forth to the world, is a learned priest, a prebendary and member of the council of the archdiocese of Santiago; nor let it be supposed that he is alone in maintaining such extravagant opinions. He is only one among a large number of educated and conscientious men possessing the same ideas, and apparently belonging to that numerous party in the Catholic Church, upon whose banner is inscribed those talismanic words "*non possumus,*" and who with a faith indelible in the ultimate dominion of their Church, wholly disregarding the signs of the times, and obstinately closing their eyes to the events taking place around them, look steadfastly forward with as great a certainty as the dispersed sons of Israel do to the advent of their Messiah, to the glorious time, when the whole of the Christian communities will return again to the fold from which they have strayed, and will resign themselves with all meekness and submission to the spiritual direction and guidance of the only true and holy Catholic Church.

The author, or perhaps more correctly speaking the compiler of the following pages, for he makes no pretension to their authorship, has by a singular circumstance been enabled to avail himself of the services of a most powerful and eloquent pleader, whom he has brought forward to vindicate the cause of outraged humanity, from the insult offered to it, in the book of the learned and reverend prebendary. This advocate is no less than the Inquisition itself, which offers in its own handwriting and with its signature attached, proofs which cannot be impugned, to show and render evident the falsehood and utter absurdity of the wild and reckless assertions of the reverend gentleman.

Should any one take up the present work under the impression that in Francisco Moyen he will find one of the ordinary sensational novels, so much admired at the present day, he will certainly be disappointed, in it there is nothing of mystery, nothing sentimental, no plot, no love affair, nor even a single female among its *dramatis personæ.* It is nothing more than a sad but true history of the personal sufferings of a gay and thoughtless young man, immured in a dungeon and loaded with fetters, during a long course of years, and only for a trifling indiscretion of speech. This severe punishment was inflicted upon him by that barbarous and cruel tribunal, which a Christian clergyman at the present day holds up to the world, as one deserving our veneration and respect for its *mildness and humanity!* This sad and mournful tale is narrated by that tribunal itself, in, as already stated, its own handwriting, and in its own words, or if I may be allowed the expression, it is the Inquisition turned author.

The meaning of the above will be understood, when I state that the authority for this history of Francisco Moyen, is the documents of the criminal process carried on against him, by that tribunal blasphemously called *holy!* The writer of this work, in which his sufferings are recorded, in the year 1860 was residing in Lima; and in one of his visits to the public library of that city, he lighted upon by chance an immense quantity of law papers, which formerly belonged to the Inquisition, and among which were those of the whole of the suit against Moyen. At a considerable expense of time and labour, he copied with his own hand many of the documents entire, and made copious extracts from others, most all of which are given in the body of this work, and with a fidelity and adherence to the originals almost carried to an extreme, for although in some parts of them the sense is obscure, and in others one or two trifling circumstances are stated evidently erroneous, nevertheless the writer has preferred to give them to the public, literally as they were written, than to disfigure them, by making any alterations or corrections of his own.

These documents, in the original Spanish, are written in a style extremely quaint and barbarous, the purport of their words is obtained more by the sound than by their orthography, several of them being oftentimes joined into one, while others are divided and their separated parts united with those which precede or follow them, clearly showing that if the Inquisition was the means of promoting literature, as asserted by the Chilian prebendary, the familiars of the one established in Peru had not availed themselves of its fostering care and encouragement. Of course their uncouth phraseology could not be preserved in a translation, but I have transferred their meaning into English, in a sense as literal as their strange peculiarities would admit.

The apparition of such a work as the present one in a country where the priesthood holds a most powerful influence over the minds of a large portion of its inhabitants, consequently produced a considerable degree of excitement, and as it came out in distinct portions in a periodical which perhaps has the most extensive circulation in Chile, or even in South America, it was impossible for the clergy to prohibit it from being read, which they might have done, had it first made its appearance in the form of a book or pamphlet, although their prohibition would have had very little force with the liberal part of the community, and it is very satisfactory and gratifying to every one who earnestly desires the improvement and mental progress of his fellow-men, to know, that in Chile there is a far greater amount of illustration and intellectual acquirements among her population, joined to an independency of spirit and impatience of clerical control, than what in Europe they are generally given credit for.

The resurrection of Francisco Moyen from among the dusty archives of the Inquisition, created more particularly, and as might be expected, a lively commotion in the Ultramontane party in Santiago, and brought down some severe invectives upon the head of its author, several refutations of his work have appeared in the clerical organs of the press, particularly one from the pen of the clergyman whose extravagant eulogy of the Holy Office first gave rise to the controversy; this last amounts to twelve long letters, each occupying several columns of a good size newspaper. But his *refutation* is nothing more than a most tedious and prolix repetition of his former arguments, all of which may be comprised in the following propositions.

1st. The Catholic Church, having received its power and authority from God, was fully justified in establishing the Inquisition to preserve and maintain the purity of the faith.

2nd. If the civil tribunals inflicted punishments upon those who committed offences against human laws, how much more ought the Church to punish those who transgressed the law of God. The logic of which is, that if the civil tribunals are justified in hanging a man for *robbery* and *murder*, how much more so is the Church in burning one, who differs from her in *points* of *doctrine*.

3rd. That the Church, in punishing heretics with death, did no more than what God commanded his holy people to do to those who endeavoured to draw them away from the true worship; this may be seen in the Bible, book which Protestants themselves acknowledge to have been written by the divine inspiration of God.

4th. The Inquisition was more merciful in all its proceedings than any other tribunal of the same period; and also that the Protestants applied more cruel punishments to those who differed from them in opinions, than ever were employed by the Holy Office!

In the so-called *refutations*, attempts have been made to cast doubt and suspicion upon the authenticity of the documents from which the author has extracted his materials for the history of Moyen, the consequence of which has been the production of the two following letters, one of them from a respectable gentleman residing in Lima, and the other from the worthy librarian who has charge of the national library, where are deposited the above-mentioned documents, and which letters must for ever set at rest all doubts, and ought to satisfy any one even the most sceptical:—

"Lima, 11*th August*, 1868.

"Dear Friend and Sir,

"I received your estimable letter, dated 20th of July, and in answer to it, I inform you that upon examining the book in which letters are copied, belonging to this library, I found that, on the 18th August, 1849, I passed a note to the treasurer of the establishment, for him to give to Don José de la Rosa, the sum of 8 dollars and 4 reals, for the large pile of memorandums to which you refer, and which since then has been deposited in this library. He who doubts may examine for himself, or by any one he may commission for that purpose.

"When the *Independiente* (newspaper) says that Vigil would not have given a quarter of an ounce of gold for a bundle of memorandums containing any thing favourable to the Inquisition, he is doubly mistaken, for although that pile of memorandums contains nothing favourable to the Inquisition, the motive which induced me to buy it, was the same which induced me to send to Chile to purchase the book, La Inquisicion,— *Rapida ojeada sobre aquella antiqua institucion, por el prebendado, Don José Ramon Saavedra*. This class of documents is of great importance to the cause of progress, in the history of which, errors fill many a page, whatever might have been the sincerity of their authors.

"With respect to what you indicated to me, to certify to the accuracy of the copies, you will be satisfied with the enclosed paper. I requested a friend, one who knows you, and who has laboured upon the same subject, to compare them, with the assistance of one employed in the library. The persons whom you proposed, one is very much occupied in one of the chambers of the Congress, and the others are not in Lima. Let those who doubt the authenticity of the copy go themselves and compare it with the original, to them belongs the task.

"Coming back to the panegyric of the Inquisition, it is almost incredible that in the 19th century, in the latter third of it, and in our America, such a book could be written. You have done very right to impugn it. On one side are labouring the friends of progress, while on the other are their eternal enemies; and these last are not aware, beginning with those at Rome, that they are giving help to the cause of liberty and sparing us half our work by rendering themselves odious.

"Yours affectionately, &c.
"FRANCISCO DE P. G. VIGIL.

"Señor Don B. Vicuña Mackenna."

"Lima, *August* 10*th*, 1868.

"HONOURABLE SIR,

"The talents and liberalism of Señor B. Vicuña Mackenna were known to me; proscribed, he offered to Peru the brilliant pages of his first essay of the *History of the Revolution of Independence;* and now he sends us, as a remembrance from Chile, a book, the subject of which is sad but fruitful in instruction: *Francisco Moyen, or the Inquisition as it was in America.*

"Being dedicated for some time to the study and investigation of the national history, I have made use of all the books, papers, manuscripts or pamphlets treating on that subject, and contained in the library over which you so worthily preside; among them I found one day a large book of memorandums or records, which had belonged to the archives of the Inquisition of Lima, I read hurriedly over the principal part, but never thought that an absurd panegyric and antihistorical paradox would render necessary the publication of extracts of this inquisitorial process, which is more properly an accusation against the judges than against the culprit.

"Nevertheless, with the work of Señor Mackenna before me, I have again examined this voluminous mass of judicial records, and I have convinced myself more of the fidelity of the copier.

"You request me to give you my opinion in writing upon this subject, and also concerning the authenticity of the process.

"The book to which I refer is one in folio, 30 centimetres in length, 21 in width, and 17 in thickness; it is bound in parchment, and has a table on the back on which is written *Penitenciado, No. 78*. It not only contains the suit of Moyen, but also those of six others, that of Pedro Fos, likewise a Frenchman, and those of Manuel Galeano, Pascual Estacio Vargas, Juan Pablo Rodriguez de Soto, Fr. Matias Ponce de Leon, and José de Medina. That of Moyen occupies from 800 to 900 leaves, which is two-thirds of the volume; the writing is very clear and legible; the identity of the signatures, and the impossibility of falsifying so much without motive, removes the least shadow of doubt about it; the ink, paper, the character of the letter, the binding, even the similarity of this book to others of the Inquisition which are in the library, all tend to invalidate the criticism of the Hardouins,* notwithstanding they are sufficiently credulous;

---

* John Hardouin, a French Jesuit, who wrote a work, the object of which was to show, that almost all the writings under the names of the Greek and Roman poets and historians, are the spurious productions of the 13th century.

witness the miracle of the cross when Pedro de Candia leaped on shore on the coast of Peru in 1530, a miracle fabricated to canonize the conquest, and to make heaven the accomplice of the violation of justice.

"Several individuals hold in their possession bundles of old papers, the judicial records of the Inquisition: one friend of mine has the process of Madam Castro. He was kind enough to show it me, and even allowed me to copy it; he found it by chance in the great chest which the people could not carry away in the sack of 1821.

"These relics are so much the more valuable on account of their rarity, and therefore should be completed wherever it is possible.

"The atrocious oath of secrecy taken by the inquisitors, and all those in their service, never to reveal, either by words, acts, or gestures, the least thing relating to the Holy Office, and the zeal of some, like that of the R. P. Dominical Seminarist, who, to guard the secret, burnt the papers confided to him, show that the homicidal Inquisition endeavours to shroud itself in darkness from the light of the age in which we live.

"From 1548, the year in which took place the first *auto de fé*, until 1570, three public *autos* were celebrated by the Archbishop Don Francisco Jeronimo de Loaisa, and it requires the patient labour of a chronicler to discover any traces of these acts, that not even Señor Palma was enabled to do for his "Annals of the Inquisition."

"Señor Mackenna has done a service to our national history, as well as to the liberal cause; he has written truthfully and conscientiously, and copied the autos without variations of any kind, carrying his scrupulosity and fidelity so far as to retain the orthography, or more properly speaking, the method of writing used by the inquisitors.

"I am sorry that the shortness of time, in consequence of the near departure of the steamer, does not allow me to enlarge more upon the subject, but I believe that I have complied with your request.

"I am, yours, &c.,
"José Toribio Polo.

"S. D. Francisco G. Vigil."

With respect to the merits of this book I shall offer no opinion, the works of the writer (and, as may be seen in the biographical sketch appended, they are not a few) have been well received by his countrymen, and thinking it might afford some interest to a portion of the British public, I have translated it into English; and although perchance I may not have been able to do full justice to the author in transferring to another language the terseness and energy of style of the original, nevertheless I have followed his meaning as faithfully as the difference in the two idioms would permit.

J. W. D.

VALPARAISO, 18*th September*, 1868.

A BIOGRAPHICAL SKETCH OF THE AUTHOR.

THE author of the following pages, Don Benjamin Vicuña Mackenna, an eminent Chilian writer and politician, whose name is not entirely unknown to the British public, was born in Santiago the capital of Chile, in August, 1831, and is descended from an ancient and honourable family of Biscaya; his grandfather Don F. Ramon Vicuña, in 1829 was President of Chile, and died in 1849. The name of Mackenna he derives from his grandfather by his mother's side, who was an Irish gentleman from the county Monagan, and held the rank of General in the Chilian service, in which he assisted the patriots in their successful struggle for Independence. Don Benjamin, in his early years received the ordinary education usually given to children at that period, and in 1841 entered as a pupil in the college of Santiago. Here at first his progress was rather slow, owing most likely to the want of application to his studies, for it appears that the time which should have been employed in them, he often spent in the perusal of works more congenial to his taste, and to the reading of which he was much devoted; nevertheless, at the age of 17 he passed his examination with success and received his degree as Bachelor of Laws. In this same year (1848), he made his first attempt as an author, in publishing a historical essay relating to the siege of Chillan, a town in the south of Chile, (*Recuerdos del sitio de Chillan*), and although it was a work of no great extent, it met with great success, being well received by his countrymen. His career, however, in the law was soon brought to a close, principally in consequence of the revolution which broke out on the 20th April, 1851, and in which he took an active part, but being made prisoner by the Government troops, he was confined for some time in various prisons, until at last from one of them he made his escape, disguised in the attire of a female, and directed his steps to Serena the capital of the province of Coquimbo. Here he joined another revolution headed by General Cruz and which extended throughout the country. He was appointed to the command of the vanguard of the army intended to march upon the capital, but which, having arrived as far as the valley of Aconcagua, was met by the forces of the Government, and a battle ensued near Petorca (14th Oct. 1851), in which the revolutionists were defeated.

In consequence of the triumph of the government party, Señor Vicuña had to leave the country. He sailed for California, and thence travelling through Mexico, the United States and Canada, he arrived in England, where he remained a whole year (1854), during which time he occupied himself in study in an agricultural college at Cirencester. The knowledge and experience there acquired by his patient industry and perseverance, he presented to his countrymen in the form of a publication on European agriculture. (*Estudios sobre la agricultura europea.* Valparaiso, 1854.)

After leaving England he went on the Continent and remained some time in Paris, yet notwithstanding the gaieties and attractions of the French capital, the generous exile appears never to have lost sight of the object he had most at heart, viz., the interest and prosperity of his beloved country, for even there he wrote and in a foreign tongue, a small work, the publication of which he considered would be conducive to her advantage. (*Le Chili considéré sous le rapport de son agriculture et de l'emigration europeenne.* Paris, 1855.) This small work has been honoured by the approbation of the illustrious Michelet, who has spoken of it in terms of great commendation. The author also was, during his stay in Paris, made a member of several literary societies.

After an absence of three years, Señor Mackenna returned by the way of Buenos Ayres and the Pampas to his native country, and in Santiago, he commenced an active literary career. He assisted in the reorganization of an Agricultural Society, and was appointed by its members to be its Secretary; he also became the editor of their Journal. In 1857 he was admitted as a fully qualified member of the legal profession, and which he exercised for some time with considerable success. He also published a history of that portion of the Chilian struggle for independence which is comprised in the romantic adventures of the brothers Carrera, (*El Ostracismo de los Carreras*. Santiago, 1857); a narrative of his travels, and a life of his grandfather, General Mackenna. In 1858 he became an active opponent of the Chilian President Montt's administration, and advocated in a newspaper, of which he was the editor, the convocation of a Constituent Assembly to reform the Constitution. In January, 1859, Vicuña, with his friends, Don Custodio Gallo, and two brothers of the name of Matta, one a poet of some eminence and the other a Deputy of Congress, convoked a meeting of Liberals in the Philharmonic Hall of Santiago. The Government forbade the meeting, and the four friends were arrested and thrown into prison. After a confinement of three months, they were taken down to Valparaiso, and put on board the English barque *Louisa Braginton*, the captain of which had been paid 2000 dollars to land them in Liverpool. They suffered very much during the voyage from wretched accommodation, and bad provisions, and, on their arrival in England, they brought an action against the captain for false imprisonment. It was during this compulsory journey to Europe that Señor Vicuña visited Spain, and ever intent upon all that related to his native country, spent a great part of his time among the public archives in Madrid, engaged in the laborious occupation of searching for materials for a life of Don Diego de Almagro the discoverer of Chile. Among other original and inedited manuscripts, in the National Library, which he investigated for that purpose, was one named in the catalogue as "*Libro de la vida de Don Alonzo Enriquez de*

Guzman," and to which he called the attention of a friend, Clements R. Markham, Esq., and that gentleman considered it to be so curious and interesting that he translated it into English, and it was published by the Hakluyt Society in London, 1862.

In December, 1859, Don Benjamin returned to South America, and established himself in Lima, where he wrote a life of General O'Higgins, the hero of Chilian independence. (*El Ostracismo de General Don Bernardo O'Higgins, escrito sobre Documentos ineditos y noticias autenticas.* Valparaiso, 1860.) He also wrote a history of the first two years of the war of independence in Peru, the first edition of which was sold in a few days. It was during his indefatigable exploration to find materials for this work, in the National Library at Lima, that he came accidentally upon the voluminous mass of law papers, which had formerly belonged to the Inquisition, and it is from these interesting documents that he selected the process of the unfortunate Frenchman, which has served as a basis and authority for the present work.

On the election of Don José Joaquin Perez, at this present time President of the Republic, Señor Vicuña returned to Chile (1861), where he again commenced the practice of his profession, but which he soon abandoned for the purpose of carrying on uninterrupted the proceedings he had instituted against Don Manuel Montt, the late President, for his summary and illegal transportation. He also employed his talents and occupied his time in writing upon the history and politics of his country, more particularly upon that of the late administration, a history of which he has already published, in seven volumes, (*Historia de los diez años de la administracion Montt.* Santiago, 1862.) In 1862 he was admitted as a member of the University of Santiago, and during the following year he conducted, as editor, the Valparaiso Mercury newspaper. In 1864 he was elected a member for Congress, and chosen Secretary for the Chamber.

In consequence of the war with Spain (1865), and the

unprotected state of the Republic, caused by its deficiency in the indispensable articles of ships and guns to carry on the contest, Señor Vicuña was sent to the United States in the character of confidential agent, for the purpose of exciting the sympathy of the northern republicans on behalf of Chile, and also to assist Señor Astaburuaga, the Chilian Minister, accredited to Washington, in the purchase of the warlike articles which Chile most required. In his patriotic endeavours for that purpose he had to contend with an immense number of difficulties, sufficient to have overcome the constancy of any one of a less energetic and determined resolution, all his actions being constantly watched, and to a great extent thwarted by the emissaries of the Spanish Government. Nevertheless he succeeded, and the guns which he sent to Chile are now placed upon the batteries which crown the heights of Valparaiso, and which it is to be hoped will prevent Spain from repeating her unjustifiable act of the 31st March, 1866.

During the whole of his eventful and active career Señor Vicuña was never married until last year (1867), when he was united to his cousin Señorita Victoria Subercaseaux, and in the same year he was re-elected to Congress as Deputy for the provinces of Valdivia and Talca; he also holds the post of Secretary to the Chamber, and has been appointed General Secretary to a National Exposition of Agriculture, which is intended to be held in Santiago in the year 1869.

Besides the works already mentioned, he has published several others on history, biography, agriculture, &c., among which is one in English (*A Sketch of Chile expressly prepared for the use of Emigrants from the United States and Europe to that country.* New York, 1866). He has also collected a quantity of interesting materials for the purpose of writing a life of Don Diego de Almagro, but which, from his multifarious occupations, and his warfare amidst the hurricanes and stormy seas of political strife, he has not been able hitherto to arrange and prepare for publication.

TO THE

MEMORY OF THE ILLUSTRIOUS

SEÑOR DON MANUEL VICUNA,

FIRST ARCHBISHOP OF SANTIAGO.

To his immaculate virtue, his sublime humility, to his infinite charity and holy teaching, who guided us from our childhood in the path of tolerance and love, eternal base of true religion. These pages, which, by a sad contrast of past times, remind us of the execrable abominations of hatred and absurdity, I dedicate with profound and sincere veneration.

THE AUTHOR.

SANTIAGO, *May* 15, 1868.

PREFACE.

On the 17th of August, 1862, with the object of being admitted a member of the Faculty of Humanities of the University of Chile, we read before that honourable Society a historical discourse, bearing the title, *What was formerly the state of the Inquisition in Chile?* and in which was given to the public, one of the most interesting and honourable episodes in the history of the Chilian Church, which two years before we had disinterred and brought to light from among the dusty archives, deposited in the treasury at Lima.

This transaction, which was lost to the world, having never been mentioned by any one of our historians, derives its interest from the noble, illustrious and courageous resistance, which, about the middle of the seventeenth century (1634-1640), the ecclesiastical chapter of Santiago, composed entirely of members of the Chilian clergy, made to the encroachments of the Inquisition of Lima, represented by the Dean, Don Tomas de Santiago, a Spaniard by birth, and acting as its Commissary-General in Chile.

As the origin and principal reasons of that dispute was an affair of rapaciousness and spoliation on the part of the Holy Office, we had applied to its ministers, more than once in our thesis, the term *impious plunderers*, and had likewise denounced some of the most detestable crimes ever committed on American soil, by that infernal institution.

Our humble essay, although intended in a great measure to the glorification of the ancient clergy of Chile, did not, to all appearance, meet with a gracious reception from the men most eminent among our modern priesthood, for they accused us, although secretly, of having falsified history, of having calumniated the Holy Inquisition, and of having committed serious errors in our appreciation of facts, and they even went so far as to deny the existence of the documents which had served as the ground-work for our narrative, but which most fortunately we yet hold, having preserved the originals.

Nevertheless, for more than six years these criticisms were not made public, they only came to our ears occasionally, and had no more authority than being reported to have been said, in the course of *conversation*, the weakest of all testimony, and obtained with the greatest facility in this noble and capital city of Santiago, where all of us spend the best part of our lives in nothing else than *gossiping*.

But lo and behold, towards the end of last year, was announced the appearance of a work which no one would have thought to be possible, its title was the following:—" *The Inquisition. A rapid Sketch of that Institution, by the Prebendary Don José Ramon Saavedra,*" and consisted of a book in quarto, containing 128 pages of good typographical matter.

We were astonished, but we bought the work, and not only bought it, but we read it (amongst us two very different things), and when we had read it, we remained still more astonished. The *rapid sketch* was not a timid defence, a modest justification, or an excuse for the past. It was a highly extolled, enthusiastic, and almost fanatic panegyric of an institution, which for several centuries had filled the world with horror. " Not only will I defend," says the clerical writer, " the Ecclesiastical Inquisition, *I will trace and verify its panegyric,*" (page 5) ;—and he has kept his word with an ardour truly heroical.

As for ourselves, he has dedicated to us now and then a passing remark, just to point out and demonstrate our errors, our aberrations, and our calumnies.

Yet, notwithstanding all this, the instinctive feeling of good sense overcame our susceptibilities of wounded self-love. It appeared to us an idle waste of time, nay, insulting to the civilization of our fellow-citizens, to come before the public at the present day, in the latter third of the nineteenth century, for the purpose of refuting a work which its own author has had the boldness to call a *panegyric of the Inquisition*. We held in consideration, that, if the canons of the seventeenth century had kept within bounds the executioners of the Holy Office, and their venerable bishop, the illustrious Villarroel, had placed in irons the Commissary-General, it would certainly be an anachronism to repeat their work, in the age of enlightenment and justice to which we have arrived. It is true, nevertheless, that to entertain this extreme opinion, we had consigned to oblivion the fact that our high clergy had just been celebrating the *centenary* or hundredth anniversary of the expulsion of the Jesuits, and that the lay-orator who had the good fortune on this occasion to pronounce their eulogium, in two months after was elected by a majority of votes an acting member of the same University which we had entered some years before, and without any other right than by a humble decree of the Government.

Upon seeing the work of Señor Saavedra it occurred to us, that perhaps he wished to prepare the way for the celebration of the *centenary* of the abolition of the Inquisition; but as that could not be carried into effect until the same year in which the Republic would complete an age of its existence, (for together in the year 1810 were joined the tomb of the former with the cradle of the latter,) we again resolved to sacrifice the punctilio of vanity which mortified us, and resign ourselves to await the commemoration on our soil of the fires of the Inquisition, when our ashes would sleep forgotten in its bosom.

The abnegation of our silence went yet still further. Two months after that the treatise of Señor Saavedra had seen the light, the INDEPENDENT (a politico-religious newspaper of the capital) published, with the signature attached of one of its illustrious editors, an extensive article or critique on that work, and in which was decreed the palm of triumph to its author, while to that of ours was awarded the contemptuous scorn of the vanquished. "Yes, we believe," said in effect the critic (and calling *conspiration of silence* what perhaps was nothing more than Christian meekness,) "it is a great deal easier to *declaim* against the horrors of the Inquisition than to *discuss* them, and it costs *much less to be silent*, than to refute arguments and assertions founded on history. Honour nevertheless has its claims as well upon those who wield the pen as upon those who wield the sword. The adversary who challenges us to a fair contest, we must either conquer or else resign to him the field. Nothing is gained by turning upon him our back, and ridiculously affecting to treat him with contempt."*

These words, given in the name of the writer, seemed then to all appearance to be intended for us, and were equivalent to the challenge of the ancient herald. The "honour of the soldiers of the pen," to which neither for good nor for evil did we ever cowardly turn our back, constituted a provocation almost irresistible. But even yet, we must confess, we were reluctant to enter the arena. Was it fear? Was it magnanimity? We cannot tell: but it appeared to us, that to occupy ourselves with the Holy Office was a thing so out of date, so rancid and so useless, as it would be to prove the truth of Galileo about the earth's rotation, or as ridiculous and beyond all reason, as to write books like that famous one which Father Garcia gave to the world, concerning the *origin of the Indians*, and in which he proves that the Auracanians are the descendants of the Phenicians, or like that of our Dean Tula-Bazan, Professor at the Royal University of Saint-Philip of Santiago, Chile, about the inconveniences and sin of the ladies in wearing dresses with *long tails*. Moreover, it was then summer, and although the spirit had been willing the flesh rebelled, and would not

---

* The INDEPENDIENTE (newspaper of Santiago), March 26, 1868.

willingly accommodate itself to an invocation of the fires of the Inquisition; besides, the bookseller from whom we bought the above-mentioned panegyric of the Inquisition, to read during the dog days, informed us that the copy for which we had just paid him was the only one he had sold, and therefore it occurred to us that we, being the only reader, both our fault and our defeat would remain hidden and unknown.

This idea, or, if it pleases any one better, they may call it *conspiracy of silence*, became then an irrevocable determination, and we resolved to leave triumphant the Inquisition, which the Prebendary Saavedra had revealed to us, and defeated and condemned that which we had described, for in the language of our critic, " The arrow had pierced our heart, and we had measured our length on the ground." Was it possible to show more Christian humility, or a stubbornness in our modesty more meritorious?

At the last moment, however, an unexpected circumstance has occurred, which has dissipated and scattered to the winds all our intentions of reserve. A few days ago, or to speak more correctly we might say a few hours, information reached us, and that through a channel which does not admit of a doubt, being forwarded by persons who were eye-witnesses to the fact, that the work of Señor Saavedra has been chosen as a manual or text-book, by the directors of the College of Jesuits established in Santiago, and that a considerable portion of it is read to the children every day during the time they are at dinner, which plan is most probably the best that could be adopted, or at least the most economical, to demonstrate to them the usefulness of torture, and excite their admiration of the stake and faggot.

A novelty like this was worthy of the most serious attention, and changed completely the ground of the controversy, to which in vain we had been challenged by exciting our personal susceptibility as a public writer. It was no longer a question of historical facts, and was still much less a personal one; it was a question of actuality, affecting the present state of things, it was a question of propagandism, of proselytism, and perhaps one with a prospect of a *centenary* celebration. And for this we have called it a question of actuality; a logical appreciation, inasmuch as the panegyric of the Inquisition has been published with the express approbation of the authorities of the archdiocese.*

From this moment our position has become completely changed, personal feelings must give way to public duty, and to our responsibility for the future. To these calls we have not hesitated to respond, and in consequence we have unrolled our bundles of old papers, and lo the *inanimate corpse*, with "the arrow pierced through its heart," as apostrophized by the writer of the INDEPENDENT, here presents itself to accept the challenge of its triumphant antagonists.

Notwithstanding this alteration, which frees us from the disparagement caused by our silence, still would remain the difficulty of publicity, an embarrassment more serious than the other.

How is it possible to invest with novelty, to make attractive, or even to plead an excuse, for a work written at the present day about the Inquisition? We do not ask, Who would buy our book? That is not the consideration, but we do ask, Who would read it? We fear the fate of our adversary, as also of our own, he who during the heat of summer found no other purchaser for his pamphlet than ourselves, and we

---

* Within the cover of the pamphlet of Señor Saavedra, is the following authorization:—

"SANTIAGO, *November* 19, 1867.

"With the information given by the official Vicar-General Don Rafael Fernandez Concha, licence is conceded for the printing and publishing the book written by Señor Prebendary Don José Ramon Saavedra, entitled, *The Inquisition. A rapid Sketch of that eminent Institution.*

"V. J. ASTORGA, Secretary.

"Let it be registered. VARGAS."

who have more than once met with a copy or two of our books in their primitive and perfect original condition, in a corner of some bookcase, where, having been received *gratuitously*, they had been deposited and despised.

To overcome this obstacle, however, we had an excellent expedient which we will explain.

In the public library at Lima, founded as well as our own by San Martin,* there exists an immense body of *autos*,† which, were the *cuadernos* placed one upon the other, would measure half a yard in thickness; one of these accumulations of records has upon its cover the following title: *Penitenciado—Cuaderno 78—Don Francisco Moyen, de nacion frances, por proposiciones* ;‡ and this, as it is, was bought for half an ounce of gold by the worthy librarian, Presbyter Don

---

* General José Don Martin, born in Paraguay, served in Spain against the French; leaving the Spanish service he entered into that of the patriots of Buenos Ayres, he was appointed to the command of an army intended to liberate Chile, then in the power of the Spaniards. He crossed over the Andes, 1817, at the head of 5000 men, and defeated the Royalists at the battle of Chacabuco, but the following year was defeated in his turn by the Spanish General Osorio, and who from most unaccountable neglect in remaining inactive after his victory, allowed the Chilians to get together an army of upwards of 5500 men in little more than two months, with which they attacked the Spanish army, totally routing it, with a loss of 1000 men killed, and more than 3000 prisoners. This decided the emancipation of Chile. In 1820, San Martin headed an expedition against Peru, to free it from the Spaniards, and after a victorious campaign of eight months, entered with his army into Lima, and six days afterwards constituted himself Supreme Dictator of Peru.

† *Autos* (Acts.) In all Spanish countries, civil and criminal, processes are carried on by means of writing, so that in law-suits of long continuance, these writings called *autos* amount to an immense quantity. Several sheets of these writings stitched together, and forming a good-sized book, is called a *cuaderno*, the covers of which are mostly a piece of skin or parchment, scarcely thicker than paper.

‡ Condemned, 78 cuadernos. Don Francis Moyen, a native of France, for propositions.—*Notes by Translator.*

Francisco de Paula Vigil, from a poor woman, to whom it had been bequeathed after the famous sackage of the record office of the Inquisition at Lima, on the 3rd of September, 1813.

Being in that capital during the year 1860, and dedicated to historical investigations for the purpose of occupying the idle time of our banishment, we had leisure to read in its old-fashioned character the whole of that large heap of papers, and with our own hands we made extracts, copying literally many of its autographical pieces, written to all appearance with the charred brands of the fires of the Inquisition.

Those papers, partly eaten by the worms, and despised by the vulgar, (another species of worm not yet classified by naturalists,) contain within themselves a true drama by which an opinion may be formed of the Inquisition in all its horrible plenitude.

With the reproduction then of this drama, we will reply to Señor Saavedra. The Holy Inquisition shall be judged by the process itself, the same by which it judged its victims, and we, in disinterring the memory of one of its martyrs, do no more than imitate that pious example, so much lauded by the author of the panegyric, and which consisted in exhuming the ashes of the heretics, for the purpose of casting them into the burning pile.

We are not going to make a book of polemics; we do not possess the vast erudition ecclesiastical, historical, and theological of our opponent. On the contrary, we are going to accept a public challenge, without any other cuirass than an old parchment; and if at times it should happen by chance that we make use of an extraneous quotation, it will not be with an intention of displaying our learning, but only on the grounds of its referring to the question in an American point of view, because it is certain that in the old world a book about the Inquisition would be simply an absurdity, but in ours perhaps it may find an excuse for its novelty.

The authors of *Inez de Castro*, and of *the Grand Inquisitor*, (both American novels,) have adorned their pages with the colouring of fancy. Llorente, the terrible historian of the same institution, of which by his office he was the depository of its archives, has represented it, to the horror of the world, by applying to its dungeons the brilliancy of its own fires.

We will adopt a very different method, and one which at least has not yet hitherto been tested. We are going to try how history may be made to furnish its aid to polemics, and with no other attributes than that of its truth and the force of its documentary evidence.

The attempt in a literary point of view may be a daring one, and perhaps it may fail in our hands, but in the alternative of offering to our readers a dry work of diatribe, or a hybrid one animated with narration and discussion, we have preferred the latter.

Nevertheless, with the object of discarding as much as possible all that is purely doctrinal, we shall precede the narrative of the process against Moyen by a short exposition of the *Rapid Sketch* of the Prebendary Señor Saavedra.

A dernier proposition of courtesy in the noble contention of literature, another guarantee of loyalty in the polemic, we have to offer to our respectable adversary.

We have already said that the original documents which served us as a starting point, and of justification for our University discourse of 1862, exist still in our power, from to-day henceforth they will be at the disposal of our opponent. They are bound together in a convenient volume, and with covers of a fiery reddish colour, and thus bearing some analogy to their contents. With respect to those we shall now quote from, it has already been said where they may be found deposited, how they were preserved and how they are kept. Should those who expressed their disbelief in the existence of the former documents, have also a doubt of that of the latter, let them send to Lima a literary or ecclesiastical requisition, or, if preferable, an inquisitorial one; and if there can be proved against us an error, in only one instance, a mistake in only a date, or even in one comma, we agree beforehand to deliver up our reputation as historiographers, as well as this poor and hastily-written essay, to the vengeful flames of the Holy Office.

INTRODUCTION.

It was an ancient custom among the gladiators to salute each other before entering the arena, and we, who still admire the nobleness of ancient manners, have to make by way of salutation, before rushing to the combat, a declaration as an act of justice which we consider due to the prebendaries of Chile.

This declaration is, that we are fully persuaded of the ardent sincerity, of the irresistible good faith, and of the almost feverish but deep-rooted enthusiasm in the soul, with which the ecclesiastic to whom we reply has undertaken his strange task. And of a truth how could it be otherwise? For only a highly excited passion could be able to infatuate a mind whose nobleness and rectitude are beyond all doubt, to that point of frightful fascination of which an example is shown in every page of his work by the vehement eulogist. For him the Inquisition is a deity worthy of all adoration, its tortures a bed of roses, its hideous delation holy advice, its atrocious secret a tender intimacy, its robberies evangelical charity, and, to finish, its burning pile the halo of its own martyrdom! He acknowledges himself to be its friend, its vindicator, its champion, " Shall we not (says he, page 3,) eulogise the heroism of him who rushes intrepidly upon a crowd of assassins to liberate a man, who, pierced by their daggers, falls almost inanimate at the feet of his murderers?"

" The Inquisition is that poor victim of *calumniators* and others who hate it."

In this we behold the explanation of the enigma.

Is it possible to conceive without this profound hallucination of the mind, that a learned man, a famous theologian, in short, a modest and Christian clergyman (as it is affirmed by every one that the Prebendary Saavedra is,)—is it possible to believe that he could raise the banner of propagandism in the name of the Inquisition ? a name cursed and abhorred by all nations and by all men, and that shattering the urn in which posterity had confined its secrets and its horrors, together with its rank and fetid ashes, had caused to draw near the neophytes of his doctrine, and as in the days of the Church's mourning, to anoint with its dust the foreheads of innocent children ! No, let us be just, the clerical writer and his abettors (for it is well known that he has some) evidently belong to that class of men, who thus are martyrs as well as immolators, and who carry hidden in their own simple but terrible ingenuousness the only possible absolution for the abortion, truly monstrous, engendered by their delirious ravings !

Having first given this manifestation of our convictions *ad homine*, let us enter into an examination of the theories advanced by the defenders of the Holy Office.

The Prebendary of Santiago commenced by giving a definition of *heresy*. This being the logical and historical source from which the Inquisition derived its origin, and immediately in conformity likewise to history he divides the Inquisition into two categories. The Ecclesiastical or Papal Inquisition, instituted long anterior to the one commonly known by the name of *Spanish*, is the one about which he occupies himself the most; and although he says that by his pen the latter will not be shown in so favourable a light as the former, nevertheless, the definitive result of the whole of the context of his treatise is, that he is as blind a worshipper of the one as of the other.

He next explains the nature of heresy subject to the ecclesiastical jurisdiction and to the stake, which for certain is not that which lies hidden in the retreat of the soul, and which alone God from his radiant throne can judge. The heresy termed inquisitorial is the *external*, or that of word and deed, and this is the only kind which has been prosecuted.

Up to this point there is nothing extraordinary in the opinions of the illustrious writer, because they are simple derivations from philosophy and history.

In the lines following he proceeds to demonstrate the right which society holds to punish heresy, and from that right he deduces the necessity, the justification, the fruitful results, in short, the panegyric of the Inquisition.

His dialectic in this part is the same as that which is as old as the first lesson at school, it is of the basket containing rotten and sound fruit mixed together, and the consequence is, that these last by their contact with the bad, become rotten also; or that of the sapling, which if not straightened whilst young, will grow up irremediably deformed and crooked. The consequences of all this is, that the soul of man, born to have holy aspirations for the good, for the beautiful and the infinitely perfect, should be treated as rotten fruit, or as wood from the tree destined to serve as fuel for the furnace. The example, the precepts, and the mildness of the Gospel, the discussion which is to creeds as light to our ideas; the divine mercy, which is the most consoling of our dogmas; hope, which is the symbol of Christianity; repentance, which has been termed second innocency; and, in short, all the attributes of love, of perfection, of the creation, and of Christianity; the two great revelations of God to the human race, are, before that theory of fire and terror which the Prebendary Saavedra embraces in preference, mere accidents, weaknesses perhaps of our frail minds, and that neither God who has endowed us with life, nor Christian society which is at the same time judge and tutor of its own free will, have right to follow any other road than that which leads to punishment and extermination by fire.

"The establishment of the Inquisition," says the author whom we impugn, "was then a natural expression of the nature of Christian Society, and of the nature of man. Up to this there is nothing that does not harmonize perfectly with the principles of natural right, to which are adjusted the proceedings of the Governments of every country."

"But it may be said that capital punishment, the infliction of which occurs in civil society, should not be used in the society of Christians because it is incompatible with the maternal mildness of the Church. But fathers, however affectionate they may be, do they refrain from using punishments to their children? Indeed it may be said, 'that their natural love itself imposes this obligation, and that they would be considered cruel if they did not observe it.' Actually, notwithstanding the extreme condescension on this point, the civil codes still bestow the power upon fathers to disinherit their sons in certain cases. Would it be said for that, that they do not love them, and that the laws authorize cruelty? Civilized Governments prohibit the disembarkation of persons affected with cholera, fever or plague, and would we bestow praise upon the authorities, who, from love to the sick, would not subject them to quarantine, and thus become the cause of infection throughout the whole of the country? By the same rule we must judge the Church. Her love to some of her disobedient children ought not to allow her to forget the claims of the others to be preserved from the contagion of heterodoxy."*

* *Rapid Sketch* (page 16). The Señor Saavedra, as may be seen in the paragraph above mentioned, is strong in comparisons, which in matters of science have the same effect upon us as rhymes in participles and gerunds in poetry. At any rate, if it is not the most powerful mode of arguing it is the most convenient. "Whatever attempt has been made," he says, speaking of the irruption of the perverse modern ideas (in page 2 of his treatise), " to restrain the impetus of the impulse given to the understanding, has been as useless as the raising of a curtain to still the hurricane, or to oppose a bank of reeds to the violent current of an overflowing torrent." And speaking of the danger of opposing this torrent, he exclaims, "Unfortunate is he who attempts to hoist the standard of truth and to cause it to be saluted with reverence!"." He would be considered as an emissary from hell, and tossed

The learned author of the *Sketch* in his exordium explains at some length the different kinds of Inquisition, which have existed in all ages, and also of the antiquity of its origin, which he traces back to Theodosius the Great; but in this part, it would have been better for the Prebendary and for us also, for him to have been more comprehensive and to have left us with the opinion of the Mexican friar, Juan de Torquemada, who in his *Monarquia Indiana* (vol. 3, page 371,) informs us, " that if the Holy Office of the Inquisition is observed well from its beginning it will be found to be so ancient that its origin may be deduced from the creation of the first man, because, in a few hours from the said creation, we find that he sinned, breaking the commandment of God, and as a transgressor was sought for, and as the Holy Scripture informs us, was judged by this same God, and sentenced for his crime."*

And hence from this paternal love of Torquemada and Philip the Second for the Christian world, is derived the opinion of the Prebendary Señor Saavedra, that " the establishment of the Inquisition was rational and just," (page 47); that " the good order and well being of society demanded its establishment," (page 14); that, according to that courtier of

about like straw by an infuriated mob;" and he concludes in these terms (page 3) : " This reaction which has taken place in the old Continent, has hardly been felt in the new. This world of Columbus received later, and without much attention, the anti-social movement as the rocks on the shore are mildly lashed by the murmuring and broken waves of the stormy sea."

* Better still was the Peruvian Bermudez in his famous work entitled : *The triumphs of the Holy Office of Peru,* for he says (page 8) that, " God as the first Inquisitor tried the cause of Adam." This nonsense reminds us of that Court Friar, compatriot and contemporary of Dr. Bermudez, who in the reception of an accountant general in Lima, in his sermon maintained that God himself was the first accountant, because in the act of taking the rib from Adam with which he formed Eve, he had made the first *subtraction* and the first *multiplication!*

kings and royal concubines, Capefigue, "it was the first tribunal which proclaimed equality before the law!" (page 118); and that also, according to the Protestant Ranke, "it became extremely popular in Spain, so much so that the people revered it as a national institution."

And certain it is, it was so, and we are of the same opinion as Ranke, that the Spaniards liked the *Autos de fé*, precisely as they liked the bull fights, and thus their ancient and modern barbarity is accounted for as eminently national.

Another of the traditional justifications for the *Inquisition* is the *right!* which the Church holds to take out of the hands of the civil power the sword of Justice. Kings burnt heretics: well, why then should the Church not do the same? "The attitude assumed by the civil governments," says Señor Saavedra, "towards the heretics was another cause which impelled the Church to establish the Inquisition. We have already seen that according to the regulations of the Roman law then in force in Europe, and which regulations have been recently renewed!—heretics were condemned to the punishment of death. For them were only two tribunals, the civil one, and that of the sacrament of penance. But the latter could only exercise its jurisdiction over those who came voluntarily to confess their faults, while the former oppressed without enlightening the understanding, wounded the heart without improving it, and destroyed life without inspiring remorse, and without procuring reconciliation to God. The Church, in its desire to rescue heretics from the punishment of death, and to restore them to God and society, conceived the idea of a *mediate tribunal*, one that would search out the guilty, instruct them and produce in their hearts feelings of remorse, would change their punishments into penance, and at the same time would modify their sufferings according to the degree of their contrition and repentance, until at last it converted the scaffold itself into the means of salvation. Was it a good or an evil, that the church should substitute love, education and penance for the sanguinary executions of the civil law?"

"Ah! How much is the 19th century extolled and magnified for having conceived the happy idea of the penitentiary system. The Church had conceived it 600 years before, and not only conceived it but realized it, and realized it to prevent thousands of heretics from suffering the punishment of death, and this *benevolence* has produced only curses and contumely."

But this is not all. It was not only *benevolence* to establish secret dungeons and burning piles for the victims of involuntary error, doubt, or even of truth itself. The magnanimity of the Church went much further than that. The Inquisition was established in *favour* of heretics themselves.

"Another reflection presents itself to show more clearly the advantages of the Inquisition," adds Señor Saavedra. "The Church established it not only in defence of the Christian faith and of public order, but also for the benefit and individual security of the heretics themselves. The continued outrages of the schismatics had already produced a great fermentation in the minds of the faithful and had provoked reprisals."

"The Church thus establishing," continues the logical eulogist (page 21), "the Inquisition, delivered the schismatics from being massacred by an infuriated populace or cut to pieces by the swords of the sbirri, and thus whilst giving to the people a lesson of moderation and humanity, and pointing out to kings the path of mercy, made known how much she valued the lives of men, although they were those of her enemies."

"Ah! all ye who fully appreciate the importance of the life of man, and so much esteem the institutions which offer themselves for its protection, how is it ye do not intone hymns of praise and gratitude to the Catholic Church for having instituted the Inquisition as a most precious guarantee of human life. But what shall I say? How can I explain the phenomenon that ye load her with reproaches for having established it? Did she do wrong to offer an *asylum* to heretics, to save them from being torn to pieces by a turbulent and furious mob?"

Is this credible? Is this the logic with which the triumphant Prebendary of the *Independent* has vanquished us? Is this the arrow with which, so much lauded in his criticisms, he has pierced our heart? Is it even a serious argument in the face of history,—history which in times not far remote the Inquisition had converted into one immense burning pile, or even before that frigid and gloomy theology itself, which served as the torch with which scholastic fanaticism applied fire to the faggots and set them in a blaze? Nevertheless the apologist of the pyre does not believe thus; for, according to his creed, the reason why hitherto the Inquisition has not been understood in its divine mission (page 4) " is, that those who *falsified history* for the purpose of serving their own sinister plans, have misled and deceived the modern populations; they have succeeded in stupifying them with their continued vociferation of crimes, tortures, burning piles and hecatombs, and thus it has been easy to imbue their minds with rancour and hatred and lead them on to frenzy."

The dignified Prebendary of Santiago shows himself in this part violent and implacable with those who have profaned with *falsehood and calumny* the beloved deity of his adoration. To him the Inquisition, which burnt alive and in effigy near 40,000 human beings, and inflicted torments and other horrible punishments upon a number six times still greater, was a tribunal of *mercy*, of *benevolence*, of *protection*, in short an *asylum* for those same heretics whom they burnt with a slow fire, whom they tore limb from limb upon the rack, and whom they caused languishingly to die by misery and terror. The charitable Prebendary, like the boatman of

Maule,* who boasted of having saved a shipwrecked Englishman, because while with one hand he held submerged the unfortunate wretch, with the other he baptized him and with the same water in which he was suffocated,—attributes in his conscience a profound admiration, a respectful and tender love for that mother of the Christians, who if she tortured and reduced them to ashes, it was only out of benevolence to protect them against the civil law, against the kings, against the populace, in short to restore them to the celestial spheres, without having to pass through the flames of hell.

Good heavens! In no other manner, fortunately for humanity, could he defend in these times the most horrible, the most inhuman, and the most impious of all the aberrations that has darkened the ages of mankind in their infancy of reason and right, of faith and religion.

Another argument *ad homine* of the zealous Prebendary is, that the Inquisition is hated because established by the Church. If its founder had been, not a Pope with a purple robe like Sixtus IV., who granted the bull of institution to the Catholic kings, or a Dominican friar with a black hood, like Tomas de Torquemada, who burnt alive 8000 heretics! but a man with a coat and wig, a philosopher like Diderot, or a statesman like Campomanes, the Inquisition would have merited applauses from all freethinkers.

"Ah! if some enemy of the Church had conceived and realized the idea of the Inquisition," exclaims its eulogist, "we may be sure that words would be wanting sufficiently to applaud the founder of such a noble and magnificent institution. All the choicest things of the talent and art of the present day would throng around a name so venerated, a hundred dramas would proclaim his glory, and thousands of statues crowned with garlands of ivy exhibit him to future generations, while the streets and public squares would

---

* A small seaport, now known as Constitution, some 90 leagues south of Valparaiso.

resound with the voices of bards singing the praises and grandeur of the dramaturgo."

But it is not alone the atrocities of the Inquisition which incites its eulogist in its defence. Whatever belongs to it, as we shall presently see, is an object of his esteem and reverence, the most unheard of absurdities, condemned by the Church itself, become in his judgment articles of faith immediately he is convinced that they are favoured by the notice of the Holy Inquisition. Witchcraft, necromancy, compacts with the devil, &c., all this monstrous spiritual cosmogony of remote ages, is resuscitated by him with an irresistible splendour, and with a force of conviction incomprehensible. The Inquisition for example burnt witches and sorcerers, *ergo*, we must believe in witchcraft, and with a faith irrevocable. No matter that the Synods of Chile have declared it mortal sin to have faith or belief in the superstition of the conjurors of the aborigines, those same *machis*,* whom Pedro de Valdivia ordered to be exterminated, giving a commission for that purpose to the historian and soldier, Góngora Marmolejo, and in that of those who yet preside in Arauco at the auguries of the Indians, and also of those who preside at the auguries of the lower orders in Santiago. No matter either that their practices have been condemned by our captains in their proclamations, and by our bishops in their diocesan laws. Did the Holy Inquisition believe in them? Well then, its excited and inconvincible admirer believes in them also. "In fact," says Señor Prebendary Saavedra (page 10), " there are many things to discuss in the present case, (that of sorcerers, wizards, and persons possessed of the devil.) 1st. Are there or can there be witches? 2nd. If there are, do they merit the punishment of death? 3rd. Would it be cruel to burn them? 4th. Has Catholicism approved of that kind of punishment?

* The medicine men, or conjurors, among the Indians of Araucania, are so called; they perform all their cures by spells and incantations, and have great influence among the aborigines.—*Note by Translator.*

"The first point in the opinion of our learned and choice spirits of the present day is not worthy the name of question, before even taking their seats in the classes at college they decide in a most dogmatic tone against the existence of witches, and go strutting about and with great gusto relishing the fruits which the conquests of the civilization of the present age have procured for them. Should they be asked what motives they have for denying that witches still exist? They can give no reason whatever, but with a disdainful smile will tell you that the times are gone by for such antiquated notions. This is not a conviction arrived at by means of profound studies; it is a pure negation which they inherit from the naturalists, systematically incredulous, and which pervades the social atmosphere, and like others of the same kind, insinuates itself into the minds of inexperienced youth and of the ignorant multitude, without any one being able to assign the reasons upon which it is grounded."

"Luther," he adds, appealing to rather dangerous testimony, "believed in the existence of commerce carried on between the devil and mankind, even to an extent approaching the ridiculous. José Gorres, to whose great talents and vast erudition Napoleon the First rendered homage, styling him 'an European power,' acknowledged also this kind of commerce;* and a French advocate, M. Bizouard, maintained the same doctrine, in a voluminous work just published in France, with the title 'Connection of Mankind with the Devil.' I pass over in silence a great number of writers upon demonology belonging to former times."

"After all this, will it still be asserted that the belief in witchcraft is based on ignorance? Would it not be more rational to declare that only the ignorant, and those who have deserted Catholicism, deny the possibility of its existence?"

* He says that devils had commerce with women, and that the children of these unions required and drained the milk of six nurses.— *Bizouard.*

In the face of all this, we ask, it being now our turn to question, we demand of all sensible persons, of all clergymen of sound doctrine, of his own bishop, heir to the pastoral staff of the illustrious Alday, the most eminent of our religious legislators, can it be admitted as a serious work, that of the Prebendary Señor Saavedra? Were we or were we not justified in declining to occupy ourselves with his 'Rapid Sketch' of the Inquisition? In short, can it be objected to our superstitious fear that some wizard must have fascinated the illustrious Canon with the evil eye, to inspire him with such a theme for his erudite lucubrations?

But more astonishing still, more incredible, if it were possible, than this doctrine of demonology of the Prebendary Saavedra, is that of the ten propositions of his treatise (page 105), in which he actually and literally expresses himself in the following words:—

"It is said that the Spanish Inquisition operated as an obstacle to science. But history says the contrary, for it was exactly only but a short time after it was established, and during the period of its development and while in its greatest vigour, that the sciences began to flourish, universities were founded, and the art of printing introduced; it encouraged the study of the classics, it favoured poetry and the fine arts, books were imported, men celebrated for their learning were invited from foreign countries, the nobles dedicated themselves to studies which had been for a long time neglected, and throughout Spain there reigned an activity for scientific investigation very remarkable. The epoch in which Spanish literature shone with its greatest splendour was from the latter part of the 15th century to the end of the 17th, and this likewise was the period in which the Inquisition displayed its greatest energy and power. Cervantes, Lope de Vega, Calderon, Fr. Luis de Leon, Solis, Santa Teresa, Luis de la Puente, Rivadencira, and the three greatest historians of Spain, Pulgar, Zurita and

Mariana, belonged to this time, and their works were printed with the licence of the Inquisition."

What! History! History, which holds exactly in this part a compact uniformity in demonstrating that the Inquisition was created exclusively for the conservation of the faith against all reforms (and especially that by Luther), according as Señor Saavedra himself assures us, in relating to us its origin and its early progress, how then does history say the *contrary?*

What! The Inquisition, which was founded to investigate the thoughts and conscience, to scrutinize and analyze them in their most secret and hidden recesses, to reduce them to the restrictions of the iron rule of dogma and theology, gives for its results the expansion and freedom of these very thoughts!

What! Because the discovery of printing was made during the time that the Inquisition flourished, but which it placed beneath its ferule of charred brands, by its censure and previous licence as the eulogist himself tells us;—the Inquisition gave impulse to the freedom of written thought, and encouraged the publication of books that were not like the Politica de Bovadilla, or the Dos cuchillos of the Bishop Villarroel?*

What! The Universities, the councils of learned men who in Salamanca opposed the voyage of Columbus to discover another world, and who in Pisa and in Rome condemned as heresy the eternal truths of Galileo. What! this Inquisi-

* Bovadilla was a Spaniard, and wrote a fulsome work on politics, for the purpose of demonstrating that kings govern by divine right. Don Gaspar de Villarroel, bishop of Santiago two centuries ago, composed two large volumes in folio, to establish the prerogatives of the Church and State, for which reason they are called the *dos cuchillos* (two knives), that is to say, the civil knife and the ecclesiastical one. And pretty sharp ones they are sometimes, as many have found to their cost.—*Note by Translator.*

tion was it, which " invited men celebrated for their learning from foreign countries?"

And because Cervantes, imprisoned, maimed and in obscurity gave to the world his admirable story of Don Quixote; because Lope de Vega and Calderon represented without being burnt at the stake their celebrated *autos sacramentales*, which are nothing more than our innocent farces of Duarte-street;* because Santa Teresa wrote her letters in a state of extasis, and because there flourished the "three great historians of Spain, Pulgar, Zurita and Mariana,"— mere chronologists of the kings! and, as learned men, entirely devoid of interest to the progressive movement of their age, —for all this, which signifies nothing more than that the human intelligence is destined to advance in knowledge and to live eternally as the stars in the immensity of space,—for this, the champion of the Inquisition declares it to have been the protector of the sciences, of the arts and of progress!

And the inquisitorial persecution of the Fathers Isla and Feijoo, who did not write an ideal romance like Cervantes, but occupied themselves in delineating with the art of masters the society in which they lived, why has it not been mentioned by Señor Saavedra as another proof of the generous protection afforded by the Inquisition to literature? Why has he not also mentioned the five years imprisonment in the *Secret* of Valladolid of the illustrious Luis de Leon (likewise a monk) and his sublime "we said yesterday to his disciples,"† when he escaped from the hands of those apostles of ignorance, to the glory of whom Señor Saavedra dares to

* A street in Santiago, where there is a small theatre.

† Fray Luis de Leon was a professor in the University of Valladolid, he was imprisoned five years in the dungeons of the Inquisition; upon his release he resumed the delivery of his lectures to his pupils, and the first words he addressed to them were, "As we were saying yesterday," as though his instruction to them had only been interrupted a few hours.—*Note by Translator.*

name as a shining light, the same learned man who was but only their victim?

And the Roman Index, a vivid catalogue of the proscription of the human mind, was that instituted, we ask, in favour of freedom of thought and liberty of the press? Oh! Why does not Señor Saavedra tell us that the gag was invented to enable us to use the tongue with greater facility in expressing our sentiments and thoughts, or that the prohibition of the FERROCARRIL* by the *confessional* was only with the pious object of increasing the number of its subscribers.

But what did it respect, we ask Señor Saavedra,—to shorten this useless polemic,—what did the Inquisition respect in science, in learning, in progress, or even in religion itself, unless it was the religion of the stake and faggot? In science did it even respect Don Felix de Azara or Olavide of Lima, accused of one hundred and sixty-six heretical propositions, for having made in Spain, with the royal sanction, the first attempt at practical religious toleration? In poetry, did it even respect the mellifluous Melendez Valdes, the ingenious Iriarte, or even his colleague, the fabulist Samaniego? In politics, did it respect the only eminent men who governed Spain, from Florida Blancha to Jovellanos, from the Conde de Aranda to Urquijo, and to Macanaz? But what shall we say, did the Inquisition by any chance respect the reverend writers themselves whom its excited eulogist invokes to prove its tolerance? Was not Mariana himself shut up in its dungeons?† Was not also Santa Teresa

---

* A liberal daily newspaper of Santiago.—*Note by Translator*.

† It is a fact that Mariana called the establishment of the Inquisition *salutary*, but not for this did he the less manifest the feelings of repugnance with which it was received by the Spaniards. He says, "But what most of all surprised them was that the children should suffer for the sins of the parents, that it was not known or made manifest who were the accusers, nor were they confronted with the accused, nor the evidence made public. In every thing the contrary to what was formerly the custom in all other tribunals. Moreover, it appeared

persecuted as an illuminator by the inquisitors of Seville?
—The saints themselves, and those whose fraternity appears to be so beloved at the present day by the admirers of cen-

to them a new and strange thing that such faults should be punished with death!"

"In giving a rapid glance," says a modern writer, (the learned Peruvian Garcia Calderon, of whose competence in Catholic matters we will speak more hereafter,) "and judging the same as Mariana of the establishment of the Inquisition, the mind becomes confused and the heart oppressed in reflecting upon the number of abuses which the Inquisition might commit, and in fact which it did commit. On the other hand, in *politics* it gave the opportunity to accuse of heresy all those who appeared to be enemies of the government or professed liberal ideas; in this manner the Inquisition, which had no other object than to preserve the purity of the faith, served in reality to sustain the absolute power of the kings of Spain, to oppose all progress and improvement, material and intellectual, and to establish the dominion of a few individuals and enable them to enrich themselves. Thanks to the Inquisition the populations remained submerged in ignorance, in slavery, in fanaticism and in superstition."

But it is not only during a cycle of three centuries that this harmony of opinion amongst Catholic writers is observed. The most modern historian of Spain has written of the Inquisition in the same way as Mariana. But Pulgar himself, whom Señor Saavedra cites as a witness in his favour, did not hold a different opinion—"Hernando del Pulgar, (says Torres de Castilla, in his 'Political and Religious Persecutions,' Vol. I. page 672,) contemporary with the establishment of the Inquisition, manifested his opinion in the 'Chronicle of the Catholic Kings,' founders of the Inquisition, by saying that some of the relations of the prisoners remonstrated because that the Inquisition in its executions 'was more rigorous than it ought to have been,' and that in the manner in which the processes were carried on, and the sentences executed, the ministers showed hatred and passion!"

"In private letters quoted in the work entitled 'Celebrated Men of Castile,' and addressed to the Cardinal Mendoza, at that time Archbishop of Seville, he speaks more clearly, maintaining 'that the crime of heresy ought not to be punished with death, but only by pecuniary fines, as St. Augustine declared, in treating of the case of the Donatists, and of the laws against them, promulgated by the Emperors Theodosius I. and Honorius I. his son.'"

tenaries. The saints of the company of Jesus were they not persecuted, ill-treated, and obliged to fly to foreign countries like San Ignacio the founder of the order, or judged in secret like his collaborator, San Francisco de Borja, duke of Gandia.*

Oh! that at the present day we should be reminding all this to a learned Chilian, to a member of the council of our archdiocese, which has been proclaimed, and justly so in our opinion, as the most illustrious and most respectable one in all Spanish America, is a proceeding which costs us something to believe, as it appears to us to be almost impossible that it could have happened; yet nevertheless it is most painfully true, and to an extent which defies all error, that his vertiginous ravings are most unfathomable.†

* "We may remark in passing," says the author of the 'Persecutions,' before cited, (vol. 2, page 499) "that the three first generals of the company of Jesus, San Ignacio de Loyola, Diego Lainez, and San Francisco de Borja, were victims of fanaticism and inquisitorial hatred, but which did not prevent the Jesuits from constituting themselves the firmest supporters of the Inquisition, and exhibiting from the first establishment of the order a ferocious zeal in the persecution of heretics." Does this come from the reading in the refectory, of which we have spoken in the preface to this work?

† Señor Saavedra arrives at the conclusion that the system of trial by jury (instituted by heretics as a protection to intelligence) is derived from the Holy Office!

"Notwithstanding," (says in effect the author of the 'Rapid Sketch,') "the notable decline of faith, Christian nations have not yet sheathed the sword of the law against heretics. Our laws submit the authors of heretical writings to the jurisdiction of an especial tribunal (trial by jury). That is to say they substitute another tribunal in place of the ancient ecclesiastical ones, but one that offers less guarantee of correctness in its sentence, because it is not to be expected that the members of the jury could have the theological aptitude requisite for them to decide in questions of dogma, and also for the rapidity which is usually observed in their proceedings."

And if trial by jury in offences of the press is derived from, or substituted for the Inquisition, we demand in our turn of the learned eulogist, where are the marks of consanguinity? Is it in the *publicity*

But this is not all, there exists an ancient and just prescription of the ecclesiastical law, which prohibits the minister of a God of mercy from having anything to do with sanguinary punishments. But of what importance is that mandate to the eulogist of an institution for punishments in the name of the Divinity? Openly he declares himself to be an advocate for the penalty of death, and to prove its *lawfulness*, he says (page 70); "Apart from the example of *all* nations of the civilized world, and from the most *solid reasons* of social convenience upon which this penalty (death) is founded, the two following considerations are sufficient : firstly, that God established it in the *Mosaical law*,* and secondly, that Jesus Christ said to Pilate, that he would not have the power to take away life unless it had been given to him from on high, and therefore God gives to Governments the right to take away life."

Hear! God gives the right to take away life, therefore the penalty of death is a divine right, the same as the tor-

---

instead of *secrecy*, in the proceedings of a few hours, instead of the dreadful martyrdom of years? in freedom of conscience instead of the constitutions of theology and the canons? between the theological aptitude and the irresponsible finding of the verdict? between the pecuniary fine and the *sambenito?* between the liberty of the accused and the stake? Most truly Señor Prebendary, with all due respect we cannot do less than say, that to maintain that trial by jury is a child of the Inquisition appears to us to be equivalent to telling us that a tigress had brought forth a lamb, such a comparison ought not to produce feelings of scandal,—because once in a professional examination we were asked, by an eminent jurisconsult and canon, a similar question, but in our answer we blundered sadly in a legal syllogism, and had it not been for the leniency of our examiners we certainly should have been rejected; had it been before the Holy Office we could not have escaped, as will be seen by and by, in the case of the mule of Francisco Moyen.

* "God commanded the Hebrew people to kill the man who endeavoured to withdraw them from the worship of the Lord God, so that all Israel should fear when they heard it, and that no one would even dare to do a similar thing." (*Rapid Sketch*, page 8.)

ture is a natural right. "In a double aspect," exclaims the prebendary apologist, "may be treated the question of torture (page 66), in a philosophical and in a historical aspect, considered under the first, we must examine whether society had the right to punish an accused who denies his crime, when there is a *probability* of him being guilty. What does the philosophy of right say to this? Many have believed that this method of discovering the truth (torture) is founded on the natural right which belongs to public authority; and it is this, without doubt, upon which is based the legislation and practice of so many illustrious nations which for many centuries made use of the torture in their tribunals."

Hear, O Christians! He who from the top of Mount Sinai said, *Thou shalt do no murder!* He who expired on the height of Golgotha asking *pardon* for his executioners, He that is the symbol of the highest good and of all that is just, is here presented to you as the first institutor of the scaffold, and as the executioner of his creatures. And by whom? By a minister of his own worship, a dignitary of his true Church! Is this credible? is it tolerable? is it Christian? is it even Catholic? Yes, says the Prebendary of the Inquisition—"Here it is shewn in the word of God itself (page 9), and to maintain knowingly opinions contrary to this word (that is to say, maintain that the penalty of death is not a divine right), *is to insult God and society.*"

Let us proceed a little further.

There is in life something which all nations and peoples have looked upon as distinct from the passions, as distinct from the world, as a mysterious point which connects the dust of the earth to the light eternal of the spheres; this something is the tomb, the ashes of man, which are respected by the Calmuck as by the Patagonian, by the Esquimaux as by the South Sea Islander. Well, then! the Inquisition that ransacked the graves to strew their ashes on the burning pile, did not commit an impious profanation in the opinion of its admirer; on the contrary, it gave a salutary example, "because it was natural," he says (page 73), "that such processes (of the dead) would inspire in the people's minds a greater detestation of that crime (heresy), and deter them from its commission." But we ask with the author of the *Religious Persecutions* already cited, taking up the question as mere discipline, how is it possible to convert a dead man? Does not the catholic dogma teach us that when we die we have to appear before God, that we may be judged, every one according to his works? Why then judge and condemn one who cannot repent, and whom God himself has already condemned or absolved? What blame can be attached to the heirs that they should be reduced to misery and infamy, at the same time perhaps being good Catholics, for the supposed heresy of an ancestor, of whom God alone is the legitimate judge? And where is the justice of judging a dead man who cannot defend himself?

Another question, and one that is not of religion, nor of doctrine, nor of controversy, but only of the dictionary, which says in effect that the word *sambenito* is used " for the bad mark which rests or results from some action, from something infamous." But behold the corrector of Bello's* Grammar dedicates no less than one of his propositions to show that the dictionary has said a falsehood, and that the explanation it gives is destitute of foundation.

But let us bid adieu, if only out of respect for our civilization in the eyes of foreigners, many of whom no doubt will

---

* Don Andres Bello was born in Caraccas. In the year 1812 he accompanied Bolivar to London, to assist him in negotiating a loan for the revolutionists of Columbia, in their struggle for independence. He remained in Europe some time, and then came to Chile. He was a very learned man, and established a superior system of education in Chile, and for many years directed her international relations as minister for foreign affairs. He is the author of her present Civil Code, and several text books of study; among other works, one on the rights of nations, and a grammar of the Spanish language, adopted throughout all South America and even in Europe. He died upwards of eighty, at Santiago, 1865.—*Note by Translator.*

read these pages, to this accumulation of generalities more or less absurd and puerile, and follow the eulogist into the province of practical facts.

Here we may condense with greater facility his exposition, because it does not treat about points of pure theological doctrine, but of the holy practices of the holy executioners.

The enthusiastic Prebendary himself sums up the charges made against the Inquisition under thirteen different heads,* for the purpose of refuting them in order, and his faithful extract will completely fulfil the object we have in view to exhibit the whole of the inquisitorial theory as laid down by the ecclesiastical writer, although some of these questions are already explained.

1st. "The Inquisition was not an ominous and treacherous tribunal." Because it conceded previously a term of grace for the purpose that heretics might voluntarily denounce themselves, in which case they would be absolved with a penance comparatively slight; because in conformity to its constitutions, it did not prosecute "for trifling causes, such as blasphemy, which crime is generally committed through anger" (Art. 4th of the Constitution of 1500); because heretics were previously examined by a doctor, for the purpose of certifying if they were or not in a sound state of mind; because the summary or resumé of the accusation was agreed to in consultation by a numerous body of qualified ecclesiastics; because it required an unanimity in the members of the tribunal (which at most times consisted of two, and sometimes of only one) in sentences of grave importance; and, lastly, because when Napoleon entered Spain he did not find even one prisoner in its dungeons.

2nd. "Its processes were not iniquitous nor inhuman." Because to the accused were conceded three audiences;

---

* In our exposition there are fourteen, because for the better understanding them we have divided into two the fourth proposition of the author, which treats of the exhumation of dead bodies and of the torture.

because during the session (audience) they were permitted to be seated, excepting while the charges of the fiscal were being read; because two clergymen were obliged to be present at the interrogations; because the denunciations were obliged to be made in writing and upon oath; because they read to the accused the charges one by one, granting him sufficient time to listen to them; because it was conceded to the accused the privilege of naming a defender; because the evidence was published (but without naming the witnesses); because he could challenge in a body all those he believed to be his enemies;* and, lastly, because they furnished him with writing materials for the purpose of taking notes.

3rd. "It is likewise almost entirely false that they treated their prisoners with cruelty." Because they were located in good habitations, lofty, upon arches, with light, dry and spacious, according as we are informed by Llorente himself, the most authorized denouncer of the atrocities of the Inquisition; because they were permitted to have servants; because the Inquisitors made a practice of visiting the prison every fortnight; because those confined were permitted to work in the prison to supply themselves with necessaries from the product of their ingenuity; and because when Beaumarchais was in Spain in 1764, he was surprised at the goodness of the Inquisition, and wrote to his own country that it was the most moderate of all tribunals.

4th. "That the torture made use of was not anything so terrible as it was supposed to be." Because it was not applied spontaneously, but only when petitioned to be used by the fiscal; because it was only made use of when the suit was terminated; because when the patient suffered too much

---

* In this may be seen the villany of the whole affair, for how could the accused challenge any one without knowing him. No doubt this privilege was granted to induce him to name persons with whom he had had dealings, and by so doing make disclosures which would tell against himself, or criminate others.—*Note by Translator.*

they applied another kind of torture less severe (literal); because they were obliged to state the reason why they put him to the torture; because the bishop of the diocese was obliged to assist by his presence the application of the punishment; because the confession obtained by the torture was not considered of any judicial value, unless it was ratified voluntarily twenty-four hours afterwards; and, lastly, because Philip III. limited the duration of the torture to one hour, whereas Elizabeth of England (a Queen eminently heretical), caused it to be applied an hour and a half. " His penal system, therefore, was in consequence the mildest." (Page 31).

5th. " The right to exhume dead bodies and scatter their ashes to the winds was not an act of cannibalism, as it has been called by Llorente." Because the Egyptians held the practice salutary and corrective of the justice they had done towards the deceased; and because (we go into comparison) as in like manner that civil society has the right to disinter bodies for reasons of pestilence, or other causes of public utility, so has the Church an equal right in respect to heretics. To prove this last assertion, the author has devoted no less than seven pages of his well stored treatise.

6th. "Neither was the right of confiscation unlawful." Because that right was held by the civil power; and because it was employed with lenity, and at times they restored part of the fortune of the condemned to their families.*

* Here is a clergyman of the present day publicly asserting that the Catholic Church has the right to confiscate the property of those who differ from it in opinion; the right to disinter and burn the bodies of those who in their lifetime had not submitted themselves to its doctrines; and the right to take from the hands of the civil power the sword of justice. The opinions he expresses are only the same as held by almost the whole of the great body of the clergy belonging to his church. We have lately seen the insolent and haughty attempt of the Pope to interfere in the internal affairs of Austria; and should any one wish to know more about the arrogant pretensions of the Catholic Church, he may see them fully laid down in a paper by

7th. "It is false that the Inquisition exercised any pressure upon those who were not Christians," as Montesquieu asserts. Here the 'Sketch' gives no other reason than the contradiction of the fact; founded upon this, that Charles V. forbade the Inquisition to punish the American aborigines,* and that Innocent III. ordered that the Jews should not be baptized by force.

Mr. Purcell, in "Essays on Religion and Literature," edited by Archbishop Manning, London, 1867. Now while the Catholic Church holds these opinions, considering them in the light of a dogma of their faith, how is it possible that in any country there can be free toleration of religion; that is an impracticability, for if all creeds are placed upon an equal footing, the Catholic Church is oppressed and persecuted by being deprived of her rights—viz., the rights which, according to her own blasphemous assertion, she has received from God, to interfere with and dominate over every other. In a debate in the French Senate, M. Sainte Beuve said, "he well knew that when the clerical party called for liberty, they meant predominance."—*Note by Translator.*

* We do not doubt but that they are genuine, the two ordinances of 1549 and 1638, which Señor Saavedra, quoting Llorente, attributes to Charles V., although even at the date of the last, "the *badulaque*, [a stupid person of little sense or reason] of Hernani," as Señor Saavedra calls him, speaking against Victor Hugo, was nothing more than a handful of dust. The laws of the Indies nevertheless only assign the prohibition of Philip II., dated 23rd February, 1571, and we do not know how Charles V. could have made laws for the American Inquisition, when it was established by Philip II. But we will not dispute about trifles, and both Señor Saavedra and Llorente may be right. We will be satisfied with producing the prohibition of Philip II. (which is Law 35, vol. 1, book 6 of the Code of the Indies), in which, if it is certain that it prohibits the Inquisition from taking cognizance of the idolatry of the Indians (had it been otherwise, not one of them would have been left alive), it was only to deliver them to other judges and other punishments.

Here is the law.

"On account of the Apostolical Inquisitors being prohibited from proceeding against the Indians, their punishment is referred to the ordinary ecclesiastics, who must be obeyed and their orders complied with; and the witches who kill by their spells, and the use

8th. "The representations which Llorente and other writers have made of the autos de fé is false." Because it happens that such pictures are "merely fantastical," (page 88); because it is false that they burnt the bones of those who had died; and because it is entirely false that the priests of the Inquisition ever condemned any criminal. (page 94.)

9th. "They are entirely erroneous the calculations of Llorente, secretary of the Inquisition, of the number of victims that Torquemada and his successors burnt, or upon whom they inflicted other punishments." The author reproduces all the arithmetical operations, and the data which served for the frightful demonstrations of the most celebrated of the historians of the Holy Office; and to this chapter alone Señor Saavedra has devoted eight of his ample pages.

10th. "It is certain that there were witches and sorcerers," —and consequently they deserved to be burnt.

11th. "It is false that the Inquisition served as an obstacle to the advancement of the sciences and literature,"—as in the time of its greatest severity flourished Cervantes, Lope de Vega, Calderon, Fray Luis de Leon, Solis, Pulgar, Santa Teresa, Zurita, and the historian Mariana. This point we have already slightly discussed.

12th. "The Inquisition did not debase the patriotism of the Spaniards,"—but it gave to it unity and consistence, as it has been observed by Capefigue.

13th. "The *Sambenito* did not stain with dishonour those who had been condemned to penance!"

14th. "The Inquisition was not an instrument of despotism for the kings of Spain." In proof of which he cites the case recorded by Balmes, of a reprimand being given by the Inquisition to a monk, who, having preached before Philip

of other evil practices, must be proceeded against by our royal justices."

Why, then, did the Inquisitors burn witches? Was it because they were never instruments of the civil power?

II., exaggerated the absolute right which monarchs hold over their subjects.*

Here we conclude the exposition of the theological doctrines, as well as the appreciation of history, of philosophy, of arithmetic, and even of necromancy, to which the learned eulogist of the Inquisition has devoted himself, and it now only remains for us to answer him.

But it is not our wish, as we have before declared, that our humble echo should be heard in this arduous but antiquated controversy. No, we desire that the Inquisition itself should answer; it being at the same time both accused and accuser, denouncing itself, judging itself, and inflicting upon itself its own punishment; and after having listened patiently and given an account of the depositions for its canonization, and of the brilliant conceptions for its apotheosis, we shall see from its ashes, although for ever quenched, from its dark and gloomy dungeons yet still in existence, from the unknown graves of its martyrs, and from the tombs of its most conspicuous executioners, arise spirits of those long departed, and, in the suit we will bring against it, these themselves shall bear witness to its infernal abominations.

Our answer can not be impugned. It is a victim of the Holy Office who comes forward to take our place in this polemic, and to reply to his accusers, bringing with him and holding up in both his hands the iniquitous and barbarous sentence itself, by which the ministers of absurdity and wickedness condemned the remainder of his days to an eternal horror. And for what? for only imaginary faults of conscience, and for trifling indiscretions of speech, which a simple absolution by a priest would have been more than sufficient to have pardoned.

* As a counter-proof to this enumeration, purely *theoretical*, of the arguments in favour of the Inquisition, will be seen in the appendix, the extracts from the *Directory of Inquisitors* in which all these points are treated *practically.*

In the following history our worthy friend, the eulogist of the Inquisition, will be able to find in the life, in the tortures and melancholy end of the condemned Francisco Moyen, a fit and proper solution of all and every one of the arguments we have slightly enumerated, and likewise some of those which yet remain unanswered, and although perhaps we may have used too much brevity in their recapitulation, nevertheless it has been with an inflexible loyalty of intention, rude only in form, but always irrefragable for its good faith, which, after the natural courtesy due to all, is in our opinion the first and essential condition in every work of polemics.

FRANCISCO MOYEN.

CHAPTER I.

FRANCISCO MOYEN, the hero of this melancholy story, was born in Paris in the year 1720; most all the members of his family were artists. His father, Nicolas Moyen, and his grandfather of the same name, had been musicians belonging to the royal chapel at the French court. His mother was a lady, a native of Burgundy, of the name of Elena Adin.

Young Moyen received an education essentially Parisian, and in conformity with his extraordinary lively disposition, which was at the same time of a nature open and precocious. At 15 years of age he had learned music and the mathematics, had a knowledge of architecture, fenced well, and understood the art of painting and drawing with the pen. The combination of frivolity with the useful and brilliant, which constitutes a genuine indication of all that belongs to the grand metropolis of the Seine, appeared prominent in the education of Moyen and in his character. The son of the musician of Louis XIV. was in every sense of the word a Parisian.

When Moyen was only 16 years old, he was already a man of the world. At this age, without any more luggage than his pencils and his violin, he went to the town of Nantes (1736) with the object of going to seek his fortune at Santo Domingo, at that time a French colony.

Prevented, however, by some accident from proceeding on his voyage, the boy musician remained a year and a half in that port, giving lessons upon the violin and in drawing. The precocity of his intelligence was as much developed as his adventurous spirit.

From thence he went to the military port of L'Orient, and there he embarked in a vessel belonging to the company of that station, which was bound for the distant possession of Pondicherry, on the eastern coast of Asia. The young adventurer held on board the extraordinary appointment of master of the violin to the captain of the ship.

That voyage, like his sojourn at Nantes, lasted another year and a half, and no doubt the young adventurer must have encountered serious dangers on the passage, for it was then that he made a vow to visit the tomb of the Apostle St. James in Galicia, which promise sometime later he religiously fulfilled.

Upon his return to L'Orient he directed his steps to the town of Morlaix in Bretagne, and here, abandoning his bow for the compass, he turned engineer. During his residence of six months in this place, he made a plan of the town, and also another of the district, and for this last work he was commissioned by the town council, which had discovered his notable proficiency in that profession. At this time Moyen had not yet completed his 20th year.

Influenced, however, by the love of novelty and adventure, he shook off from his spirit the lethargy of a provincial life, and in the year 1739 directed his steps to Lisbon in search of a stage more in unison with his taste for variety. In was in this journey, that Moyen, who was at the same time as pious as he was restless, accomplished the vow which he had made to visit the sepulchre of the Apostle so beloved by Spaniards. He remained two months in Santiago in Galicia, and at length embarked at the port of Pontevedra for Lisbon.

Moyen remained for one year at that court, living quietly upon the resources of his diversified and brilliant talents. He assisted a Scotch writer, by illustrating with pictures a work that the Scotchman was engaged upon for the king, who had commissioned him for that purpose. He taught fencing to the two sons of the Conde d'Ouvidor, under whose roof he had found protection, and likewise instructed in the rudiments of music the Infante Don Manuel, who was partial to that art.

About this time, March 1742, the death of his grandfather recalled him to Paris, where he remained a year, and then returned to Lisbon, no longer as an artist but as a merchant. With the fruit of his former assiduous labours, and a sum left him by his grandfather, he purchased a stock of goods, which cost him 3000 dollars, and according to the mercantile customs of those times, he expected to quadruple its value, carrying it in person himself to the Indies.

In consequence, therefore, Moyen made the best of his way to Lisbon, and there embarked in the fleet which every year carried to Rio Janeiro the whole of the supplies for its market. One entire year was employed in that voyage; and although we do not know the amount of his profits, there is no doubt that Moyen had better fortune as a trader than as an artist. It happened then exactly as it happens now, and as will probably always happen while this world is what it is.

The position of Moyen, upon his return to Lisbon in 1745, was so much improved, that the Infante Don Manuel named him "engineer and designer of his chamber."

The death of his father was the cause of another journey to Paris, for it appears that Moyen had great sensibility of soul, the soul of an artist, and that he most tenderly loved his family. His destiny nevertheless prevented him from giving one last embrace in this life to his widowed mother; for having embarked in an English man-of-war, which, meeting with a French frigate upon the high seas, engaged and captured her, he had to return with her to the port she had left, in consequence of which he found himself once more in Lisbon.*

* There must have been some mistake made by the Secretary of the Inquisition, for why should Moyen embark in an English man-of-war to go to France if that nation was at war with England? But as it was so stated in the *autos*, the learned author of this work preferred to give it literally as it was written, however absurd, rather than make the slightest alteration.—*Note by Translator.*

Here an occasion offered to Moyen of another journey to the Indies, caused by his friendship with the Conde de las Torres, a personage of importance, and the bearer of an urgent commission either to Chile or Peru, but to which we do not know.

Along with this nobleman, although it is not known in what capacity, Moyen again embarked for Rio Janeiro on board the fleet of galleons of 1746, and immediately from thence, accompanying his patron, he started for Buenos Ayres. The Conde had to set out in great haste for Chile by way of the Pampas and the Cordilleras de los Andes, which at that time was the favourite route between Lima and Madrid, and although Moyen prepared to follow, an unfortunate circumstance occurred to prevent him.

Moyen was, as a young man, as an artist, and above all as a Parisian, one of those adventurers full of courage, generosity, and thoughtless imprudence, who would as soon strike a rival with his dagger in the saloon of a café as he would deprive himself of his cloak at the corner of a street to give it to a friend or to a beggar. The fact is that he had a warm dispute with a certain Don Miguel de Landaeta, (a person who must have been of some standing, as he held the post of chief magistrate of Oruro,) and ran him through with his sword. The marvellous skill which Moyen possessed in the art of fencing, joined to his impetuous temper, unfortunately made the young Frenchman a consummate duellist; and at that time a horrible scar which marked his visage, extending from his forehead to the chin, bore evidence that this was not the first passage of arms he had had in his life.

The magistrate of Oruro did not die, nevertheless his wound was of that serious character that his adversary had to seek an asylum in the cloisters of Santo Domingo, to escape the rigour of justice. But with all that, he was taken from the place where he had sought refuge, and kept in prison for three months, until he had proved the provocation he had received, and the surgeon had reported favourably of the health of Lendaeta.

This occurrence took place about the middle of 1748, and Moyen prepared to continue his journey and seek out his protector the Conde de las Torres. He chose for the sake of having good company the route of Potosi, and on the 21st of November of that year he mounted his mule and directed his course to Cordoba and Jujui. It is of importance to relate, that upon this occasion and before commencing his journey, the pugnacious artist retired in a most christian-like manner into the house of exercises* of San Ignacio de Loyola, and there purged himself of his sins, and of the thrust he had given to the magistrate of Oruro.

We are ignorant, however, whether Moyen performed this act of devotion voluntarily from piety, or by a mandate of the law. We comply with our conscience in declaring we believe that the latter motive was the true one, because at this time he made ostentation of being a proselyte of the philosophers, who to the terror of the Church had risen up in the metropolis on the banks of the Seine. Already, on his last journey from Lisbon to Rio Janeiro, one of the companions of his voyage, and who was to be one of his executioners in the character of an informer, accused him of having read Buelo and Bortel.† During that navigation, and in the relaxation with his comrades, the incautious youth had expressed himself with entire freedom (for according to the last sentence of his judges he was "very loquacious and daring,") against the luxury of the Popes, and against their desire for making wars; adding that as they canonized men for money, (what if he had known the

* Irreverently styled by the heretics in South America, "The Whipping Shop."—*Note by Translator.*

† Inquisitorial orthography for Boileau and Voltaire.

history of Verdesi,)* so they also for money sold indulgences to commit sin. How very far was the unfortunate Frenchman from ever imagining that those words, which the sea breeze carried away through the air, would come back again and cause to grate behind his steps with jarring sound the iron bolts of the dungeon of the Inquisition at Potosi. His confidant on board the ship of the Conde de las Torres, was called Don Bernardo de Rosas, and must have been an ecclesiastic, because when he became informer at Potosi he supported his denunciation by many theological quotations, although we do not understand what connection they could have with the temporal power of the Popes. With respect to the politico-theological doctrine of Moyen, the only thing that we could be sure of is, that he would not have enlisted himself among the Pontifical Zouaves to fight against the cross of Sardinia.

Meanwhile we will follow Moyen in his itinerary from Buenos Ayres to Potosi.

The companions of his journey consisted of creoles and Spaniards from Upper Peru, who had been to make their purchases on the coast, and were now returning with their effects, which were transported upon the backs of mules; all of these persons were young, merry and of good temper, but pious and devout to an extreme. The principal one among them was a native of Burgos, called Don Diego de Alvarado, who was going to take his seat as magistrate in the town hall at Porco, to which he had been appointed.

* The 'servant of God.' Verdesi was a Spaniard belonging to the laity, who a hundred years ago was famous in Santiago as being a saint. It is asserted that upon various occasions considerable sums of money were forwarded to Rome for the purpose of having him canonized, but as the money never arrived there, they did not succeed in making a saint of him. The last that was heard of this attempt at canonization was in 1862, when a great search was made for him during several days in the church of San Francisco, in the presence of the archbishop, but without success, as they were unable to find his coffin, nor even any indication of his body.—*Note by Translator.*

In the journey to Jujui nothing remarkable occurred. On the 18th of December the party passed by Cordoba; and in the first days of February arrived at Jujui. The loquaciousness of Moyen, his violin and his animated and cheerful character made him the favourite of the company. As for his heresies against the Popes, the good folks of the road did not hear or else did not listen to them. Only the muleteers were accustomed to say whenever he passed before their mules, "there goes a Jew." The truth is, that at that time in America there were only known three classes of men: the Chapetones, which were the inhabitants of the Peninsula, or natives of Spain; the Creoles, those born in America; and Jews: to the last category belonged all foreigners, and especially the Portuguese, because it is well known, that at the expulsion of the Jews from Spain, the greater part of them took refuge at the more tolerant court of Lisbon.

In Jujui the number of these lighthearted traders was increased by the addition to their party of one of the same kind of business, but with a disposition false, obstinate and hypocritical, who, like Rosas, but beyond him and still more persevering, made himself the instrument of the ruin of the incautious and talkative Moyen. His name was José Antonio Soto, a native of Galicia in Spain; he was born in the town of Redondela, and had arrived very young in that part of the new continent, where he styled himself "merchant of Potosi, Chile and Buenos Ayres."

One day (the 10th or 11th of March, 1749,) Soto was dining with the companions of Moyen at the table of a merchant of Jujui, called Juan Tomas Perez, when they commenced a conversation very common at that time and since among Spaniards, about the sixth* commandment of

---

* The seventh of the English Church Catechism. As the Roman Catholic Church entirely ignores the second commandment of the decalogue, there would have remained only nine, but as it was necessary to complete the number, the ingenious expedient was re-

CHAPTER I.

the law of God, and between the laughing and drinking it happened that one of them made the remark that Moyen was a heretic, because he did not attribute very great importance to that prohibition. In this point the theory of the young violinist inclined more to the evangelical precept than to that of the decalogue, for he declared that between the *cresciti et multiplicamini* and the sixth commandment, the word of God was more to his liking than that of Moses.

At hearing such an irreverent remark, the gloomy Galician of Redondela arose from the table and withdrew for the purpose of interrogating the muleteers from Buenos Ayres, concerning what they had heard said by the French Jew during their journey, these assured him that Moyen was a consummate heretic, and this was asserted more particularly by a servant of Don Rodrigo Palacio, a member of the company.

From that moment Soto swore in his heart to accomplish the ruin of the Frenchman, and he resolved to watch him and observe all his expressions, while on the road which he was about to take to Potosi, he having joined himself at Jujui to the party which had arrived from the Plata.

On the 26th of February they started on the road, in the direction of Potosi, and with them Moyen, who was always the same, lighthearted, thoughtless and giddy, and of course always a heretic. It was not long before Soto, the officious familiar of the Holy Office, found an occasion of confirming his preconceived suspicions, and to commit to his memory fresh data for his intended denunciation.

During the first day's journey they entered the semi-tropical region of those parts and encamped for the night. While the travellers were resting in their tents a violent

---

sorted to of extracting a portion from the *middle* of the tenth, and calling the part so taken the ninth, and thus the Roman Catholics have *two* commandments against the sin of covetousness.—*Note by Translator.*

storm arose, accompanied by thunder and lightning, which occasioned a dispute, half theological and half physical, about the cause of such a phenomenon. This took place in the tent of the well-intentioned magistrate of Porco, Don Diego de Alvarado, where were assembled together Moyen, the spy from Redondela, a deacon, native of Salta, known by the name of Don Diego Antonio Martinez de Iriarte, who no doubt was going to Charcas for the purpose of being admitted into Holy Orders, and some others, with the servants of the first-mentioned. Their opinions were divided. The deacon declared that it was only necessary to repeat the *Quicunque* to dispel the storm. Soto had no faith except in exorcisms and in the *trisajio*; but Alvarado, who was a humourist, addressing himself to Moyen, said, " And you, *Mossiu*, do you not say that in a storm you always drink a bottle of wine and play on your fiddle?" to which he to whom the question was put laughingly answered, " Yes ;" and no sooner said than done, for while Soto retired with his muleteers to repeat the *rosary*, Moyen began to appease the fury of the elements with the harmony produced from his violin.

The sight of this gave rise to a more grave discussion among those theologians of the desert, whose profession it was to follow the tracks of their mules laden with cotton and other effects, the productions of heretical nations.

Moyen at length affirmed that no one ought to fear God in the sense that this word (*craindre*) has in French, in which idiom it implies the idea of terror, or the imminent and active fear which is felt by the mind. Such an opinion put the Galician from Redondela beside himself, and he commenced to cite texts to the heretic, concluding with the one which God said to Santa Teresa, *Teme mi ira!*—on which the Frenchman exclaimed, *stuff and nonsense.*

This last audacious act exhausted the patience of the Galician, and in the fury of his anger he declared to Moyen that he would accuse him to the Inquisition, at the same time begging of Alvarado not to continue his jokes, as they would corrupt the servants. "Ah, sirs," said Moyen to them at the end of the discussion (which occurred at a place called the Volcano, about ten leagues from Jujui), "if you had read the works written in French which I have, you would soon undeceive yourselves." To this they made the observation, that such books could not circulate, because they were prohibited by the Inquisition. On this Moyen settled the question by a tremendous philippic against the Inquisition of Lisbon, whose horrors no doubt he had had occasion to know something of. But very far was he from thinking that these and other propositions or heresies, were going to cost him a life-long punishment, decreed by that same abominable tribunal.

A few days journey more in advance, the heresies of Moyen concerning *the anger of God* acquired greater gravity by the suspiciousness and felony of his concealed informer. Having arrived at Santiago de Cotagaita, Soto invited Moyen to make a visit to the curate, Don Juan Antonio Leon, and meeting there the Franciscan father, Juan de Mata, he being advised beforehand, they commenced both of them, assisted by the theologian of Redondela, to argue upon that thesis, which, if for the ecclesiastics it was one of pure dogma, for Moyen it was only one of grammar, or more properly speaking one of a dictionary, for the signification he attributed to it.

Be it how it may, the candid Frenchman stated his opinion with his accustomed openness of manner, and when the two priests had formed their opinion, Soto requested Moyen to go and bring his portfolio of drawings to show to the curate: his object by this manœuvre was only for the purpose of consulting the curate and friar alone, and obtaining their opinion of the nature of the heresy of the foreigner. Both of them being of accord, informed him " that they considered Moyen to be a sectarian; he did not remember (says Soto in one of his denouncements) whether it was *Calvinist*, or *Lutheran*, or other *heresiarch.*" The Franciscan moreover at last recommended, that in the moment of his arrival at Potosi he should denounce him as *heresiarch* to the Commissary of the Inquisition; and promised him that he also would do the same in the next visit he intended to make to that city.

Thus assured by the opinion of the curate of Cotagaita that he was in the company of a *Jew*, the informer of Redondela noted down day by day his words as so many other heresies. One night, when the travellers were encamped in the open air contemplating the immensity of the stars, Moyen said, for example, that in his opinion those worlds were superfluous. From this expression was formed a formal heresy, which figures in the first line in the act of accusation of the Holy Office.

At another time, passing before a stone cross that was standing in the road, it occurred to Moyen to say that the only cross worthy of the adoration of Christians was that which had served for the crucifixion of Jesus Christ, as the others were but symbols of it. Another accusation, another heresy, and another *proposition* of the 47, which at last his denouncers, his judges, his fiscals, and his executioners, framed against him.

Again, one day the Frenchman, in his ostentation of theology and grammar, said that in the *Ave Maria* it ought to be said, " the Lord was with thee," and not " the Lord is with thee." This, which was no more than a simple question of speech, was afterwards *qualified* as an atrocious heresy, and offensive to the most Holy Virgin.

Upon another occasion, speaking of the Gentiles (most likely meaning the idolatrous Indians of America), Moyen, who knew by heart the following verse of Voltaire—

> " Vous qui Dieu fit naître aux portes du soleil
> Vous serez donc aux flammes condannés
> Pour n'avoir sû qu'autre fois
> *Le fils d'un charpentier expirâ sur un bois ?*"

exclaimed, " 'Tis a hard case that so many millions of men should be condemned for not knowing that the son of a carpenter had died for them."* And from this another heresy!

But Moyen for his misfortune had not only read Voltaire, he also knew some of the admirable satires of Boileau against the unbridled luxury of the clergy of his time, and when he reproached the deacon of Salta, for the richness of his saddle embossed with silver, which the owner seemed to display out of vanity, he would repeat with or without maliciousness,

> " On ne vois aujourd'hui que de gens de mitre et de crosses
> Rouler des superbes carosses
> Quand autre fois l'Eternel
> Ne montá qu'une annesse dans un jour solennel."†

But the continued and implacable espionage of the volunteer of the Inquisition did not stop here. One dark night a muleteer, with great brutality was illtreating a mule which had fallen on the road, oppressed perhaps by the weight of his burden, and Moyen who undoubtedly had a well-disposed and kind heart, reproached the fellow for his cruelty, and asked him how he could dare to illtreat in that manner one of *God's creatures?* Here was blasphemy, heresy, *a proposition;* it was this that finally clinched the proofs against Moyen, accused for the expression of *Pythagoricism* and other absurdities impossible to believe, but which we shall see in its place.

At length, after having collected this series of heretical *propositions,* besides many others to the number of 44, the caravan arrived at Potosi, on 27th of March, 1749, having

---

* This verse of Voltaire, as we have transcribed it, was cited by Moyen in his defence, and it may be seen in speaking of the son of the carpenter, he only used the same as the poet, a figure of rhetoric, so much in use at the present day, that the pupils of the seminary of Jesuits employ it without scruple.

† A verse also cited by Moyen in his defence.

taken those who came from Buenos Ayres more than four months to make the journey.

The unfortunate Moyen, upon his arrival at the imperial city of Potosi, no doubt figured to himself that a new life, full of pleasures and enjoyments, would commence for him after the fatigues of his long journey. Meanwhile his malignant persecutor had scarcely left his mules in the yard, and placed his bales of goods upon the shelves in his shop, when he made haste to the house of the commissary of the Inquisition, who was provisionally at that time the curate of the principal church of Potosi, Doctor Don José de Lizarazu, Beaumont y Navarra, &c. &c., and presented in writing his first iniquitous denouncement. This took place on the night of the 29th of March, 1749, only two days after the arrival of the caravan at Potosi from Buenos Ayres, which was on the 27th of March, as we have already said.

Here begins the atrocious drama of the persecution and martyrdom of Moyen. But for the purpose of understanding in their true light the proceedings of the Inquisition, and to be able to apply to all and to each one the measure of the eulogy of the Prebend Señor Saavedra, it becomes indispensable to interrupt, by a short digression, the thread of the personal narrative, so as to explain and make understood what was the state of the Inquisition at that time in America.

CHAPTER II.

At the time in which the Inquisition opened its doors to Francisco Moyen, in the May of 1749, it had already arrived at the first stage of its decay.

The times had long passed in which Philip II. celebrated in Toledo his marriage with Isabel de Valois (1560); the nuptial torch being the flames of the *burning pile*, and those no less ominous in which one of his grandsons, Philip IV., in 1632, made a present to his bride Isabel de Bourbon of 118 condemned persons, of which 19 were burnt alive in their presence and in that of the whole of their court.

The house of Bourbon, drowsy and indolent, brought with them to the throne, if not clemency, at least the sloth of cruelty, and the burning piles of the Austrian Kings eternally in a blaze, at last began to fade and die out of themselves. The son of Charles V. had burnt for hate for conscience and for covetousness, because his heart itself was a firebrand steeped in the mire of his filthy and shameless passions; but if the grandson of Louis XIV., founder of a new dynasty, had burnt in his turn during his reign of 46 years, more than 1500 heretics, he had done so, notwithstanding to him the Inquisition was odious, as we are assured by the most serious of Spanish historians,* because it was necessary to the plans of his policy, which was directed to consolidate and make sure the throne lately presented to him. Although a Parisian, the Bourbon knew that the Spaniards enjoyed in an equal degree the bull fights and the *autos de fé*, and for

* Lafuente, History of Spain, vol. 21, page 200.

that reason during his reign he caused to be celebrated no less than 782 of the latter.*

But under the mild dominion of his successor, the gloomy Ferdinand VI., in whose reign, 1746-59, occurred the circumstances of the history which we are relating, the cruelty of despotism, disguised by the imposture of its love to God, had commenced to lose along with the royal support, its tremendous popular prestige. During the 13 years in which that Prince dragged on his languid life of fear, love and music, there were only 34 *autos de fé*, and scarcely 10 heretics were burnt alive.

An equal falling off had been observed in the registers of the grand inquisitors. Andres de Orbe, archbishop of Valencia, had condemned during a period of seven years (1733-40) 1785 heretics; Manrique de Lara, archbishop of Santiago, in three years (1742-45) condemned 1020. But Francisco Perez de Prado, bishop of Teruel, who began his authority and concluded it along with Ferdinand VI. (1746-59), and under whose supreme jurisdiction fell the unfortunate Moyen, only exhibited at his *autos de fé* 120 condemned persons, of which not more than 10 were burnt alive, and five in effigy, less than one a year.

A long time had elapsed, as we have already said, since the days in which one Inquisitor alone (Tomas de Torquemada), had burnt alive at the stake 8,800 heretics, during the 18 years of his supremacy, while the number burnt in effigy amounted to 1,500, besides 90,000 condemned to other punishments, making a sum total of above 100,000 victims of

---

* The number of persons condemned in the reign of Philip V., according to Torres de Castilla, in his 'History of Political and Religious Persecutions,' (vol. 6, page 733), amounted to 14,076, viz.—

Burnt alive	1,564
Do. in effigy	782
Condemned to different punishments	11,730
	14076

that horrible monster, who only by uttering the greatest blasphemy against God, could be called a minister of his worship. *

* Señor Saavedra, in this part of his treatise, when he refers to statistical calculations, resolutely charges Llorente with falsehood, and gives us an inductive statistic of his own invention, very ingenious no doubt, but of which we cannot make ourselves master, owing perhaps to our stupidity in the science of numbers. But as Llorente was secretary of the Inquisition, and for many years had had at his disposal the archives of the *Supreme*, the name of the superior court of inquisitors, and in which presided the Grand Inquisitor, it appears to us only natural to suppose that his calculations are more worthy of credit than the capricious numerical lucubrations of the Chilian Prebendary.

According to the computations of Llorente, the number of victims of the Spanish Inquisition during the 327 years of its power (1481-1808) amounted to 341,021, in the manner following:—

Burnt alive	31,912
Do. in effigy	17,659
Condemned to severe punishments	291,450
Total	341,021

Torres de Castilla in his history (vol. 6, page 758) increases this amount to 356,659, giving the number of victims under each grand Inquisitor, his proportion is as follows:—

Burnt alive	34,659
Do. in effigy	17,552
Other punishments	304,448
Total	356,659

According to the same author reckoning the family of each victim to be composed of only five individuals, to whom is attached the dishonour and misery caused by the punishment of fire and confiscation, the number of direct victims of the Inquisition in Spain, not taking into account those burned in America, Portugal, and other countries, will amount to 1,705,105. The French historian of the Inquisition, Leonardo Gallois, quoted by his son Napoleon Gallois, makes the number of victims of the Spanish Inquisition, including the Moors and Jews who were banished, amount to 5,000,000 of persons.

On the other hand the Inquisition of Lima, upon which depended in a direct manner the process of Moyen, was compromised at that time in a law-suit regarding it administration, in which its ministers mutually accused each other of being thieves (which in truth they were); while the illustrious Conde de Superunda, notwithstanding the benignity of his character, united to a refined rectitude of conduct, controlled their insolence, and restrained their misbehaviour towards civil society and the throne, as we shall see in its place.

Consequently the misfortune of Moyen could not arrive to such an extreme as to bring him to the stake, for that was almost entirely abolished, and it was precisely at that time in which in all parts, and more especially in France, heresy was raising its head and making rapid progress, all which go to prove the efficiency to which the institution had arrived, so much proclaimed as *useful, just, rational and holy*, by a Prebendary of Chile, where, thanks to our ancestors, it never was established.

We will now return to the interrupted narration of the process of the heresiarch of Potosi.

CHAPTER III.

As all that was not horrible connected with the Holy Office was infamous, beginning by a denunciation and concluding with the stake :—a man who by that act alone renders himself vile, joins himself to another clothed in mysteries, and there and then, between the two alone, in secret mutually swearing the most inviolable reserve, and without responsibility, without remorse, in an anonymous and cowardly manner, plotting the ruin of a third, of a family, or the whole of a race, and with that perversity, that greedy dissimulation, that horrible impunity which so much scandalized the upright soul of Pascal and his friends.* How many secret and terrible acts of vengeance, how many assassinations in which the torch superseded the use of the knife? How many years of gloomy captivity of a husband, of a father, or of a rival owner of coveted beauty? How many fortunes ruthlessly snatched from orphans? How many dark intrigues fomented in the interior of the domestic circle, by that silent and supernatural power, that subterraneous monster, called the Holy Office, against whose mandate neither fathers, nor sons, nor friends, nor even God himself could afford protection! Kings sold *lettres de cachet,* to shut up in their dungeons those against whom any one desired to take vengeance. The Inquisition proceeded in a different manner, and offered a greater guarantee of security to speculators and to the malevolent, for it gave its orders for imprisonment gratuit-

* See a letter from an advocate of the Parliament about the bull *Unigenitus,* (1657). The complete works of Blas Pascal, (1860) vol. 1, page 224. " Do you not find," exclaimed the advocate Lemaistre, " that the Inquisition is the most convenient and sure method to ruin your enemies, however innocent they may be?"

ously, and which orders no one dared to disobey, and as it compelled its victims themselves to pay for their own persecution, the result was that while it quickly enriched itself, it benefited at the same time its agents and its informers.*

We have already said that the offended Galician of Redondela had made his first denouncement to the Commissary of Potosi on the night of the 29th of March, 1749, and from this time he had returned at short intervals to the house of the Commissary to hasten the secret preparatory proceeding, the substance of which was that contained in the charges of heresy which we have already noted, for the revelations of Soto have been our principal guide in this part of the voluminous process.

Jointly with Soto began also to give their depositions, but always with the most profound secrecy, all the witnesses whom he pointed out. One of the latest, perhaps from compassion or from nobleness of soul, was the magistrate of Porco, Don Diego de Alvarado, the jocose comrade of Moyen

* As generally those accused by the Inquisition were men of wealth, as we shall show by and by, it resulted that they had many debtors, and hence it was, that the most expeditious method, and one that cost less to cancel the debt, was to make a denunciation of heresy against the creditor. This system was more sure and efficacious than any judicial or mercantile litigation, because as the eloquent French writer, Coquerel says, "The Inquisition, the same as all other absolute powers, believed itself, or at least declared itself to be infallible; every accused person was presumed to be guilty, until he could prove the contrary; yet nevertheless the proof was impossible, because he was prevented from holding communication with any one, nor could he cite any witness in his favour, and as to assist a heretic was itself considered to be heresy, nobody was willing voluntarily to put himself into the hands of the terrible Holy Office."

It is this last circumstance which has given origin to the well known anecdote, that Philip III. (who was no other than a crowned Torquemada) having once had pity on certain condemned, who were going to be burnt in his presence, the Inquisitors to punish his heresy, not being able to burn him, compelled him to allow himself to be bled, and then threw his blood into the burning pile.

since his departure from Buenos Ayres, and who only for innocent amusement " put out his tongue," (the expression used by the accused himself in his process,) but at that time he was very far from thinking that his jokes would help to shut up the Frenchman in an eternal dungeon.

It was not before Soto had made his denunciation one month, that Alvarado came forward (the 1st of May) to make his. A week afterwards (the 8th of May) was given in the part which corresponded to the theologian Don Bernardo de Rosas, of whom we have said that he was the companion of Moyen in his last voyage from Lisbon to Rio Janeiro.

And this was the organization proclaimed to be worthy of all admiration, of the circumspect and Holy Tribunal, which, under the pretext of safely guarding the Christian faith, imposed severe and harsh penalties to the extent of converting the scaffold itself into the means of absolution. It did not use notwithstanding, according to the Prebendary of Santiago, " that secret police which watched as a spy upon all the steps of the citizen, which maintained its agents in all parts, and which introduced them even into the domestic circle."*

* Saavedra, "Rapid Sketch," page 53.—We may see, with respect to this among others, how a great historian expressed himself, and although not a Catholic, he has not the less demonstrated, along with the celebrated Prescott, that the Inquisition, so much beloved by the people according to the author of the " Sketch," was the effectual and principal cause of the rising in the Low Countries, of their religious apostacy, and change of government, when Philip II. and his worthy myrmidon, the Duke of Alva, endeavoured to establish it in those possessions.

"In the course of time," says Motley (recently minister from the United States to the Court of Vienna,) " the jurisdiction of the Office was extended. It taught the savages of India and America to shudder at the name of Christianity. The fear of its introduction froze the earlier heretics of Italy, France and Germany, into orthodoxy. It was a court owning allegiance to no temporal authority, superior to all other tribunals; it was a bench of monks without appeal, having

Denunciations poured in abundantly from all who had seen the heretic pass by their door, from all who had ever

> its familiars in every house, diving into the secrets of every fireside, judging and executing its horrible decrees without responsibility. It condemned not deeds but thoughts. It affected to descend into individual conscience and to punish the crimes which it pretended to discover. Its process was reduced to a horrible simplicity. It arrested on suspicion, tortured till confession, and then punished by fire." (The Rise of the Dutch Republic, by John L. Motley, vol. 1, page 333.)

But if this testimony should not be received (being from the pen of a heretic) by Señor Saavedra, let him listen to one irreproachable, conscientious and orthodox, one no less than the President of the last Peruvian congress, Don Francisco Garcia Calderon, the same who from his seat demanded the resignation of General Prado, in the name of the flag of Arequipa, which was the *labarum* of religion for his countrymen—" The absolute independence of the Inquisition (says, with respect to the same purpose, the learned writer of Arequipa in his 'Dictionary of Peruvian Legislation') the irresponsibility of its members, the mystery which enveloped all its proceedings, the impossibility of the accused to defend themselves, the obligation of all its functionaries to obey without a murmur the orders of the Holy Office, to respect and sanction with their presence the *autos de fé*, the mysterious aspect and gloominess of the locality in which the Inquisition exercised its functions, the torture it applied to its prisoners, the absolute uncertainty of the accused with regard to their future fate, and the importance attached to the determination of the Inquisitors, being also accompanied by the ceremonies of religion, greatly influenced the minds of the crowd and filled with fear the imagination of all the inhabitants. The Inquisition was a horrid phantom that was felt in all parts, and caused to shudder with affright even those who had given the best proofs of their faith.

" For all these reasons the Inquisition was a despotic tribunal, which gave unjust sentences in many cases, because the torture often forced from most individuals a *false confession* of the heresy of which they were accused, and the tribunal from this alone *condemned them to death*. The truth never could be made manifest, because the accused were ignorant of the names of their accusers, and also of the testimony deposed against them, and in consequence not being able to exonerate themselves, although their innocence was most positive, their condemnation was certain. And again, the Inquisition served as an instru-

heard any thing spoken about the Jew. In this is seen one of the most odious characteristics of the Inquisition: the contagion of terror. As in the time of an epidemic, every one fancies that he feels the fatal symptoms (a comparison we take from the incomparable 'Sketch,') so the dread of complicity with the accused by the Holy Office communicates itself to the hearts of all who had at any time ever addressed him, of all who had even ever heard the name of the victim. For this reason, and as Moyen had but recently arrived, the greater part of the declarations were only hearsay, yet however that did not prevent the witnesses ratifying their depositions upon oath *ad perpetuum*, and to so great an extent was the servility and treachery of many, that in a few days the verbal process enlarged itself, until it formed a file of papers containing 200 pages in folio!

In this state it was referred to the two counsellors of the

ment of private vengeance, for truly nothing was more easy than to free oneself from an enemy by denouncing him as a heretic to the Holy Office, which immediately made itself master of his person, and thanks to the system of torture and other measures observed in its processes, the *denounced appeared guilty*. Who could consider himself safe in a country in which the laws sanctioned such vicious proceedings?"

Here then, without going out of our way, and keeping our promise not to accumulate quotations from vain ostentation of learning, we present to Señor Saavedra witnesses whom we do not know how he can reject. For the present we have Motley against Van der Haeghen and Garcia Calderon for Hefelé, Rivaud, Hunter, Margotti, Cobbett, Macker, Morerti, Feller, Berault, Beriaste, Balmes, César Cantú, &c. &c. It is a pity nevertheless that among so many and learned citations from writers which the erudite author of the "Sketch" has given us, he had not remembered the remarkable Sprenger, the profound Castro, the prudent Simancas, the wise Martin del Rio, the learned Paramo, the industrious Torreblanca, the eloquent Carena, and the erudite Piñateli; all these authors have written about the sins of the Inquisition, and Doctor Bermudez quotes them with their corresponding qualifications in his "Triumphs of the Holy Office of Peru," (page 133,) a work that the Prebendary Saavedra has read as well as ourselves.

Commissary of the Holy Office, whose names we omitted to copy in our notations, but it is enough to know that they were ecclesiastics. Both of them were agreed that it was necessary to proceed immediately to apprehend the accused, but disagreed in this—one desired that the warrant should be made out in Spanish, while the other considered that it ought to be done in the language of the holy fathers.

It also required, according to the Constitutions of the Inquisition, the previous opinion of the Archbishop of La Plata, but the impatience of the Holy Office of Potosi would not allow of that delay; and although it is true that the prelate's opinion was also for the imprisonment of the accused, and that he gave his assent in Chuquisaca to that effect, still it was not until Moyen had been already a week in irons in Potosi.*

It was on the 14th of May, 1749, and when the unfortunate Moyen had completed two months of his residence in Potosi, that in consequence of what we have already related, the Commissary Lizarazu, Beaumont y Navarra, issued his warrant or definitive act of imprisonment, and which for its imperative peculiarities of form we insert verbatim.

It is expressed as follows in its textual orthography, the same we shall preserve in all the documents of Moyen's process, which we have to produce for the purpose of collating them.†

---

* Speaking of the proceedings in the act of denunciation, Napoleon Gallois, the writer already alluded to, says, "All were submitted to its terrible jurisdiction, those absent as well as those present, living and dead, sovereign and subject, rich and poor. Numerous likewise were the categories of those considered as suspected of holding opinions against the faith. It was sufficient on the slightest denouncement to drag them before the Holy Tribunal, and from the moment that the first preparatory process declared their culpability, or even the suspicion of such, the warrant for their apprehension was issued. And from which time there was no privilege or asylum for the accused, whatever might be his rank or condition."

† It being impossible to reproduce in a translation the antiquated

"We, Doctor Joseph de Lizarazu, Beaumont y Navarra, Senior Rector of the Holy Metropolitan Church of this city, and Commissary of it and the jurisdiction of its district, in the absence for cause of sickness of the proprietor. For the very Illustrious Señores Apostolical Inquisitors who reside in the city of the kings of Peru; we command you Don Bernardo Barragan, Alguazil of this Holy Office, that immediately this mandate is delivered to you, to go to the house of the Colonel Don Antonio Rodrigues de Guzman, or to others in whatever places, that is, or may appear to be necessary within or without this city, and take into custody the body of Don Francisco Moyen, native of Paris of France, and residing in this city, wherever he may be found, although it may be in a church or other sacred place, fortified or privileged, and as a prisoner and well secured, take him to the public prison of this said city, and deliver him to the chief Alcalde Alguazil, whom we command to receive him from you in the presence of the Notary of this Holy Office, and keep him confined and well secured, and not to let him go free, not even with a bond of security, without our licence and mandate. And you will cause that the said Don Francisco Moyen leaves his goods with the care necessary for their safety and guard, given them in charge to the person whom he may choose, and by an inventory before the Notary of this Holy Office, that from them he may be maintained. And for the better execution and compliance with the contents of this our mandate, should you require favour or help, we exhort and request, and if necessary in virtue of holy obedience, and under the penalty of excommunication major, *late sententie, trina canonica monitioni*, and one thousand dollars *essayed*, for the extraordinary expenses of this Holy

orthography of the original, with its quaint phrases and numerous abbreviations, I have therefore in the above, and all other documents, of which copies have been given by the author, endeavoured to render their meaning in English as literal as the subject would permit.—*Note by Translator.*

Office, we command all and whatever judges and justices, whether ecclesiastical or secular of this city, or of any other places of the kingdoms or dominions of his Majesty, that being by you required, they give and cause to be given to you all the favour and help that you demand. Should you have need of men for a guard, or beasts to carry the aforesaid, and his bed and clothes with the fetters or chains, and maintenance of which you may require at the current prices of their value without making them dearer. Given in the Imperial City of Potosi, the fourteenth of the month of May, of the year one thousand seven hundred forty and nine.

"Joseph de Lizarazu Beaumont y Navarra,
by command of the Holy Office.

"Manuel Antonio Galvete y Varela,
Familiar and Notary of the Holy Office."

CHAPTER IV.

MEANWHILE, and during the time that the Alguazil of the Holy Office was in search of Moyen, carrying along with him the terrible mandate hidden beneath the folds of his cloak, the unwary stranger was merrily passing his time among his drawings and his duels, his theological studies and his love affairs.*

The restless and laborious Frenchman had been hospitably received in the imperial city, in virtue most likely of his connexion with the Conde de las Torres, of whom he was in pursuit, under the honorable roof of the Colonel Don Antonio Rodriguez de Guzman, according as reads the order for his imprisonment which we have just given, and there, with the exception of his moments of diversion and intrigues, that man of an active and fruitful genius lived, occupied with his studies of a nature as serious as diversified.

In that which Moyen showed himself truly to be a genuine Frenchman and essentially a Parisian, was in the multiplicity of his talents, in his readiness to attempt all kind of studies, and in his admirable intelligence in mastering them. The reader may have already seen that all his heretical *propositions* (articles) were based upon a stock of not to be despised theological knowledge, of philosophy, of history, and even of physics and poetry; and of this, as we shall see by and by,

---

* In this last part it must be confessed that Moyen showed himself consistent in his theories of the sixth (seventh) Commandment, as we have already mentioned, and not without a coarseness of manner meriting censure, for he had formed a connection with a common woman called *La Pilatos*, in whose house he had had a quarrel, which terminated in a challenge, although we do not know if it was carried into effect, as the process only gives the name of his adversary, who was called Salcedo.

he gave proofs truly singular. Besides his familiarity with the arts, "and his distinguished dexterity in painting," as witnessed by the Commissary in the process, he took a pleasure in the study of medicine, of the mathematics, and in the questions which the philosophy of the age (a science which, to his misfortune, caused his ruin) had brought so much in fashion.* He also occupied himself in making a plan of the city, and taking views of the principal places, for which, besides being a heretic, they also accused him of being a traitor to the Crown, "as if Potosi had been a fortified place," said Moyen himself in his defence, "or if the King of France had been at war with his cousin the King of Spain."

Moyen, although violent and fiery—we do not say brave, because we have already said that he was a Frenchman—opposed no resistance to the warrant of the Inquisition, but allowed himself to be conducted to a dungeon, which was not an especial one belonging to the Holy Office, for not

* Among the effects which the Alguazil of the Inquisition confiscated at the time he was taken, was found a treatise on medicine, and apparently written by his own hand, another upon military fortification, and also a suspicious volume which had the following title— *Histoire des revolutions arrivées en Europe en matiere de religion, Paris*, 1687.

We ought to add in consideration of the asceticism of the heretic Moyen, that there was found likewise amongst his effects a volume of sermons by Bourdaloue, the great Catholic preacher of that period, and moreover the judicial investigations certify that the *heresiarch* of Jujui, during his residence at Potosi, had given four dollars to have masses said, applying a portion of his small gains to the maintenance of that worship whose ministers were about to condemn him.

They likewise confiscated from Moyen a treatise on international law, by Puffendorf, "and a trunk of drawings (as he himself said in reclaiming them afterwards in Lima), which I value more than all the silver of Potosi." Poor artist, they wished some time later to take away his violin, the only solace of his misery, but rather than submit to that deprivation, he made an attempt upon his life, as we shall relate further on.

having one in that part, we are inclined to believe that it was situated within the walls of the public prison, according as may be seen in the order for imprisonment.

During the first few days he was kept in the strictest confinement, for the purpose of preventing the contagion of his heresy, the Commissary of the Holy Tribunal issued four successive *autos*, prohibiting all access to his person, under a penalty of excommunication *ipso facto* and a fine of one thousand dollars. Both these comminations were nevertheless unnecessary. A *heretic* in those times was worse than a man stricken with leprosy, for every one, seized with terror, fled from his presence.

But when the process was sufficiently advanced (without Moyen having had any notice of it, or even suspecting its existence), he was permitted to communicate with a few persons, but they only visited him for the purpose of treachery and to add to the number of denouncements against him.

One of the most persevering of these miserable wretches was the son of an apothecary of the town, who delighted to visit and enter into arguments about the everlasting subject of the sixth (seventh) commandment and other propositions of the heretic, which was the great novelty of the day. One time Moyen, being tired with the impertinence of the troublesome fellow, asked him, what he understood by *heretics?* The intrusive apothecary's apprentice answered, as many others would have done at the present day, " that heretics were the English because they did not believe in the Gospel, and also that Frenchmen were not Christians, because they did not recite the prayer of the *rosary* which the Virgin had given to Santo Domingo."

Another of the arguments of Moyen with the apothecary's son, was concerning the bull of the crusade. Moyen having asked the young man if it was a sin to eat meat on the days of its prohibition, and at the same time whether the bull to eat it without committing sin could be bought for money. And as the blockhead in both cases answered in the affirmative, he shut him up with this syllogism without an escape, viz., that if eating meat offends God, and a man may buy a licence to eat meat, ergo, it is buying a licence to offend God!

An end, however, was put to the polemic in a manner rather less courteously than theologically; for one day Moyen being ill, and consequently in a bad humour, drove the logician from his presence, telling him at the same time it would not be well for him if ever he made his appearance there again.*

Another of the importunate and perfidious visitors to the dungeon of Potosi, was a Franciscan monk, syndic of his convent, who also found it a pleasure to go and provoke the ever unguarded tongue of the thoughtless Parisian; at times about the commandment with which, after the vows he had taken, he ought to have had the least to do, and at times to dispute concerning the real or substantial presence in the eucharist. One day this monk met with Alvarado in Moyen's cell, and " there, as the accused at a later period himself related before the Inquisitors of Lima, remained for the space of an hour or an hour and half, playing on the violin and drinking brandy with the persons present, he Moyen having his brain heated, although not entirely deprived of his senses."

This incident, although coarse and vulgar in itself, yet nevertheless is of serious importance in this process, and for that reason we have taken notice of it; for it appears that the monk wrote a pamphlet with the object of refuting the theories advanced by Moyen concerning the eucharist, and sent his manuscript to Madrid, and it was only some years later when they returned printed, and while Moyen was confined in the prison of the Inquisition at Lima, that he came to have the first suspicion that his conversations with that

---

* Moyen, to excuse himself for his incivility on this occasion, afterwards declared before the Inquisitors at Lima that he was sick at the time; the truth is, that the unfortunate Frenchman had a temper too hasty and irritable, not but what he had motives more than sufficient to render it so.

monk might be part of, if not the principal cause of his sufferings.

And such nevertheless was the truth, so horrible was that secret of bronze with which the *mild* Inquisition, " that surrounded itself with precautions to guarantee the innocency of the accused," guarded within its dungeons of granite and iron the body and soul of its victims. ." They slander me also even in Spain," said in effect the unhappy and astonished Moyen in one of his writings for his defence, some years afterwards, and alluding to the publication of the Franciscan monk, which by some chance had fallen into his hands, "a priest slanders me and without any foundation, except a trivial story told him by an ignorant layman ; * and without waiting for the decision of the illustrious Señors Inquisitors, he has hastened to publish and hold me up to the world as a heretic, as a despicable man, and comparing me to that miserable Atahualpa† and to others of the same kind, and not satisfied with that, he has also represented me as a traitor to the Crown, in consequence of that map of the hill I made,‡ as though Potosi were a fortified town, and that the cousins were at war one with another. And thus, Señor Doctor, if a charitable priest and missionary, without knowing me, treats me in this manner, only because he is a Galician and I a Frenchman, what hope have I to expect from my destiny in this life ?"

For the same purpose of removing from himself the responsibility which the denouncements of the Friar Syndic would bring upon him, are directed the revelations which Moyen made to his judges of the state of his heated brain, while draining their glasses he disputed with his hypocritical delator concerning the august sacraments. All this is related most minutely in the process ; but it does not tell us, whether it was the friar or the apothecary's son, who

* Alluding no doubt to the ignorant son of the apothecary.
† Atahualpa, one of the Incas of Peru put to death by Pizarro.
‡ The hill of Potosi.

supplied the alcohol to the heretic which vaporized his ideas, and gave a looseness to his tongue, and thus furnished matter in abundance for their villainous denouncements.

Meanwhile, the situation of Moyen could not be more wretched, for at the same time that his mind suffered all the tortures of doubt from not being able to ascertain or receive an explanation of the cause of his misfortune, his body also suffered torments not less severe. Moyen was by nature epileptic, and frequently had the most horrid attacks of that complaint. But of what consequence was that to his jailers? Was he not a heretic, and the epilepsy perhaps was only a symptom of that which the soul felt, like that of Carmen Marin possessed by the devil.* They kept him in a dark cell, in that severe climate, loaded with irons and without any other means to procure food and clothing, except the small sum he gained by his own labour, either because the Inquisition at Potosi had no rents, or else that the mines which had at another period furnished abundant harvests of heretics and doubloons were now in a state of decadence.† It is true, that now and then they permitted him to see a visitor in his cell, but that was almost always some new delator; and it is likewise true that they furnished him with brandy, but this last was not intended to have the same effect during his examination as the *gag* during the application of the punishment. This at least is what may be inferred from the confessions of the unfortunate victim.

Although the penal system of the Inquisition, according to the Prebendary Saavedra and the reviewers of his work *was*

* Carmen Marin was a poor woman of Santiago afflicted with epilepsy, whom the priest pronounced to be possessed by the devil. The affair caused a good deal of excitement at the time, and a great deal of controversy; they tried to exorcise the evil spirit, but it was of no use, the devil was obstinate and would not budge an inch for all their holy water, candles, &c.—*Note by Translator.*

† He maintains himself, said the Commissary Lizarazu to the Inquisitors, in a letter dated November 2, 1749, by the small sums he receives from the use of his distinguished talent in painting.

CHAPTER IV.

of the most mild character, the life of Moyen glided away in one uninterrupted torment. What drove him to desperation, caused no doubt by the chronic disease with which he was afflicted, were the chains which oppressed him. And for this, invoking the meekness of Jesus Christ, he petitioned his superior judges, the Inquisitors of Lima, to release him of his fetters, when he had already been seven months in irons.* " I may call myself (said he to them in his Gaulo-Portuguese-Spanish dialect) one of the same flock of sheep, and Jesus Christ did not put chains on its feet, but placed it upon his shoulders and brought it to where the others were." †

But in vain was his request. The *mild* Inquisition never had pity, because it never had a heart; its soul was covetousness; its spirit was fanaticism; torture and murder were the only diversions which varied the dark monotony in the life of its atrocious executioners!

Already a year had passed and the unfortunate Moyen was still supplicating that at the least they would inform him what was the cause of his imprisonment, which he conjectured to be only for suspicion. " Si je suis arreté," he wrote in his own language to the inquisitors of Lima the 12th of May, 1750, when it only wanted two days to complete the first year of his cruel imprisonment, " pour avoir eû conversations en matière de religion, je *ne savais pas que c'etait defendu*. Je supplier," he added with the most profound humility, " le conseil de l'Inquisition de me regarder en pitié, et comme je *ne demand point d'autre grâce que la justice*, qu'elle me disse le supplice que je merite, je serais mon propre bourreau." ‡

* Letter from Moyen to the Inquisitors at Lima. Potosi, 26th December, 1749.

† In this passage it is clearly seen that Moyen is alluding to the parable of the lost sheep.

‡ The proud inquisitors must have looked at each other rather awkwardly when they received this missive written in French, as there was not one belonging to the Inquisition, great or small, that understood that language, and had it not been for a Jesuit father, called

In the expression of this last phrase Moyen did by no means deceive his persecutors, for it happened that one day the notary of the town council of Potosi, under the pretext of confiscation, was going to deprive him of his violin. Exasperated, and driven to a state of desperation, which those wretches were unable to comprehend, he made an attempt on his life by thrusting a knife into his stomach. Such was the *mild* penal system and *evangelical disinterestedness* * of the Inquisition! And all this occurred when its ferocity, which had aroused the indignation of the world, was in a state of complete decay. What then must have been its *suavity* and *mildness* in the fulness of power of its ancient system? †

Francisco Gomez, who translated it, those stolid immolators of mankind would not have known that it was possible to ask for mercy in any other idiom than that of their official vernacular, or in that of their kitchen.

* Cited in a letter from the Commissary of Potosi. Moyen confessed eight years later in the audience of the 8th of July, 1757, before the Inquisition of Lima, to the truth of this fact, but not without cursing the "bandy-legged notary, Torres," for his unbridled avarice. All that the familiars of the Holy Office could realize of the few effects of the artist were eight yards of thread lace, which were sold at half-a-dollar a yard. As for the books of Bourdaloue and Puffendorf, who would have bought them in Potosi, unless it was the trader of Redondela? If in the city of the kings (Lima), there was only one friar who knew French, how many would there be in the imperial city (Potosi)?

† The prebendary Señor Saavedra, who unites at his pleasure, or separates according to the convenience of his logic, the ancient and modern Inquisition, as though in their object and practices they were not always one and the same, has the hardihood to assert against the complete unanimity of history, "That the true patriots of Spain received with *notable rejoicing* the new (Spanish) Inquisition!" We have already seen what Mariana and Pulgar, its contemporaries, and whom Señor Saavedra quotes in his favour, have said of the manner in which it was received. We have likewise quoted the opinions of Motley and Prescott, concerning the true cause of the rebellion and apostacy of the Low Countries. And although, to con-

Meanwhile the process in the hands of the Commissary dragged itself along with a most despairing slowness. Only

found such extravagance it would be sufficient to open any elementary text book of history, we recommend to Señor Saavedra to read the following passages, all of them from Spanish authors. "Meanwhile, let us observe," says Rodriguez Buron (referring without doubt to the text of the clerical Spaniard Llorente), "that notwithstanding the ignorance and superstition in which the inhabitants of these towns were submerged, the Inquisition was not established among them without meeting with a sanguinary resistance. The hatred which inspired in all parts the office of inquisitor was the cause of a multitude of Dominicans, and even several Franciscans, perishing by a violent death. We have already seen how the Abbot of Cister died by the sword of the Albigenses, and that the first severities of the Inquisition were immediately followed by the assassination of Pedro de Planedis; after which we see that the exasperated Spaniards stoned the inquisitors and killed them even at the foot of the altar." (Compendium of the Critical History of the Inquisition (vol. 1, page 35). "While the inquisitors," adds the same author (vol. 1, page 102), "endeavoured to form a holy alliance against the people, the latter united themselves against the inquisitors. The cruelties of this tribunal excited in all parts popular insurrections, which the king could not without much difficulty restrain. Disturbances arose simultaneously at Teruel, Valencia, Lérida, Barcelona, almost in all the towns of Catalonia. The resistance was so obstinate that, notwithstanding the severe measures adopted by the king Ferdinand to oppose it, it required two years to reduce those whom they called seditious, at the head of whom were found many men of the superior class. Barcelona, more especially caused itself to be admired for its brave opposition. The inhabitants of that city, as well as those of all the province, would not submit themselves to the yoke of the modern inquisition, nor acknowledge the authority of Torquemada; and it cost a great deal of trouble to introduce the reform of the Holy Office into the province and subdue the Catalonians. The same occurred in Majorca and Minorca, whose inhabitants opposed the introduction of the inquisition for the space of more than eight years, and it was not received into these islands until 1490."

"All these testimonies of an opposition so general, incontestably prove that the Holy Office was introduced into the Peninsula against the voice of all the Spaniards, and that it was imposed upon them by force and terror. The ambitious desire of power of the Popes, the

on the 9th of June, 1749, had he acquainted his superiors with the capture of Moyen, and he had delayed no less than

avarice of Ferdinand, and the fanaticism of a few monks, plunged Spain into an abyss of evils, which the people had already foreseen when they struggled against the orders of their king, and against the bulls of the Pope. The people seldom deceive themselves—unfortunate are those who despise their representations."

As the anterior quotations may be attributed to Llorente, whom Señor Saavedra accuses of being partial, an apostate and even a falsifier, let us hear what the Spaniard Rodriguez Buron says on his own account. "Of all the plagues," he exclaims in the introduction to his Compendium, "which have desolated successively the different parts of the globe, there is not one which has left its marks so difficult to erase as those of the Holy Inquisition. The existence of plagues, wars, famines, earthquakes, and volcanic eruptions, has only come to our knowledge through the pages of history.

"But in every place where the deadly atmosphere of the Holy Office has been respired, wherever this sanguinary tribunal has been established, there the most populous cities have been deserted by their industrious inhabitants, until they have only enclosed within their walls informers and their victims, gaolers and their executioners, and the lands the most fruitful have become converted into one frightful desert."

And as Señor Saavedra endeavours (resting upon distinctions purely theological, or of the difference of hierarchy, ecclesiastical or civil, regal or papal), to make it appear that the Inquisition of Rome was different from that of Valladolid, Toledo, or Madrid, let any one read what the writer, whom we have several times quoted, Torres de Castilla (likewise a Spaniard), says about the former, where he gives an account of the termination of the pontificate of Paul IV., the Italian Torquemada. "A series of persecutions," he says in the work already cited (vol. 3, page 700), "and executions signalized the pontificate of Paul IV., during which his tyranny rose to such an extreme and became so insupportable that it drove the people to exasperation, and was the cause of many disturbances.

"At length, on the death of this Pope, which occurred on the 19th of August, 1559, a formidable revolution broke out in Rome. The people broke in pieces the statues of Paul, dragging them about the streets many days, and then threw them into the Tyler, and to avoid the corpse of the pontiff sharing the same fate it was necessary to bury it without any ceremony!

half a year for the purpose of the previous qualification of the propositions, before he sent them the first copy of the summary.*

"One of the first acts of the Roman people, on the same day that Paul died, was to rush to the place of the Inquisition, break open the doors, release the prisoners of which the dungeons were full, and then set fire to the building, which was consumed, with all the books and papers it contained.

"The troops which hastened to Rome were able to prevent from being burned in like manner the convent of the Dominicans, the monks of which exercised the office of Inquisitors."

With respect to the Venetian Inquisition, equally as horrible as that of Spain and Rome, we may see what has been said about it by Sarpi and Daru, historians who treat extensively of its cruelties, proving that the Inquisition, like the cholera, or even hell itself, was the same in every place and country.

* In this is seen how, after having made allusions not the most decent, to the heresy of the sixth (seventh) Commandment, the Commissary in his first communication (the same date as above) to the Inquisition at Lima, thus expresses himself. "The *propositions* for which I am now making out a summary, are because it is maintained that the cross upon which Jesus Christ, our life, died, is the only one that ought to be adored and not any other; that the most Holy Maria and the saints should not be adored, but only held in veneration; that the infallible science of the doctors concerning the existence of future sin, is incompatible with the liberty of man to sin; that the sacrifice of the mass, indulgences, prayers for the dead, and other meritorious works, are of no avail to the souls in purgatory; that the Sovereign Pontiff is not the universal head of the Church, and that he does not hold the power to bind and absolve; that he grants indulgences, canonizes, and does anything required of him for money; that it is permitted to a man condemned to die, or in a situation in which he must die, to take away his own life; that the authority of the general councils is superior to that of the Sovereign Pontiff; that it is wicked to condemn so many (referring to those who are lost for not having heard of the Messiah), for the want of not having ever heard anything of the son of a carpenter, and various others of great gravity uttered by a Frenchman called Don Francisco Moyen.

"This, as may be seen, completes the enumeration of the heresies we have pointed out, and which the careless Moyen openly expressed during the whole of the journey from Buenos Ayres to Potosi.

"We will also make an observation concerning the heresies uttered

In consequence, it was not until a full year had passed since the arrest of Moyen, that he had substantiated and rendered intelligible, but without any intervention of the accused, or even notice of it being given to him, what might be called the body of the offence, that is to say, the *heretical propositions* of the accused, who at the same time was ignorant of, or at least had forgotten that he had ever uttered them. During the 9th, 11th, and 12th days of May, the Holy Tribunal was occupied in condensing the denouncement of the process, together with the official letters of accusation of the Commissary of Upper Peru, and with the aid of the alembic of theology, these " potent, grave, and reverend

by the foreigner among us now and then in his journeys here in America."

The Señor Prebendary relates in the 33rd page of his "Rapid Sketch," the following curious anecdote of the road, " The descendants of Luther have inherited from him his brutal sentiments against the Catholics. A short time ago, in the train from Valparaiso were seated together in the same carriage an European and a young Chilian, the latter of whom from his appearance might be taken for an Englishman or a German; the foreigner no doubt mistaking him for one of those nationalities, and believing him to be a Protestant, said to him that he hated the Catholics, and he could with great pleasure kill them all. The young Chilian replied, that he was a Catholic, to which the Protestant made answer, ' Oh, then I would spare you.' It is in this manner some of the foreigners repay the generous hospitality of Chile !"†

We might ask the question, that if the carnivorous descendant of Luther above-mentioned, instead of riding comfortably seated upon the soft cushions in the train from Valparaiso had been mounted upon the mule, upon the back of which Francisco Moyen had to perform his journey, how could he have escaped from the hands of the Catholic inquisitors, those who gave so good an account of the latter?

---

† No doubt there are numbers simple enough to believe, that a man (not insane) would suddenly address another to whom he had never spoken, in the manner above-mentioned, but that Saavedra believes such a story, I very much doubt; if he does, he must possess a much larger share of the organ of credulity than most people would give him credit for.—*Note by Translator.*

Señors," obtained no less than forty-four *heretical propositions,* some of which are already known to our readers, and which, together with the remainder, we will lay before them in their proper language* when we have fully entered into the suit.

In virtue then of that precious judgment, or as it should be termed that scandalous prejudgment, done in secret and at a distance of 500 leagues, without any judicial notification or information being given to the supposed delinquent, or even without his entertaining the remotest suspicion of such a proceeding, (all of which of course were among the formularies adopted by the Holy Office for the *protection* of innocence,) a writ was issued for the accused to be brought before the inquisitors, and in consequence, complying with the orders transmitted from Lima by the Conde de Superunda, Viceroy of Peru, the Commissary of Potosi, on the 12th July, 1750, arranged that Moyen should be conducted in safe custody, his person being delivered successively to the different magistrates of the districts along the course of the extensive route between Potosi and Lima, for in this manner was it decreed by the Holy Office, and by its mandate was the order given by the civil power.

That journey of 500 leagues occupied almost two years, and was truly a *via crucis* to the unfortunate culprit, condemned to such a penance; his long imprisonment had to such an extent broken up his robust health that the epileptic attacks with which he was afflicted had become a customary habit of his existence.† It does not appear in the writings

---

* See note 1, page 76.

† In another place we have said that Moyen was naturally subject to attacks of epilepsy, and it being our wish to be as impartial as is consistent with right, it is only just that we should state it to be our belief that this disease is in some cases constitutional, but we must add that in the writings of the process we are told that he had not suffered from any attack, until his imprisonment in Potosi. Was this then one of the benefits of the *mild* Inquisition ?

of the process, that during his journey from Buenos Ayres to Potosi, he had suffered even once from that horrible complaint; but on his road to Lima it is found that he had an attack almost daily. On the 22nd of November, 1750, he was at Chuquito, a town in Upper Peru, and from thence they wrote to the Inquisitors, "that with four men of his guards they were unable to control him during his epileptic fits." The magistrate of that district, Don Pedro Miguel de Meneses, in a letter to the Inquisitors, dated the 9th of Jan. 1751, corroborated the fact related of Moyen, and added that their prisoner had suffered "a terrible burning fever, which had brought him to the brink of the grave," but from which he was now convalescent, after having received the last sacraments. From thence the unfortunate victim proceeded by slow journeys; he was detained a month in La Paz, two months in Puno, and 15 days in Ayaviri, always suffering from his cruel complaint. It was only in April, 1751, that he arrived at Cuzco, having been attacked by the epilepsy in a bad pass of the road, where he was nearly on the point of perishing.

In that city a lawyer called Don Tomas de Lecaros, who must have been a man of great influence, interested himself in the fate of Moyen, and becoming responsible for his security, took him as far as Arequipa, with the object of having him cured by some competent physician of that place.

Unfortunate in every thing, he did not obtain much relief in that city, but from his residence there we learn another circumstance of the process. During his stay he had formed a friendship with an English hatter named William, who gave him very good advice, and full of prudence, that is to say, to become a hypocrite, for such is the great result, social and religious, of propagandism by terror, the fundamental base of the Holy Inquisition.*

* The English Catholic advised the French heretic not to mix himself up in such things, nor even to talk about them in a country where

On returning to Cuzco in company with his protector, Moyen sought an asylum in the village of Urcos, eight leagues distant from that city. We are ignorant if it was on account of his health or that he wished to escape from the

there was an Inquisition, to leave purgatory on one side with his meat and his fish, &c., and to do as he did, that is go and hear mass at six o'clock in the morning.

In Lima, Moyen being closely pressed by the interrogator of the Inquisition, had the weakness to make those useless revelations, which were equivalent to a denunciation, and consequently to the ruin of the poor hatter.

This artizan no doubt was the Englishman of whom Ulloa and Juan make mention in their *secret memoir*, as the inventor of the hats made from the wool of the vicuña, so much in fashion about the middle of the 18th century. According to those authors Don Guillermo had strictly guarded the secret of his invention; but we do not know whether his indiscretion with Moyen permitted him to go on manufacturing hats and hearing artificial masses at six o'clock in the morning!

Nevertheless, this anecdote illustrates another phase not much elucidated, of the benefits produced in Catholic society by the Holy Office, that is to say, the habit of reserve, of distrust, and what is still more serious, that of hypocrisy. The illustrious Buckle, speaking of this says, "We hear much of martyrs and confessors—of those who were slain by the sword or consumed in the fire, but we know little of that still larger number, who, by the mere dread of persecution have been driven into an outward abandonment of their real opinions, and who thus, forced into an apostasy the heart abhors, have passed the remainder of their lives in the practice of a constant and humiliating hypocrisy. It is this which is the real curse of religious persecution. For in this way men being constrained to mask their thoughts, there arises a habit of securing safety by falsehood, and of purchasing impunity with deceit." (History of Civilisation in England, by H. T. Buckle, vol. 1, page 136.)

Yet notwithstanding these profound truths, which may be easily verified by any one who for only a day has visited Spain, the Prebendary Saavedra, guided by that *faiseur de libres* Capefigue, has the boldness to maintain that the Inquisition, the symbol of Spanish degradation in the times of Philip II. and Ferdinand VII. was the palladium of its patriotism and independence. "Nevertheless," ex-

persecution of that terrible Brotherhood commissioned to watch all his movements, but certain it is that his person

claims a Chilian statistician, (Don Mariano de Egaña,)* whose orthodoxy is beyond all doubt, "Oh Spain! thou disgrace and dishonour to all that has ever been, these are the doctrines which have reduced thee to the state in which thou art at the present day, and in which thou wilt remain for many years to come!"

"Although enormous were the material losses to Spain," says an eloquent French writer, (M. Coquerel,) speaking of the expulsion of the Jews and Moors, exclusively the work of the Inquisition, " they were nevertheless but of little moment in comparison to the moral injury which the Inquisition brought upon her, while at the same time that it suffocated all activity of spirit, and all liberty of thought, it degraded the character of the people by the influence of terror, which is the vilest stimulus that can affect the human mind. Its spies and its sbirri were to be found in all parts, and as they belonged to all classes of society, they transformed a most shameful delation into a true social institution. More than one proud Castilian had to resign himself to this shameless character to avoid the danger of suspicion, and in this manner the Inquisition has come to be one of the most active causes of the sad and long degeneracy of Spain since the time of Philip II." (" L'Inquisition a été ainsi une de cause le plus actives de la triste et longue decadence de l'Espagne depuis Philippe II.")

" Every one became a persecutor," exclaimed in his turn a still more distinguished modern writer, (the illustrious Michelet, Guerres de Religion, page 194,) " to avoid being persecuted; none were left to the Inquisitors unless they burnt each other; there were no Jews or Lutherans for the burning pile. The ravenous Inquisition was obliged to seek for victims far off in the Low Countries. Every moment vague denunciations were arriving at Hamburg. From whom? From Andalucia; from the Inquisition at Seville?"

But returning again to our proper ground, and answering the beati-

---

* Don Mariano de Egaña was a minister of Chile, chief and oracle of the conservative party, very devout and religious, but enlightened and well informed, hence his feelings of disgust for the Inquisition. In 1824 he was appointed minister for Chile to the Court of St. James's, and while in London he arranged the payment of the loan made in 1822 to that Republic. He died in Santiago, 1846.—*Note by Translator.*

CHAPTER IV.

being demanded to be presented in Lima in the peremptory term of two months, under the penalty of excommunication major to any one who should endeavour to prevent it,* the commissary of Cuzco, who was the precentor of the cathedral, Don José Alvarez de Adriasola, ordered his notary to go and take him; who, as he himself says, "executed the order punctually, notwithstanding the resistance he made, threatening with a dagger the said notary."†

fied Capefigue with Dr. Egaña, we ought to mention that the exclamation we have alluded to, of the ascetic Don Mariano, is to be found in his own handwriting, upon the 134th page of a copy in his library of the work already mentioned of the Peruvian Doctor Bermudez, the title of which is the " Triumph of the Holy Office of Peru ;" the said book was found in the year 1839, among the papers left by Don Francisco Valdivieso at his death, and presented by his son to the Señor Bello, who in his turn made a present of it to Doctor Egaña. But more in advance we shall give an account of this inquisitorial curiosity; and we regret not being able to do so immediately, from a work recently written in Spain, after ten years of assiduous labour, with the title of " A General History of the Archives of Simancas," or the recapitulation of all the ferocious and infamous acts of the " Demon of the South," (Philip II. the hero of Señor Saavedra,) but the publication of which has been prohibited by the illustrious government of Gonzales Bravo, in virtue no doubt of the habit of freedom of thought left by the Inquisition. According to a correspondence of the 4th of last April from Madrid, we learn that the work is going to be published at Brussels or in Germany; and thus, in consequence of the protection afforded to literature by the Inquisition, we shall have sent to us this proof of its liberality by way of contraband! Oh! if we were Don Mariano de Egaña, should we not here exclaim of Capefigue: "Oh! courtly buffoon! if the patriotism of the Spaniards depended upon the existence of the Inquisition, when they were conquered by the French, might it not likewise have been attributed to their bull fights, cock fights, royal lotteries, and other Spanish institutions contemporaneous with the Holy Office?"

* A letter from the Grand Inquisitor, Don Mateo de Amuzquibar, to the commissary of Arequipa, dated 4th September, 1751.

† A letter from the commissary of Cuzco to the Inquisitors at Lima, dated 6th October, 1751.

When the sbirri of the Holy Office apprehended Moyen by force, they found upon his person a manuscript book in his own handwriting, with the following title *Philosophy of Epictetus*, or the *Inquiridium*. Three months after a Belemite friar called upon Juan de San Miguel, residing in Cuzco, and wrote secretly to the Inquisitors, that Moyen persisted in his doctrines and spread them publicly about in Cuzco. In this we behold another of the fruits of the wise, just, and rational Inquisition. That light-hearted and giddy youth, enthusiastic only for the arts, carried away by those passions which are the sad heritage of his birth, converted by means of the *salutary* correction of the Holy Office into a stubborn fanatic, into an obstinate and firm philosopher, in short into a man capable of encountering martyrdom for his belief. And this and nothing else can be the result upon those whose natures are rich in moral force, and in gifts of intelligence, of that atrocious institution which endeavoured to compress within its grasp of iron the most noble attributes of the soul which thinks and the conscience which discerns.

At length, on the 26th of March, 1752, a muleteer called Ventura Bejar, delivered Moyen as a prisoner within the gates of the Holy Office at Lima, for which, and for having conducted him from Cuzco, he received sixty-five dollars. The Inquisitor, Amuzquibar, had ordered that he should be brought in irons at his expense,* but happily the barbarous instructions reached their destination too late, the impenitent offender had left Cuzco two weeks before they arrived. He was immediately shut up in one of those horrible vaults situated in the public square which yet retains the name of the Inquisition; they also caused an inventory to be made of his miserable luggage, most probably for the purpose of ascertaining whether he had brought with him anything of

* A letter from Amuzquibar to the commissary of Cuzco, dated 17th February, 1752.

value,* and they assigned to him five reals a day for his maintenance.†

About three years before that time Moyen had arrived at Potosi, young, gay, brave, full of talent, and fervently glowing with all the passion of gallantry. He was then, according to the description of his own comrades,‡ of well-proportioned stature, stout, round face, a beard full and black, white skin, Roman nose, thick lips, large, sharp, and blue eyes, and with the mark of a cut across the jaw to the extremity of the mouth.

Now the man behind whose tottering steps they had drawn the bolts of the Holy Office was but the shadow of that robust youth of nine-and-twenty years,—emaciated, cadaverous, with the hair tinged with grey, says the scanty register with which they described him in the process at the time of his reception. Moyen had lived in three years a whole life of pain and misery. In the prime of his life he had already the signs of premature old age, produced by the combined torture of the flesh and spirit. Such, then, were the inevitable fruits of the *mild Inquisition!*

The incarceration of Francisco Moyen in the prison of the

---

* All that Moyen possessed when he was shut up in the Inquisition at Lima, was a bed, four shirts, five waistcoats, four pair of drawers, six pair of stockings, a cloth cloak, a black hat which had been given him, a bronze crucifix, a violin, a box of paints, some portraits and a book with the title of *Compendium of Meteors.*

† The five reals assigned to the accused were to be expended in the following manner: three reals for food, one and a half for spirits, and a half real for *mate*, (tea from Paraguay). The head jailor of the Inquisition, Don Francisco Ximenes, was charged to see that this division was faithfully carried out. It may cause surprise that in this distribution there should figure so large a proportion for a liquor foreign to the austerity used towards the accused by the Holy Office, but perhaps it might have been for the purpose of consuming the spirit that was produced on the estate of the inquisitor Amuzquibar, situated in the valley of Majes, in the wine province of Arequipa.

‡ The first denunciation of Soto, in March 1749.

Inquisition of Lima, in the third year of his persecution, marks the intermediate point of this narrative and of his process, which now commences in its more complete form, and gives an appropriate place to the documents characteristic of its nature and object.

But before conducting the unfortunate artist before his terrible judges, it will be necessary to inform our readers who these judges were, and how they came to establish their power in America.

CHAPTER V.

WE have no room in this history to relate in what manner the Spanish Inquisition was founded; whether it was by the fanaticism of the first Isabel, or by the covetousness of her husband, Ferdinand of Aragon; for, according to one historian, it was enough for him the hopes of augmenting his riches by confiscation.* Nor is it for us to say whether the

* Whether *faith* was the pretext and gold the true motive for the establishment of the Spanish Inquisition, the same as it was for the conquest of America (in virtue of which they are now proposing to canonize Christopher Columbus) is a question which history has already answered. It is well known that Alfonso de Ojeda, prior of the Dominicans in Seville, and Philip de Berberis, inquisitor of Sicily, advised Ferdinand the Catholic to establish the Holy Office almost exclusively against the Jews, which, according to a learned article in the *Penny Cyclopedia* (vol. xvi. p. 407) were considered the richest men in Spain.

" By means of the restitutions (that is to say, the property seized by the inquisitors themselves)," says Rodriguez Buron, speaking of the first advantages gained by the Holy Office, and the pecuniary fines which they imposed upon those persons whom they had reconciled, " Torquemada established the revenues of the Inquisition, to which may be added the expenses of the salaries of a great number of spies spread abroad all over the face of Spain. This last measure, sufficient to infuse terror into the minds even of the old Christians, was enough to cause the grand inquisitor to be hated, and from that moment his life was in the greatest danger."

With regard to Charles V., for whom Señor Saavedra professes so much admiration, notwithstanding he had sacked Rome (which Garibaldi has not done), it is known to all that he must have required large sums of money for his eternal and sacrilegious wars. So poor was his treasury that the ceremony of his abdication had to be performed, for the sake of economy, in the saloon of mourning, covered with black curtains taken from the royal palace!

As for Philip II., the fact of his bankruptcy is still more evident.

Spanish people, who stoned to death Pedro de Carideta, the inquisitor of Barcelona, and poniarded the inquisitor Arbués in Zaragoza, received with content, as the prebendary Saavedra assures us, the creation of that monstrous tribunal, which in the name of God committed all the horrors which before had been delegated to the executioner. The investigation of all this we shall leave without regret to the learned prebendary, author of the panegyric on the Inquisition.

It is enough for us to know that the Inquisition was ordered to be established in America, the 7th of February, 1569, by the royal letters patent of Philip the Second, it being eighty-eight years after the time that Pope Sixtus the Fourth had given to the Catholic kings the permission of St. Peter to light the first burning pile. In consequence of which were created the three Grand Inquisitors of Mexico, Carthagena, and Lima, to the last of which was assigned the jurisdiction of Chile. One year later, 9th February, 1570, the first Grand Inquisitor, Servan de Cerezuela, made his solemn entry into Lima, invested with all the majesty derived from being the double representative of Pope and King.

Nevertheless, the harvest of fire reaped by the American inquisitors at first appeared to be rather scanty. The place for the celebration of the *autos de fé* was only adorned on the

---

and for which the Holy Office had to compensate. According to Michelet, in the first years of his reign he had not sufficient, upon one occasion, wherewith to pay the expenses of sending a courier to Rome, and it was necessary for the Cardinal Granvella to defray them from his own pocket. The Spanish deficit, according to the same historian, was *nine millions* out of *ten millions* of estimates. "In the time of the inquisitor Valdez" (adds Rodriguez, in his work already quoted, vol. ii. p. 25), "who was contemporary with Philip II., it was then, with contempt of the rights of nations, and of the existing treaties between the King of Spain and the other powers of Europe, that the Holy Office seized, judged, and *condemned to death as Lutherans, English, French, and Genoese merchants*, who had gone to Spain with *rich cargoes of merchandize*, and which the Inquisition confiscated without the least scruple!"

days of festivals, such, for instance, as the solemn entry of a viceroy, or to commemorate the feast days, particularly the days of the Virgin; but, on the other hand, the harvest of gold was immense, inexhaustible, in virtue of the holy right of spoliation which those rapacious executioners arrogated to themselves. And why not? In America there were no heretics. Its recent conquest had been accomplished as much by the cross as by the sword. The soldiers of Pizarro and of Hurtado de Mendoza were like the soldiers of Tancred and Godfrey de Bouillon, both of them rushed to the conflict against the Mussulman or the Indian with the same war-cry: *'Tis the will of God, 'tis the will of God!*

But, on the other hand, if there were no unbelievers, there were abundance of men of large fortunes, such as those who had received the ransom of Atahualpa, and those who had thrown the dice for the massive golden sun which covered the front of the temple in Cuzco dedicated to that luminary!

At that time Potosi was in the height of its greatness, and its insatiable masters had bestowed upon it, in exchange for its *royal fifths*,* the title of the Imperial City. Such, then, being the state of things, were the learned inquisitors to sit at ease under their canopy of green velvet to idle and doze away their time, without having even one single process to occupy their leisure? Why should those who were the highest functionaries of the Church and State, owners of the lives and properties of all the inhabitants, not be able to participate in the general opulence? If the gloomy Don Francisco de Toledo had cut off the head of the arch-millionaire of Puno (Salcedo), who, according to the tradition, is said to have offered to pave the side walks of the streets of Lima with bars of silver in exchange for his life,

---

* Before the independence of South America the fifth part of the produce of all the mines belonged to the king; and as Potosi, at the time referred to, was exceedingly productive in silver ore, the revenue derived from it must have been great.—*Note by Translator.*

why should not the inquisitors also melt down in the Acho* some of the millions accumulated by the merchants of the city of the kings, which for its marvellous riches was worthy of the name?

As for Chile, it was different,† nothing was derived from thence except a small quantity of wheat to supply the bakers along the coast, and some tallow which served to light their streets and dwellings, and it was this safeguard of poverty to which we are indebted for the benefits, social and political, that we are enjoying at the present day, and if we did not remain entirely free from the insult of the *sambenito* at least we escaped the horrors of the burning pile.

Among the 29 *autos de fé*, which the inquisitors celebrated during the 250 years of its existence (1570-1820) as we have already said, ‡ the most famous and solemn was that

---

* The public square at Lima was so called, in which was situated the *quemadero*, or place for burning heretics, and also the amphitheatre for the bull fights.

† What the inquisitors received, direct from Chile, was very little in comparison with the immense spoils obtained from Upper and Lower Peru, at that time in the height of their opulence.

‡ The first auto de fé at which any one was burnt took place in Lima, on the 29th of October, 1581, for the purpose of celebrating the entry into that city of the viceroy, Don Martin Enriquez; in it were burnt Juan Bernal and other heretics, and the last took place in 1776. According to Fuentes, the number of those burnt during that period of 195 years were, fifty-nine burnt alive, eighteen in effigy, and the bones of nine others, in all eighty-six.

Of the butcheries of the Inquisition of Carthagena, which was one of the three in America, we have not been able to obtain any account; but of the opulent Mexico, which stands first in the category, it is well known that it displayed a greater degree of luxury in its executions than that of the Holy Office of Lima. According to Juan Torquemada (*Indian Monarchy*, vol. iii. page 379), from 1574 to 1593, a term of only nineteen years, were celebrated nine *autos de fé*; in the first of which were present sixty-three penitentials, of whom five were burnt alive. In the tenth *auto de fé*, celebrated in honour of the Immaculate Conception of the Virgin, on the 8th of December, 1596,

which Juan de Mañosca celebrated on the 23rd of January, 1639, and in which were burnt twelve Portuguese merchants, and, as it happened, by a curious coincidence they were present sixty penitentials.* In another, celebrated 25th of March, 1602, the number exceeded one hundred.

Juan de Torquemada, we do not know if he was a descendant of the famous Thomas (although both were monks), who published his "Indian Monarchy" in 1723, appears to have been a great enthusiast in the burning of heretics, and the picture he has given of one of those *festivities*, of which he appears to have been an eyewitness, is so characteristic of his ferocious but ingenuous simplicity that we cannot do less than copy some parts of it as a specimen.

He says:—" The place selected was the town-hall, being in the principal square of the city, where was ordered to be erected a sumptuous seat. Its base was on a level with the balustrade of the balcony, which formed a running cornice, with curious mouldings, in the clear of which they placed the seat, raised in form of a dais, with sufficient room for the chairs of the Viceroy, Inquisitors, and the Town Council, above which was the canopy of the tribunal, which, with its silk curtains, and the beautiful worked and rich carpets, spread all over the spaces and flooring of the dais, made a most majestic appearance.

" It was quite a marvellous thing to see the people who crowded to this celebrated and famous *auto;* they were in the windows, and every place, which they filled even to the house and doors of the Holy Office; and to see the singular procession and accompaniment of the relaxed and penitentials, who came out with ropes about their necks and pasteboard caps on their heads, with flames of fire painted on them, in their hands they held a green cross, and each had a monk by his side, who exhorted him to die well; they had also familiars of the Holy Office for a guard. The reconciled Jews with sambenitos, those twice married with caps, upon which were painted objects signifying

---

* This could have been nothing in comparison to that splendid *auto de fé*, in honour of the Immaculate Conception of the Virgin, or as she is styled by the Catholic Church, the *Queen of Heaven*, on the 8th December, 1863, when upwards of 2000 persons were burnt alive! If the prophet Jeremiah denounced the Jews for offering incense and drink offerings to the Queen of Heaven, what would he have said if they had offered her sacrifices of human beings?—*Note by Translator.*

were the richest men in Lima!* One of those alone, Don Manuel Bautista Perez, owner of the regal residence in their crimes. Those accused of witchcraft with white caps on their heads, candles in their hands, and ropes about their necks. Others for blasphemy, with gags in their mouths, half naked, their heads uncovered, and with candles in their hands, all in order, following one after the other; those for lesser crimes going first, and in the same order the rest, the *relaxed* following behind, and the dogmatists and teachers of the law of Moses as captains or leaders, the last with their trains on their caps, rolled up and twisted to signify the false doctrines they taught, and in this manner they proceeded towards the place erected for them, which was in front of the seats for the tribunal, at the foot of which were also seats in the form of steps, upon which were seated the familiars of the Holy Office, each according to his seniority.

"As for the scaffold, or framework for the seats of the condemned, it was *marvellous*, because in the middle of it was a half pyramid, surrounded by semicircular steps up to the top; upon these were seated in their order the relaxed, the dogmatists upon the highest steps, and the others in gradation, and in this order also were the effigies of those who were relaxed, but who were either dead or absent. The reconciled, and other penitentials, were seated upon low benches in the open space of the scaffold. The head jailor of the Holy Office had a chair placed for him at the base of the scaffold, a pulpit was also placed upon the right of the Holy Office, from which a sermon was preached by the Archbishop of the Philippine Islands, Don Frai Ignacio de Santivañes, of the order of my glorious father San Francisco. Two other pulpits were placed, one on each side of the tribunal, from which were read by the reporters the sentences of the condemned, but which, for the sake of not being too prolix, I will not give here; it will be enough to say that there were many of those obstinate Jews, who each one might have been a Rabbi of a synagogue. All this was celebrated with *great majesty*, the immense majority of the people not being a little astonished at the rites and ceremonies, as well as at the enormous crimes, an account of which they had just heard read to them, of these judaizing heretics."

Are these the marvellous exhibitions to which the *centenaries* would treat our people?

For the edification of those interested will be found in the Appendix

---

* According to Rodriguez Buron, Llorente gives an extensive description of this *auto de fé*, so much spoken of even in Europe.

Lima, which yet bears the name of the house of Pilate, possessed a fortune equivalent to a million of dollars at the present day, and it was the sequestration of his effects, held by those who were indebted to him, by the rapacious myrmidons of the spoilers, which gave origin to the disturbances in Santiago and Coquimbo, which some of our readers may remember to have read an account of, in a pamphlet we published concerning the robberies committed by the American Inquisition.*

Another of those who were burnt in that *auto de fé* was the *judaizing* (for thus they called the Portuguese when they were rich) Don Diego Lopez de Fonseca, whom they accused of having a crucifix placed beneath a stone in the threshold of the door of his shop; and as his informers asserted, any one upon entering to purchase goods, who would tread upon that stone, he would sell to them for half the price of what he would sell to another.†

But it was not alone the Portuguese, to whom the inquisitors afforded the pleasure of being burnt to make their king heir to their robberies. When they could they robbed the king himself, and as they could not burn him, as it is proved that upon more than one occasion they wished to do, they abstracted from the royal share all that their insatiable voraciousness could grasp.

To such a height did this state of things arrive in the opulent city of the kings, that at last the inquisitors, Don

---

an extract of the account of the celebrated *auto de fé* of the 23rd of September, 1736, and of which the Doctor Bermudez was the historian, and whose work is quoted abundantly by Señor Saavedra. As in this *auto* were concerned some of the judges of Moyen, and in its relation details are given, which we had not the advertence to copy from his process, they will be interesting from their novelty.

* Quoted in the preface of a work called "What was the Inquisition in Chile?" 1862.

† Richard Palma.—Studies relating to the Inquisition of Lima, published in the *South American Review*, Valparaiso, 1861.

Cristóval Calderon and Don Diego de Unda, were denounced to the supreme council of the Inquisition at Madrid, as known swindlers, and a scandal to the Crown; this was at the time when the Conde de Villa Garcia was viceroy in Peru, and the Archbishop of Santiago, Don Manuel Isidoro Manrique de Lara, General Inquisitor of Spain (1740 to 45).

This last was obliged to send to Lima in quality of visitor, and invested with the most ample powers, no less a person than one of the three councillors of the *supreme*, Don Antonio de Arenaza, whom we shall see figures in the qualification of the process of Moyen (1750). But although it was considered certain, says the illustrious Manso in his memoir to the king, speaking of this scandalous proceeding, yet they (the Inquisition) have so well concealed their treasures, that with all the diligence practised, and all the activity of the visitor, nothing has been gained except the formation of a large accumulation of *autos* (law writings).

But what is certain is, that both Calderon and Unda were removed from their posts for being *thieves*, and that, of the property of the last, which was confiscated to compensate the Holy Office for his robberies, there existed at the time of its first suppression (1813) a sum of 2047 dollars in jewels.

As for Calderon, after having given a bond jointly with his colleague, of 50,000 dollars, he retired to one of his estates, and "the affair remained without advancing any further, because, as stated by the Viceroy Manso, they could not agree about a question of etiquette, which consisted in the manner the senior judge should be admitted into the Inquisition, he insisting upon entering with his hat and cloak, and the inquisitors on the other hand that he should not be received unless he would enter with a cap and gown, each party sustaining their determination as though it were a matter of the utmost importance."*

* In the memoir cited by Manso may be read these and other characteristic details of the state of the Inquisition at that period. The Viceroy Amat, successor to Manso, and the most implacable

Such was the state of the Holy Office when the unfortunate Moyen arrived a prisoner to its dungeons. The corruption of the highest order of the clergy from among whom were chosen his judges, under the pompous title of Qualifiers of the Holy Office, (a position by many eagerly coveted), was upon a par with that of the jailors themselves. From the evidence of two persons* residing at that time in Peru, and who, as we may suppose, were well qualified to judge, being commissioned by authority to scrutinise the proceedings of the clergy, we learn " that the ecclesiastics of Peru may be divided into the secular and regular, and that both one and the other of them lead a life of licentiousness, attended with a deal of scandal and independent of all control; and although there are frailties in all men, and faults in all nations, as well as errors and weaknesses in the inhabitants of Peru, yet it appears to be a peculiar institution of those churchmen to exceed all other men in perversity of manners and in disorderly conduct!"

And these are the kind of men who are going to carry on a process against a man, rational, intelligent, and a Christian, and to keep him year after year bound to a chain, only because he said that a mule was *one of God's creatures!* and had changed the *is* in the *Ave Maria* into *was.* Good God! was such the infamous tribunal to which an honourable and virtuous Chile clergyman has erected altars for its justification! strewing them with flowers, and offering up incense to purify it from the disdain and disgust with which it is regarded by every right-minded and honest man.

enemy to the ecclesiastico-political element in Chile and Peru, compelled the heirs of the inquisitor Calderon (as he mentions in his memoir), to refund the sum of 30,000 dollars! Such was the calibre of the rapaciousness of those wretches!

* Don Jorje Juan and Don Antonio Ulloa, both lieutenant-generals in the Spanish navy. *Secret Memoirs,* page 490.

CHAPTER VI.

At the interruption in our narrative of the personal movements of Francisco Moyen, we said that on the 27th of March, 1752, he had been delivered into the hands of the head jailor of the secret prisons of the Inquisition, one month after which his trial before the Holy Tribunal commenced in earnest. The three years which he had already passed in a state of martyrdom, were nothing more than the preliminaries in receiving informations, and the judicial transportation of his person to his superior and legitimate judges, a short initiative of an endless punishment not considered by them and his jailors of any account.

We now commence a part the most important, most characteristic, and most terrible in this dark episode of the history of our civilization as a political people and as a Christian community, and for that reason the most interesting to us, as we were at that period politically and socially nothing more than a humble appendage of Peru!

Before proceeding it will be right that we give some explanation concerning the grounds of the process. And for the reason that it is so variable in itself, at one time serious and profound, at another frivolous and trifling, so characteristic of the men of the time of which it treats, that we shall constitute ourselves as simple expositors.

The Inquisition had no reporter, or, if it had, he does not appear in the process.

Let us be permitted then to occupy his vacant post, and in doing so, should our voice be tremulous with horror, we must beg the indulgence of the spectators, who may be present in the gloomy precincts in which the debate is going to be sustained.

The first audience to which Moyen was admitted before the inquisitors, took place on the 4th of May, 1752, those who held the office at that time were Don Mateo de Amuzquibar, successor to the "honourable Calderon," and Don Diego Rodriguez (unknown to us except by name) successor to Unda, who was already dead, and whose property even to his household furniture, and for aught we know perhaps his coffin, had been laid under an embargo for the purpose of making restitution for his fraudulent administration!

At the commencement, the cause took a course of unaccustomed activity, no less than ten sessions (examinations) being held from the 4th of May to the 21st June following.

In the first of these they confined their investigations to the origin, or more correctly speaking, to the ethnology of the accused, and the external signs of the religion he professed. Moyen had to give a most prolix history of his grandfathers, brothers, and all his relations, to prove the purity of his race, because, according to the constitutions of the Inquisition, one may be born a heretic. Judaism, for example, is a heresy constitutional and hereditary.

But in this part the Parisian and Burgundy lineage of Moyen came out triumphant; for he proved, so says the respective act, to be of a good race and generation, without any mixture of heresy, Mohammedanism or Judaism.

After that they made him cross himself and repeat the prayers in use among Catholics.

In this the accused was less fortunate, because he only crossed himself on the breast, without being able to do so in the face, and although he correctly said the *paternoster* in Latin, he did not know a single word of the *salve*, and also stammered continually in saying the Commandments of God and the Church.* In the three years in which Moyen

---

* All this was in conformity with the ancient practice and constitutions of the Inquisition. Marchena, commenting upon the *Directory for Inquisitors*, by Almerico, already quoted, and of which we shall give a full account in the Appendix, says, "The accused is to be asked

had been a neophyte of the Inquisition, and in the hands of one or other of its familiars, not one had had the compassion or kindness to teach him to recite his prayers, or to cross himself in a proper manner; and this when, according to the assertion of Señor Saavedra, its principal object was the improvement, and not the punishment of the accused, and for which the scaffold had been converted into the means of absolution.

The second session was occupied by Moyen, in giving a relation of his life from the moment of his birth, up to the time in which he was then speaking; but, as it was getting late, he was interrupted at his arrival at Puno, where, after his imprisonment at Potosi, he was conducted to Lima.*

At the third session, which was held upon the 9th of May, 1752, the nature of his process was insinuated to him for the first time. The inquisitor asked if he was aware of the cause for which the suit was carried on against him; and the only answer made by Moyen, was, that he attributed it to his conversations with the Franciscian Friar of Potosi, whose printed book, in which he was compared to Atahualpa as in a former part we have mentioned, no doubt the accused had read—the first ray of light coming to him from across the ocean. So great, so horrible, and so profound was the secrecy which was imposed even to the very walls by the *mild* Inquisition!

After this, seven consecutive sessions were devoted to a

whether any of his family had been inclined to Judaism, or if any one had been condemned by the Holy Office, because those who have not the blood pure, are more likely to offend against the faith. He also is to be ordered to repeat the Lord's prayer, the Ave Maria, the Creed, the Articles of Faith, the Commandments of God, and of the Church, the Sacraments, and other prayers; and should he not know them, or make a mistake in saying them, it is a most vehement indication of his not being a Christian.

* From the personal revelations of Moyen in this part of the process we have taken our authority for the incidents of his life, which are given in the first pages of our history.

vague and inconsistent elucidation, apparently intended to analyze and explore the spirit of the accused, concerning various of the theological questions which served as a basis for the heresies of which he was accused by the delators of Potosi, and which, at the proper time, had been qualified by the Holy Office.

This discussion being exhausted, they gave the prisoner to understand in the tenth conference, that by the inquisitorial constitutions, they were bound to make him three admonitions, with the object that he should reserve nothing which might influence his defence, or rather his inculpation, because for the former he did not require a judicial compulsion. Moyen acknowledged himself as satisfied with this first canonical advertence, and declaring that he had nothing left to add, he placed his signature to the act of the day with a steady and firm hand (as it always appears to be in every page in which it is found written), together with that of the notary of the secret, Don Gaspar de Orúe.

The second and third admonitions were made to him four months later, the 13th of October, 1752.*

And what was the accused doing all this time?—delivered up to the *mild* penal system of the Inquisition, with shackles on his feet, which had worked deep wounds into his flesh, in a dungeon dark and damp, where he suffered in silence his immeasurable torture? We were going to say

* The ceremony of the admonitions was also an ancient practice of the Holy Office. " The accused, against whom had been issued an order for his imprisonment," says Marchena, " for any of the causes which require a secret summary by the Holy Office, is to be heard three times by way of admonition. In these three audiences no especial charge is to be made; he is only to be asked, whether he knows for what cause he has been imprisoned, giving him to understand at the same time that the Holy Office apprehends no one without a just motive. If in the three audiences the accused should confess any other crimes than what are contained in the *autos*, they are to be added to those with which he is already charged!"

that the inquisitors invented hell long before Dante and Milton—but we are simple expositors, so let us pass on.

In the last session of October 13th, 1752, they gave Moyen to understand that the fiscal had already drawn up the act of accusation against him, and therefore, in consequence, he should lose no time in making his last declaration; for which purpose they admonished him, because they would then be able to use towards him the *clemency* that the Holy Office *was accustomed* to use to those who made a *good confession*; but if he did not, they advised him, that the fiscal would be heard and justice done.

This took place, as we have already said, on the 13th October, 1752; but two days before this the fiscal (who was a doctor called Grillo, and apparently worthy of his name*) had already concluded his task, and which was so enormous that its contents occupied forty Pages of inquisitorial matter, that is to say, obscure and crowded closely together.

That document was a terrible one. We will only give its conclusion, that an opinion may be formed of it :—

" I beseech and demand of your worships," says the agent of the executioner,† " that holding my relation for true, inasmuch as it is necessary, you will be pleased to declare the said Don Francisco Moyen to be a *heretic, formal, obstinate, and sequacious of the said sects of Luther, Calvin, Sacramen,‡ Jansenius, Quesnel, Manichæus, and Mahommed, and most vehemently suspected of Judaism,* and approver of other errors and heresies, and as such has incurred the penalties and ecclesiastical censures, condemning him to those which by common right are the laws and royal ordinances of these kingdoms, and the custom of the Holy Office, established against such delinquents, and punishing them with the

* Grillo, *anglice*, shackle or handcuff; it also means a cricket.

† See Note of the Translator, p. 76.

‡ Sacramen, who was he? His name is not to be found in Mosheim. Surely Grillo did not mean the English Sacheverell. I should rather suppose he meant Savonarola.—*Note by Translator.*

merited execution, and delivering him to the civil power as an impenitent convict, and a feigned, denying, and fictitious confessor, and declaring his estates confiscated, and ordering them to be appropriated by the royal fiscal; for all which, and whatever else may be necessary, I make this petition as it may best agree with the justice I ask; and I also swear by God our Lord and this + that I do not proceed from malice, but to comply with the obligations of my office, &c.

"Moreover, in case that my intention is not considered as well proved, and if necessary, and in no other form, I demand that the accused be put to the *question of the torture*, in which it is provided, that it be repeated as many times as it may be necessary until he shall declare the entire truth. I demand as above under the corresponding protest, &c. Secret, 11th of October, 1752.

"BARTHOLOMÉ LOPEZ GRILLO."

One thing is prominent in this frightful mockery and atrocity, showing of what the sophistry of man is capable, and that is, that the fiscal who demands the confiscation of goods and the application of the torture, repeated as many times as it may be necessary,* does not demand death nor point to the burning pile!

* We say, in the extracts of the *Directory for Inquisitors* given in the Appendix, that the first inquisitors prohibited the *repetition* of the torture; but, at the same time, they invented a horrible formula to escape this prohibition, which was to say at the end of each application of the torture that it remained suspended. The commentator Marchena, giving an account of this infamous fraud, says literally:—" If the accused, having been put to the torture, should persevere in his denial, it may be repeated several times, the judge inquisitor taking the precaution to declare that the torture has been commenced but not concluded." (*Process of Juan Salas in the Inquisition of Valladolid*, 1527.)

Here are a few other rules, as abominable as hypocritical, concerning the application of the torture established by the Holy Office, according to the instructions of Torquemada, promulgated in Seville, 29th October, 1484, and commented upon by Marchena:—

"Although the accused should confess all that may be imputed to

He only asks to have the prisoner delivered (relaxed) up to the arm of secular justice as a convicted impenitent.

What is the reason of this?

It is because the Inquisition was essentially hypocritical as it was essentially treacherous and cruel. Its inquisitors

him, and given undeniable proofs of candour, still the fiscal ought to require that he be put to the torture, this being an indispensable requisite of the fiscal accusation."—*Instructions*, Arts. 21 and 22.

"Although, according to the jurisprudence of the ancient Inquisition, it was necessary that at the least there should be two indications for the application of the torture; in the present Spanish one this requisite is not necessary, it being entirely arbitrary; the judge being able to order it in every case in which he considers it advisable; and therefore there is no other rule in this matter than the prudence of the inquisitors who may be concerned with the suit. (*Idem.* Art. 48.) For the application of the torture the law says that the previous determination of the inquisitors and councillors is necessary; but in practice the decision of the judge charged with the summary is sufficient; and this is the practice of all the tribunals of Spain."

"In applying the torture to the accused, he is not to be asked any especial question, not even upon the points which may have been the motive for its application; for should he declare any other crimes than those of which he is accused, or discover any other criminals against whom there has not been any suspicion, a cause may be substantiated against them, or the punishment augmented of the accused who is upon the rack." (*Idem.* Art. 49.)

"The heretic convicted and confessed can and ought to be put to the torture, *in caput alienum*, that is to say, that he may declare his accomplices."

"Although in the civil tribunals the only torture made use of is that of the rack, the Holy Office makes use of many others according as it may be convenient. The before-mentioned Salas, after giving him eleven *tratos de cuerda*,* placed over his face a piece of fine linen made

---

* The hands of the accused are placed behind his back and tied fast to one end of a rope, which is then passed over a pulley, and the unfortunate wretch is in this manner suspended and raised to a certain height; he is then let fall, but before reaching the ground he is suddenly checked by a stop upon the rope. It is needless to say that both arms are dislocated by such horrible treatment.—*Note by Translator.*

were mostly ecclesiastics, and, as such, they were by the canons prohibited from the shedding of blood. It is true they burnt thousands of persons, but they never condemned any one to death!

It is from this that the Señor Prebendary has taken his

wet, and then poured into his mouth and nose half a gallon of cold water, which, in passing through the linen, fell drop by drop. This operation was repeated after giving him two more *tratos de cuerda* in both feet."—*Process de Juan Salas ut supra.* (This was the same torture applied to Antonio Perez, Secretary of Philip II.)

Now what does the Prebendary Saavedra say to these authentic and constant practices, so opposed to his mild theories? Let us hear him:—

"What use," says he, "did the Spanish Inquisition make of this torture?

"1st. The torture could not be applied except to offenders against the faith" (that is to say, the only offence for which no man ought to be punished).

"2nd. The torture could not be applied until the suit was concluded and the accused had made his defence." (The Señor Prebendary is answered by the fiscal Grillo demanding the application of the torture to Moyen before his defence was heard,)

"3rd. To decree the torture it was necessary to have a *semi-plena* proof of the offence, and that the accused had been of bad reputation." (Agreed: For the full proof two witnesses were sufficient, although they were infamous, false, heretics, &c. What, then, must have been the semi-proof?)

"4th. The torture was applied at the petition of the fiscal, and not by the command of the inquisitors." (Agreed: Some one had to ask for it. Would the Señor Prebendary have the accused ask for it himself? And the fiscal, was he not also one of the inquisitors?)

"5th. It was requisite to have the unanimity of the inquisitors." (Agreed: But how many were there? Generally two, never more than three, and many times only one.)

"6th. The accused could appeal when it was unjust." (But to whom could he appeal? for example, in Lima, when the inquisitor whose turn it was went in a bad humour to visit the secret dungeons and commenced to put in use the rack. Should he appeal from one inquisitor to another, from one executioner to another executioner, from the thief Unda to the thief Calderon?)

grand and principal argument. "The inquisitors," he says, "could not condemn any one to death; *ergo*, the Inquisition was not cruel and sanguinary; and those who say the contrary are nothing less than calumniators and shameless

"7th. Before applying the torture to the accused they gave him to understand the reasons for its application." (But we have already seen that to do so is prohibited by the 49th Article of the Instructions of 1484. And how could they say what it was they wanted to force from him, when this was exactly what they did not know? This is the logic of those who try to defend the Inquisition.)

"8th. When the accused declared that he could not bear the torture they applied to him, they changed it for one of a milder kind!" (What refinement in cruelty, *mild torture! ! !)*

"9th. Paul III. gave orders that the torture should not be applied more than one hour, when Elizabeth of England caused it to be applied one hour and-a-half." (Granted likewise: the Prebendary Saavedra is, as we are informed, for we have not the honour to be acquainted with him personally, young and robust, and we will take the liberty to ask him, for how many minutes, nay, how many seconds, would his reverence like to bear the torture of the *rack?*

"10th. The Bishop of the diocese was obliged to assist at the application of the torture, along with the inquisitors and councillors, to moderate its rigour." (Let the Señor Prebendary read in the Appendix the judicial power granted by the authority of the Bishop of Santiago, in 1806, to the Inquisition at Lima to apply the torture *ad libitum*. How could it be otherwise? In no case could the Bishops of Santiago, Buenos Ayres, or Chuquisaca, assist at Lima, to moderate the rigour of the torture applied to any of their flock.)

"11th. The torture could only be applied once." (It is true, it was so ordered, but we have seen that with a slight precaution it might be applied twenty times, and supposing it were so, how is it that Grillo demanded that it should be repeated as many times as it was necessary? —*Nota bene.)*

"12th. The confession under the torture was not valid unless it was ratified by the accused twenty-four hours after; this left him in full liberty, and it cannot be said that his confession was obtained by force." (Agreed: but how was it obtained? Was it not by the mild persuasion of the rack?)

It was prohibited to torture the *Moors*. "Unheard of mildness!" exclaims in his enthusiasm the Señor Prebendary, and we also say— Indeed it was!

slanderers, and consequently declared enemies of the catholic religion."*

To which we answer, it is true such is the *formula*. It says at relaxing the accused, that is to say when they deliver him up to the executioner (whatever he may be called, whether jailor, magistrate, viceroy, &c.), we beseech and charge you to be considerate with him.† but with that

And here the apologist concludes his defence of the torture in the following words, page 68: " See then, ye stubborn enemies of the Spanish Inquisition, in what manner it made use of the torture, which the practice of the European tribunals and the national laws had formed to its hands. See how it surrounded its application with *charitable precautions* (the one hour of Paul III. for example) that the accused should not suffer too much."

We have expatiated rather long upon this subject, perhaps to the tiring of our readers and at the risk of repetition, but it is without doubt the most odious phase of the Inquisition, and it must be seen that the enumeration alone by Señor Saavedra of its *charitable precautions* has exposed it in all its repugnant and naked horrors.

In another point of view the above exposition may be taken as a specimen of the dialectics of the reverend apologist, who impelled by his singular determination to justify, coûte qui coûte, an institution which nothing can justify, has believed that he has fulfilled his object in a most triumphant manner, by bringing forward theories and doctrines taken merely from liturgies and books of theology, or from those of sectaries and casuists and that with sophisms and absurdities he has been able to overthrow all history and philosophy, truth and logic. It is for this we have believed that for those to condemn the Inquisition who did not know it, it would be sufficient for them to read with a little attention the *Rapid Sketch* of the Señor Saavedra.

* *Rapid Sketch,* page 121.

† Fuentes, in his statistics of Lima, page 128, gives the complete formula. The commentator of the *Directory for Inquisitors*, in his annotations, translated by Marchena, concerning the fiction of humanity so admired by Señor Saavedra, expresses himself in the following terms, truly worthy of the Inquisition : " Let the inquisitors observe great caution, he says, not to omit making this request to the civil power, not to shed human blood, so that they may not commit an irregularity. or this purpose a most useful precaution is indicated by Covarrubius,

beseeching and charging the most part went from thence to the burning pile. "An exception purely nominal," exclaims an illustrious modern writer* in reference to this artful fraud, " seeing that the inquisitors held at their disposal the torture and power of relaxing the accused, which carried with it the declaration of heresy; a crime which the laws condemned to the punishment of death, and whose sentence the judges could do no less than carry into effect when the Holy Office delivered up to them the criminal." Moreover, if the judge, in compliance with the hypocritical supplication with which they concluded the sentence, viz. that he would treat the prisoner with humanity, did not burn him immediately, the Inquisition would judge *him* as being suspected of heresy, founded upon his negligence in complying with the civil laws against heretics.

The fiction was a coarse one, but it served its purpose, it quieted the legal scruples of the tender-hearted and humane inquisitor, the blood of the victim was not upon *his* hands,

and which is, that instead of using the word *deliver (tradere)* to the civil power, it would be far better that the Inquisition should condemn the criminals in presence of the civil judges, and then immediately expel them from the ecclesiastical jurisdiction *(damnatos a propria jurisdictione dimittere),* that there and then *ut denique statim* they may be received by the secular power, and suffer the punishment of death *judex sæcularis eos recipiat, et ultimo supplicio adficiat,* and in effect such is the practice."

The intercession made by the inquisitors to the civil power, when they delivered up a heretic being, as we have seen, a mere formality, gives occasion for the following question, Can an inquisitor make such an intercession without any scruple of conscience, taking into account that there are many laws prohibiting any one from interceding for a heretic? To which I answer, certainly it would not be lawful to intercede for a heretic, when by doing so it would be of service to him, or tend to prevent the punishment of his crime; but it is permitted when it has no other effect than to avoid an irregularity, which without it the inquisitors would incur. (Annotations upon the second book of the *Directory of Aymerico.*)

* Torres de Castilla.

nor was his holy robe stained with the saliva which issued from the foaming mouth of the dying wretch in his last convulsive moments of pain and anguish.

But if in consequence of the torture it should happen, as it frequently did, that the accused expired under it, they did not then have recourse to the artifice of words but to the infamy of hypocrisy. The formula they used in sentencing any one to the torture was in effect the following; " to which (the torture) we command that you be put and kept such time as it shall seem right to us, and if you should die or in any way be maimed it will be *your own fault and charge* and not ours, in consequence of your not being willing to tell the truth."

Here we behold the scholastic sophistry, in all its brutal nakedness, brought face to face with history, and confronted by our daily experience, and which every one may contemplate before his eyes, or feel within his conscience to be the inevitable logic of reason. To maintain as the truth, that the Inquisition did not condemn to death, would be the same as to contend that the tribunals of our republic at the present day do not intend that punishment should be inflicted, because pointing out the laws which prescribe it, they delegate its being carried into effect to the commandant of police, and by him to the executioner.

Such is the casuistry and absurd logic of the Señor Prebendary!

Again, they declaim against Llorente because he says that *to relax* is equivalent *to kill*. But we, who have not read the work of that critical historian, being content with the perusal of a compendium of it by Rodriguez Buron, do not require his authorized testimony. It being simply a question of common sense, of good faith, in short one of a dictionary. In effect Escriche, in his 'Dictionary of Legislation,' says "Relaxation is the delivering up of the criminal, made by the ecclesiastical judge to the civil one, for the purpose of carrying into effect the sentence, in the execution of which blood has to be shed." "Relaxation to the secular power," adds the commentator Marchena, "is the last punishment to which any one is sentenced by the Holy Office, and it is the civil judge who decrees the ordinary punishment. It is true that the civil judges would be excommunicated and treated as heretics, if they did not order the criminals delivered to them by the inquisitors to be executed immediately;" and he also says that the inquisitors affirm that "they are in no manner responsible for the death of the heretics, because the laws which condemn them to that punishment are carried into effect by the civil power."*

Concerning whether relaxation is equivalent to death, and death by fire, we have the opinions of the eulogists and oracles of the Inquisition themselves. "No one doubts," says Peña, "in his commentaries upon the 'Directory for Inquisitors,' but that heretics should suffer capital punishment; but it is asked, what kind of punishment should that be? Alfonso Castro, second book *de justa hæreticorum punitione*, believes that it is of little consequence whether they are put to death by the sword, or by fire, or by any other method; but the Cardinal de Ostia, Godofredo, Covarrubias, Simancas, Roxas, and others, consider that it is indispensable, and of an *absolute necessity* that they should *be burnt in the fire;* because as the first one of the above-named very justly observes, that fire is the natural punishment of heresy, for the Evangelist St. John, chap. xv., says, 'Si quis in me non manserit mittetur, foras, sicut palmes, et arescet, et colligent cum, et in ignem mittent, et ardebit.' 'If any man abide

---

* There have been juriconsulists, says the commentator Peña, who have maintained that the civil judges, to whom have been delivered the criminals relaxed by the Inquisition, have the power not to sentence them to the ordinary punishment; but all the canonists refute this opinion, grounding their authority upon the constitutions of the pontiffs Boniface VIII., Urban IV., and Alexander IV. So that if the judges should delay the punishment of the criminals, those who may be guilty of such a great crime would be considered as the abettors of heresy, and prosecuted as such!

not in me, he is cast forth as a branch, and is withered; and men gather them, and cast them into the fire, and they are burned.' And this opinion is sanctioned by the universal practice of the republic of Christ. Simancas and Roxas add that they ought to be burnt alive, but before burning them it is necessary to take the precaution *to tear out their tongues*, or put a gag into their mouths, to prevent them by their blasphemies from giving scandal to the spectators." (Peña, Annotations to the second book of the Directory.)

But, finally, does not the apologist of the Inquisition himself endeavour to make manifest in every one of his pages the inconclusiveness of his bloodless theory, with the undeniable reality of facts? Does he not himself refer to St. Augustin, where that saint asked of the Conde Marcellino mercy for the heretical Donatists, saying, in the *name of Jesus*, " We desire that they may be corrected, but not that their lives be taken away"? Does not the same author put into the mouth of Gregory the Great those noble words of the ancient Church : " The Church defends criminals from the punishment of death, so as not to be a participator in the effusion of blood"? And those other words of the Pope St. Leo : " The Church confines herself to pronouncing spiritual punishments by the mouths of its ministers, but it never sheds human blood"? And, in short, does he not himself point out, as though he would with a breath overthrow the unsubstantial fabric of his sophistry, the historical date in which the Emperor Frederic II. of Germany, prescribed to the civil judges that " they should deliver to the flames those whom the inquisitors had condemned as heretics"?

With his own confessions before him, how is it credible that the same writer, who had just noted them down, should in the next line ask us a question like the following :—" Have you still the pretension to make us agree that the Inquisition ever sentenced any one to death? Why that would be the height of folly."

Yes, Señor Prebendary, it would be the height of folly to

deny that the Inquisition, which knew that to *relax* was equivalent to *kill*, (because in a legal sense they were identical, the same as they were in practice), which knew that the civil judges were compelled to deliver up to the flames " those whom the inquisitors had condemned as heretics ;" in short, knew that it was a mere fiction of formula to say, *I relax*, instead of *I condemn to death* ; and finally, which prosecuted the officers of the civil power themselves, as accomplices of heretics, when they did not immediately burn the *relaxed*, as your own work itself tells us ;—to deny all this is indeed not only the height of folly, it is the height of madness!

Yes, Señor Prebendary, it is the height of folly to endeavour at the present day to maintain such sophisms of contradictions. Our globe has grown too large to be held in the sleeve of our father, St. Francisco, or for any one to believe, not even the disciples of St. Ignacio, in the "He did not pass here"* of the casuists. "The Inquisition," says a writer, a Christian and a ultramontane Catholic, but enlightened and sincere, † "as an ecclesiastical tribunal ought to have limited itself to the judging of heretics and to the imposition of spiritual punishments, such as excommunication, fasts, and other penances, that would make them voluntarily abjure their errors, and return to the bosom of the Catholic Church; nevertheless, it did not proceed in this manner. The Inquisition not only excommunicated, but it also condemned to death, to prison, and to the galleys, and in general imposed at its pleasure the punishments it thought

* It is said that one day, a thief took refuge in a convent, the provincial of which was the great San Francisco, and that when the agents of justice who were in pursuit arrived, they addressed themselves to the saint, who was standing in the doorway, and asked him if the thief had entered the convent, he replied, with his finger pointing to the loose and ample sleeve of his dress, "He did not pass here." And thus he believed, that while he had saved the thief, he had not compromised himself by telling a falsehood! How many saints of the present day narcotize their consciences, by acting in a similar manner? —*Note by Translator.*

† Doctor Garcia Calderon, president of the last Peruvian congress.

proper; and thus was put in practice the principle that heretics had no right to inhabit the surface of the globe!"

M. Haureaux, who certainly is not the most severe enemy of the Inquisition (for he has more than once justified it, praised it, and like our Prebendary, almost canonized it), says, "that when the inquisitors relaxed a criminal and recommended him to the clemency of the civil power, they knew but too well that the pile was already lighted." If blood caused them such feelings of horror, they ought not to have condemned more than their first victim, and at the sight of the first blood shed by their verdict, they should have renounced a power which others exercised with so much cruelty. But is it not well known that they opposed the clemency which they themselves asked for? Is it not known that before the establishment of the Inquisition, Rome had seized the sword and had wounded and killed with it? The neo-Catholics, says the impartial French writer, and pointing as it were with his finger to the men of the school of the chief Prebendary, ought not then to persist in maintaining this miserable theory, but ought to acknowledge the participation, direct or indirect, that the Romish Church has had with the *autos de fé* which have imbrued in blood France, Spain, and the Low Countries.

"What! the Church has horror of blood?" says M. de Coquerel, "the inquisitors could condemn to death but could not behold its infliction; they had executioners to torture the prisoners in their dungeons, but not to execute them upon the scaffold."

But let us proceed with the process.

The fiscal Grillo, in his extensive writ of accusation, (which it is needless to say was an immense accumulation of nonsensical jargon and absurd pedantries, according to the style of that period) condensed the articles of it into the 44 heresies recorded against Moyen as they had been *qualified* by the Holy Office, and added two more of his own accord, only for the purpose of showing his personal zeal, and also a third for *perjury*, in consequence of the accused having denied all the charges, so that the heresies summed up were altogether forty-seven.

In what did they consist?

We have noted down in the course of this narrative, the character, the occasion, the tendency and even the explanation given of some of them by the accused.

But arriving at this part, the most important and serious of the whole process, inasmuch as it involves the *cuantum* of the question, and therefore it is necessary should be heard and understood by our fellow-citizens, (among whom has been circulated the glorification of the Holy Office with the express sanction and approbation of our ecclesiastical authorities), the mournful and terrible debate in its own phrases with its peculiar terminology, and if possible with its quaint and contracted orthography, the same almost as though we had photographed each page of the writings of this horrible summary.* And thus the figure of the victim will be exposed more to our view in the obscure recess in which he is going to be judged.

It is not possible to transcribe one by one all the accusations and their respective answers;—were we to do so this work would extend to volumes. But when, eight years ago in the library of Lima, we made with our own hands these extracts from the process, we selected, with the object of preserving the unity of the whole, those which we considered as being more connected with the original denunciations, and also as containing less of theology and logic.

We thought then that perhaps at some future day we might make a small book which could be read with advantage by our countrymen. But now it goes forth to the world clothed with the yellow robe of polemics, although not for that is it one *iota* altered from the original, it is the same terrible process of one condemned by the Inquisition.

Behold then the series of the *propositions* which are copied

---

* See note by the translator, page 76.

from the original documents, according to the order in which they were qualified by the Holy Tribunal.*

In order to render the picture more compact, which in any other manner would have presented itself in great confusion, we have placed at the foot of each charge the answer given to it by Moyen, that is those of which we have preserved a copy or an extract.

Behold then, the gloomy hall of the Inquisition of Lima, with its curiously ornamented but lugubrious and obscure ceiling, its large crucifix working upon hinges,† its lighted

---

* The 13 propositions we have transcribed correspond in the same order in which they were found marked in the process with the numbers 1, 2, 15, 20, 28, 29, 31, 32, 33, 34, 37, 39 and 40.

† The traveller Stevenson, who took an active part in the sackage of the Inquisition at Lima by the populace in 1813, assures us that he saw this crucifix, and that it had a groove in the upper part of the neck by which a man placed upon a ladder behind the canopy could move the head as he pleased. "In how many instances," indignantly exclaims the witness of such an artifice, "may appeals to this imposture have caused an innocent man to own himself guilty of crimes he never dreamt of! Overawed by fear, and condemned as was believed by a miracle!" (Stevenson's Twenty years' Residence in South America, vol. 1. page 368.)

Stevenson, who came to America in 1804, and afterwards served as secretary to Lord Cochrane, 1820, was obliged in 1806 to appear before the Inquisition (when it was already in its last stage of decay) in consequence of holding a conversation, rather free, in a café with a Dominican friar called Bustamonte, about the Virgin of the rosary, for which he was denounced, and conducted to the Inquisition by its last alguazil major, the Conde de Montes de Oro. "I turned my eyes," he says, "to the dire triumvirate, seated on an elevated part of the hall, under a canopy of green velvet, edged with pale blue, a crucifix of a natural size hanging behind them, a large table was placed before them, covered and trimmed to match the canopy, and bearing two burning green tapers, an inkstand, some books and papers." (Work above quoted, page 271).

This description corresponds exactly with what we have been informed by a respectable gentleman residing at Santiago, and who a short time later had to assist with his presence a *little auto de fé* for having read a book prohibited, but who, however, was innocent.

tapers of green wax, with its three sombre looking judges seated beneath a rich canopy of silk and velvet; the head jailor in a coat embroidered with gold, the fiscal, or attorney-general, the four secretaries of the confiscation and of the secret, the familiars, the notaries, the acolytes and the executioners of the torture, all are in their places, seated upon rows of seats, in the form of steps. The unhappy criminal in the dress of a penitencial, sitting upon a bench, scarcely able to express himself in their language, and loaded with shackles, is seen alone, haggard, wan and wretched, reduced to that condition by his long imprisonment and the tender mercies of the *mild* Inquisition! in front of his accusers, his judges and his executioners.—*Ecce homo!*

Let us now commence the reading of the pieces announced in the process.

QUALIFICATION.

" In the Holy Office of the Inquisition, in the city of the kings, on the days ninth, eleventh and twelfth of the month of May, one thousand seven hundred and fifty, the very illustrious Señor Counsellor, visitor general, Doctor Don Pedro Antonio de Arenaza, y Gárate, and the Señor Inquisitor Doctor Don Matheo de Amuzquibar in their audience of the morning, gave orders to admit the R. R. P. P. Fray Francisco Xavier Torrejon, y Velasco, of the order of our Lady of Mercy, and ex-provincial of his order; Fray Agustin Espinosa, of the monastery of San Augustin and Metropolitan of his order; and father Joseph de Paredes of the company of Jesus, qualifiers of this Inquisition, to whom had been delivered the extract thirty-four days before for the purpose of becoming acquainted with its contents, and having time to study the different points of the said extract, and also having read it over again the days ninth, eleventh and twelfth of the present month, they pronounced to each head the following censures.

I. PROPOSITION.—THE FEAR OF GOD.

" A certain European of the French nation, said before

several persons that we ought not to *fear* God, and being contradicted by the bystanders he repeated his assertion, and declared that God was incapable of being angry or of changing his intentions, and consequently of punishing mankind, because he was benignant, and to do so was contrary to his almighty goodness. A proposition which he repeated several times in that conversation, without conceding or being convinced by the many reasons given to him to the contrary, particularly by a certain ecclesiastical doctor; till at length one of the bystanders enraged, said to him that it was heresy he defended, and that he appeared to be a Lutheran, to which he replied that he was not a heretic, and what he said was not heresy, and that he defended only what he had read, and what in reality was the truth.

"They said they were agreed, and that the charge contained a proposition scandalous, temerarious, and heretical, and which constituted the accused a formal heretic, and a contumacious Lutheran."

ANSWER OF THE ACCUSED.

Although the proposition censured, contains in this case the explanation given by Moyen himself to his words, he moreover asserted in the audience of the 24th of May, with respect to this charge the following :—

"That the really true Christians have no cause, nor ought to fear God, because God is incapable of doing an injustice, and having received from His Majesty all the good we possess, we ought not to fear him but to love and adore him, and for this reason in the first precept of the Decalogue it does not say fear God, but love Him above all other things."

II. GOD AND TEMPESTS.

"A Spaniard in company with others having asked the said Frenchman if he was afraid of tempests, upon an occasion in which it thundered, by which they were frightened; the said Frenchman replied that he did not fear God nor ought to fear him. And that proposition being impugned principally by the same ecclesiastical doctor referred to in the first charge, he said that he affirmed that they ought not to fear God, for with respect to the man who was predestined to glory, whether he feared God or not, he would be saved, and he who was predestined to hell, whether he feared God or not, would be condemned.

> "They said they were agreed, that the first point of this charge confirmed the censure given to the antecedent, and that the second point contained a new proposition erroneous, scandalous, theologically false and Lutheran heretical, and which constitutes the accused a formal Lutheran heretic."

Answer.

The answer made by Moyen to this proposition was by ratifying it, as being true, says the act cited of the audience of the 24th May, 1752, that the tempests are occasioned by natural causes, the order of which is designed by God for the good of the natural world.

XV. The Pontiffs.

" Upon another occasion in the presence of various persons, the said accused repeated the same proposition as in the last charge, adding that the Pope canonized, or did any other thing for the sake of money, because it is known that his Holiness does not canonize many that are canonizable, because there is no money forthcoming.

> "They said they were agreed, that the first part of the charge had the same censure as the one antecedent, and that the second part contained scandalous doctrine, temerarious, heretically blasphemous and formally heretical, and injurious to the Pontiffs and to the Church, constituting the accused a heretical blaphemer, and formally a heretic."

Answer.

Although we have not preserved an especial annotation of

the answers of Moyen relative to the anterior proposition, nevertheless as it is concerning the Popes, and is one of the most important points of the accusation and defence in the process, we insert the following passages in his notes made in the year 1758, for the purpose of serving as a basis for his advocate in his allegation of defence.

"The first argument that I had with the *Serranos** concerning the Pope, was upon an occasion when he was called the Universal Head of the Church, which title the Pontiffs, who have been acknowledged as saints, refused to admit; because St. Gregory says, that the Pontiff who takes this title is a precursor of Antichrist, and exalts himself above his brethren, and has renounced the faith; and in which case the other bishops would not be each head of his Church, which is heresy; but it is manifest to all, that they are true bishops in their dioceses, established by Jesus Christ over a number of Christians in the order of hierarchy, all of whom are under the command of the Pontiff, who is the first of the bishops, and also the Bishop of the Universal Church, but not the Universal Bishop of the Church, as St. Gregory says.

"The government of the Universal Church was delivered to St. Peter, who is the prince of the Apostles, but he never was called the Universal Apostle, and none of the Pontiffs have been willing to receive this title. This is what the accusers affirm. I have said, and it is true, that they are words translated from the history of the Schism of the Greeks, written by the Father Luis de Maimbourg, of the company of Jesus, vol. 1, book 1, page 76 and 77; and if to my misfortune I have persisted in this difference of saying 'the universal head of the Church, or head of the universal Church,' which is the distinction made by St. Gregory, it is very different and very well explained. He says that he

---

* He refers to those who denounced him at Potosi, and whom he calls in one of his declarations, the Doctors of the Sierra, (ridge of mountains) in contradistinction to the ancient Doctors, whose canonical and theological authority was the only one he admitted. . . . . .

who calls himself Universal Head, may be compared to the devil, but he who calls himself Head of the Universal Church may be compared to St. Peter; that there is a great difference between the two, and thus I have understood it as explained by St. Gregory, and I have done nothing more than repeat what the holy Doctor said, and therefore it appears to me, Señor Doctor, that this accusation will not stand.

"For having said that there have been Popes unworthy of that Holy Office, I ought not to have been accused to this Holy Office, it is what history says in the Schism of the Greeks, (vol. 1, book 3, page 256). It also says that the Roman Emperor made use of Alberic, king of the Romans, who held the Pope John XI. shut up in a room like a slave, and compelled him to give satisfaction to the Emperor contrary to justice, and that such a Pope was unworthy of that supreme dignity; and such was that miserable John XI., whom the infamy of his mother had placed upon the chair of St. Peter.* This I said upon an occasion in which I

---

* Moyen must have been well read in history, and appears to have had more knowledge, education and sound sense than all his bigoted persecutors put together. We may see the degraded and infamous state of the Popedom at the period to which he refers, in the 49th chapter of the Decline and Fall of the Roman Empire. "In the frequent schisms," says Gibbon, "the rival claims were submitted to the sentence of the Emperor, and in a Synod of Bishops he presumed to judge, to condemn, and to punish the crimes of a guilty Pontiff. Otho the First, imposed a treaty on the senate and people, who engaged to prefer the candidate most acceptable to his majesty; his successors anticipated or prevented their choice; they bestowed the Roman benefice, like the Bishops of Cologne or Bamberg, or their chancellors or preceptors; and whatever might be the merit of a Frank or Saxon, his name sufficiently attests the interposition of foreign power. These acts of prerogative were most speciously excused by the vices of a popular election. The competitor who had been excluded by the Cardinals appealed to the passions or avarice of the multitude; the Vatican and the Lateran were *stained with blood*, and the most powerful Senators, the Marquises of Tuscany and the

remarked that the señors curates and clergymen went about with so much grandeur, with their dresses trimmed with fringes, when in Spain, France and Portugal the ecclesiastics go about so moderate in their dress; and if in this there is blame, it is the truth, and therefore it can be nothing more than Catholic indiscretion which cannot offend the Holy Tribunal.

Counts of Tusculum, held the Apostolic See in a long and disgraceful servitude. The Roman Pontiffs of the ninth and tenth centuries, were insulted, imprisoned, and murdered by their tyrants; and such was their indigence after the loss and usurpation of the ecclesiastical patrimonies, that they could neither support the state of a Prince, nor exercise the charity of a Priest. The influence of two sister prostitutes, Marozia and Theodora, was founded on their wealth and beauty, their political and amorous intrigues; the most strenuous of their lovers were rewarded with the Roman mitre, and their reign may have suggested to the darker ages the fable of a female Pope. The bastard son, the grandson, and the great-grandson of Marozia, a rare genealogy, were seated in the chair of St. Peter; and it was at the age of *nineteen* years, that the second of these became the head of the Latin Church. His youth and manhood were of a suitable complexion; and the nations of pilgrims could bear testimony to the charges that were urged against him in a Roman Synod, and in the presence of Otho the Great. As John XII. had renounced the dress and decencies of his profession, the *soldier* may not perhaps be dishonoured by the wine which he drank, the blood that he spilt, the flames that he kindled, or the licentious pursuits of gaming and hunting. His open simony might be the consequence of distress; and his blasphemous invocation of Jupiter and Venus, *if it be true*, could not possibly be serious. But we read with some surprise, that the worthy grandson of Marozia lived in public adultery with the matrons of Rome; that the Lateran palace was turned into a school for prostitution, and that his rapes of virgins and widows had deterred the female pilgrims from visiting the tomb of St. Peter, lest, in the devout act, they should be violated by his successor."

Moyen has told us that St. Gregory says, "that he who calls himself universal head of the Church may be compared to the devil, but he who calls himself head of the universal church may be compared to St. Peter." History does not inform us, I believe, what the above mentioned worthy successors of St. Peter called themselves, but I

"Afterwards I remember that they accused me of having denied the absolute power of the Holy Father. I had no intention to offend the respect due to His Holiness, and the distinction I made between the spiritual and temporal, was that the only obligation of the Pontiff was to maintain the doctrine of Jesus Christ, and to govern his religion as one who had received this charge from Jesus Christ himself, when he made him the first Bishop of His Universal Church and delivered to him the keys, a proof that the Holy Father ought to occupy himself in the affairs of Heaven, without maintaining troops and carrying on wars, which is the business of kings to whom God has committed the government of men in what relates to temporal affairs, and who ought to give to His Holiness troops sufficient to guard his person; this indiscretion I have not made out of disrespect, and it does not appear to me that I have offended against religion, and if I have done so I am ready to retract, because it has been through ignorance.

"Señor Doctor, the misfortune I had in entering into an argument with that clergyman, who told me that he had a good mind to smash my face with a candlestick,* was not my fault. The first witness had told him of the abdication of Pope Benedict IX.† and the said clergy-

can well picture to myself the rage and indignation which the devil must have felt at the outrageous insult offered to his character, should anyone ever have had the ignorance to compare the son, grandson, and great-grandson of the *virtuous* Marozia to his Satanic Majesty.—*Note by Translator.*

* The curate of Cotognita.

† The worthy clergyman above mentioned, who seemed to be so fond of striking arguments in his discussions, would perhaps not find in his veracious catalogue anything like the following: "But very different from them, as a most flagitious man and capable of every crime, was their successor Benedict IX. The Roman citizens, therefore, in the year 1038, hurled him from St. Peter's chair; but he was restored soon after by the Emperor Conrad. As he continued, however, to be as bad as could be, the Romans again expelled him in the year 1044; and gave the government of the church to John, bishop of

man told me it was a lie; that never any of the pontiffs had abdicated his seat; that I talked like a declared heretic; that it was not written in the catalogue which he had. And with respect to the other part, the second witness had told him, that I believed God had more power in purgatory than the Holy Father. He asked me if I was ignorant of the authority that the Popes held in purgatory: and as my intention was not to deny it, only that he should prove it to me by argument, I asked him if the soul was not sent there by God to suffer for its sins. He answered, Yes. I immediately deduced the consequence that as for God there being no time, and as his determination must be fulfilled in the object of it, which is the soul; and as the time of being in purgatory is determined by God, how can the Pope deliver that soul? The power of man cannot prevail against the decrees of the Divinity, and consequently if I had to give ten or twelve thousand dollars to the Holy Father to deliver a blessed soul from purgatory, which he was not able to do, it would be better for me to keep the money. Not being able to answer otherwise, these mild words came into the priest's imagination, and he said "that he would break my head!" And although these were not the words a clergyman ought to use, yet it is the truth, and I bore them only from the great respect I have for the holy religion and its ministers.

Sabina, who assumed the name of Sylvester III. After three months Benedict forcibly recovered his power, by the victorious arms of his relatives and adherents; and Sylvester was obliged to flee. But soon after, finding it impossible to appease the resentment of the Romans, he *sold* the pontificate to John Gratian, arch-presbyter of Rome, who took the name of Gregory VI. Thus the Church had two heads, Sylvester and Gregory. The Emperor Henry III. terminated the discord; for in the Council of Sutri, A.D. 1046, he caused Benedict, Gregory, and Sylvester, to be all declared unworthy of the pontificate; and he placed over the Romish Church Suidger, bishop of Bamberg, who assumed the pontifical name of Clement II. (Mosheim's Ecclesiastical History, vol. 2, book 3, part 2, chapter 2).—*Note by Translator.*

"If he had asked me, did I believe in purgatory, if I said prayers for the dead, if I bought the bull of confession, if I believed that the Pope was a saint before dying, should I not have made those answers in a Catholic manner, which he at the expense of his understanding mistook for heresy, telling the other *serranos* to make me talk of those things which are prohibited by the Holy Tribunal, and as a Catholic he should not have asked me nor answered me. If without knowing I have asked questions, and as a foreigner I may have erred in that without offending the Holy Tribunal; and it is these questions (which he first asked me) that are the whole of the arguments theological, physical, metaphysical and historical, which I have had with those of the *sierra*; and this was enough for that said witness to be made a muleteer in the service of the Holy Office, and a great deal more he has concealed of his lying calumnies."

XX.—THE AVE MARIA.

"In like manner the accused, in presence of several persons, frequently and at various times said, that when they repeat the *Ave Maria* they ought not to say, The Lord *is* with thee, but, The Lord *was* with thee.

> "They said they were agreed: that this charge contained impious, scandalous, and offensive doctrine, injurious to the most holy Maria, temerarious, erroneous, and formally heretical, and constitutes the accused a formal heretic."

ANSWER.

We have no note or extract concerning this charge, probably because we considered it unnecessary.

XXVIII.—THE EUCHARIST.

"The said Frenchman being at sea, in a voyage from Europe to the Indies, a certain person said to him that God was in all parts, by His essence, His presence, and power. The accused denied this, and said that, although

God was everywhere by His essence and His power, yet not in His presence, because, if He was so, He would be visible to man; to which the said person replied to him, saying that God was a pure Spirit, and consequently not perceptible to the corporeal senses; and it being easy to the Divine power that Christ, our life in body and soul, should make Himself visible, how could he find it repugnant that God, being a pure Spirit, was not perceptible to the bodily eyes? The accused maintained his opinion without giving in to this and other reasons with which the said person endeavoured to convince him.

"They said they were agreed: and that this charge contained scandalous doctrine and false theology, erroneous, and formally heretical, and which constituted the accused a formal heretic."

ANSWER.

The explanation given by Moyen of this charge is contained in the following declaration which he made the 29th of May, 1752:—

"I declare that in the above-named conversation with the syndic (the Franciscan friar) he asked me whether I believed that Jesus Christ was in the host, it being consecrated; and the deponent, believing that what he asked him was whether what he saw with his eyes after the consecration was the body of Christ, he answered that it was the body of Christ mystically but not physically, not knowing that the term physically could cause any surprise; to which the said syndic replied, How was it that the body of Christ was not in the consecrated host physically?—was He not the same as in the heavens? And this deponent answered, Yes; and that was what he said. And as they were drinking, this deponent was playing on the violin, and being asked by Don Diego de Albarado to go on playing, the conversation upon that subject dropped; but what this deponent wished to make understood, in saying that God does not exist physically in the eucharist, is that which our religion teaches us, according as I have understood it, that after the consecration of the elements there remains only the appearance of bread and wine, being the physical or material of what is transubstantiated into the body of Jesus Christ; for I always believed, do believe, and shall believe that in the holy sacrament of the eucharist Jesus Christ exists in the same manner as He does in heaven, in body, and in spirit, and in His divinity; and, expressing more my mind, I add that what I wish to say is, that after the consecration of the Host the body of Jesus Christ is not seen physically, but only the appearance of the elements, but that by the transubstantiation they are no longer physical or material."

XXIX.—THE APPEARANCE OF JESUS CHRIST ON EARTH.

"In like manner the accused, in a certain conversation in presence of several persons, said that the apparitions of Christ our life to men were false and chimerical, giving to understand that these apparitions were other spirits; and also that neither could angels appear in a corporeal figure, because they did not possess bodies, and that Christ having suffered, died, and rose again, and ascended into heaven as an adult man, He could not appear again as a child. With which he wished to satisfy the answers made to him that Christ had appeared in this figure to St. Christopher and to St. Antonio.

"They said they were agreed: and that this charge contained three propositions formally heretical,* .... the heresy of the Sacramentarios,† which constitute the accused a heretic, formal and contumacious."

ANSWER.

We have preserved no extracts concerning this proposition.

* A word is wanting here, it being unintelligible in the original document.
† Those who deny the Real Presence in the Eucharist.

XXXI.—Simony.

"In the same conversation alluded to, the accused added that the sacrifice of the Mass being spiritual it was simony to give money for it; and although they answered him that the stipend for the Mass was not the price of it, but only a contribution, or a species of charitable offering which the faithful gave for the purpose of supporting the priests, he would not retract his opinion.

"They said they were agreed: and that this charge contains scandalous doctrine, offensive to pious ears, contrary to the practice of the universal Church, and erroneous, and constitutes the accused vehemently suspected of the faith."

Answer.

Neither to this charge have we preserved any notes or extracts; but we consider it a proper time to bring to mind what we have already said in a note (page 80), that the process of Moyen informs us that he had given in Potosi the sum of four dollars for the purpose of having Masses said. If it was so, the answer to the charge could not be more practical.

XXXII.—Astronomy.

"The accused being one night in company with several persons, and one of them having referred in terms of praise to the beauty of the starry heavens, the accused made answer and said that so many stars were superfluous; giving them to understand that God had erred in the creation, for that with one He could have produced the same effect as with many.

"They said they were agreed: and that this charge contains a blasphemous and heretical proposition, constituting the accused a heretical blasphemer."

Answer.

We have not preserved any notes or extracts concerning this charge, as at the time very likely we thought it was best to give it without any remarks.

XXXIII.—Geology.

"Upon another occasion the accused said that our globe had never been created, but that it had existed from all eternity; this opinion was impugned by one who was present and heard it, nevertheless the accused persisted in his assertion.

> "They said they were agreed: that the charge contained a formal heresy, which constituted the accused a formal heretic."

Answer.

We are in the same case as in the last proposition.

XXXIV.—The Luxury of the Clergy.

"The accused, in a conversation about the ecclesiastics, several times spoke of them in general in a mocking and disrespectful manner, particularly of the pomp and ostentation of the Señors Bishops, Archbishops, and the Holy Pontiff, wondering that they rode in rich coaches and had large incomes, when St. Peter and the other Apostles and Evangelists went about covered with poor clothing, asking alms and preaching the Gospel.

> "They said they were agreed: that this charge contained scandalous doctrine, offensive *piarum aurium*, insulting to the Pontiffs, to the Ecclesiastical Prelates, and to the State; temerarious, partaking of the heresy of Wickliff, and constituting the accused vehemently suspected in the faith and of the Wickliffian heresy."

Answer.

The answer to this charge by Moyen is found in his first representation to the inquisitors, in which may be read literally as follows:—

"With regard to what I said at that time, concerning the Ecclesiastics, it was not from contempt, nor aversion either, because I have always held that respect for them, which is due to those persons who are dedicated to God, and who represent Jesus Christ in the sacrifice of the mysteries, but it came to be spoken in this manner: The clergyman, whom the Señor Commissary of Potosi has qualified as a Doctor, sometimes talked with me about the poverty in which the Apostles lived, and at the same time while doing so he always drew aside the folds of his dress that I might see the embroidery and silver ornaments beneath it. It was then I spoke of the ostentation and vanity of the bishops, cardinals, and *monigotes*,* who went about in coaches and upon mules, when Jesus Christ only once rode upon an ass one day at Easter; and that to teach religion and celebrate the mysteries it was enough to be learned in theology, and be humble and virtuous, and not necessary to have an income of twenty or thirty thousand dollars, nor to dress, some in scarlet, some in purple, and some without shirts, others with great beards, and here the curates in rich dresses with fringes; that the Gospel did not teach all this grandeur; and suppose that in this description the clergy beheld their picture, and did not like it, my indiscretion did not offend the law, as I did it only for my diversion."

In this charge is also included the verse of Boileau, mentioned at page 65, having taken it from the notes made by Moyen for his advocate.

XXXVII.—THE CROSS.

" Upon another occasion, certain persons who accompanied the said Frenchman, having made reverence before a cross, he said to them that they ought not to venerate any cross, except that upon which Christ died, because the one in that place was only a stick of wood in the form or figure of the true one.

> "They said they were agreed: that this charge contained doctrines opposed to those received by our Holy Mother Church, offensive *piarum aurium*, subversive of good habits, impious, and formally heretical, which constitutes the accused a formal heretic."

ANSWER.

The refutation of this charge is seen in the following

* Monigote, lay brother of a religious order.

words taken from the notes made by Moyen for his advocate:—

"Señor Doctor, I have confessed before the Holy Tribunal, that when I said that they ought not to adore the stone crosses erected along the roads, I did not pretend to speak of the adoration due to the sign of the cross, but it was of the material I spoke; this distinction the accuser ought to have comprehended, that is, if he had had understanding; because confessing adoration for any piece of the holy wood, was confessing to the adoration of the sign of the cross, which if it was not for the sign or form it had, would not be called holy; not that I was ignorant that that adoration is not a precept of the law, but only a proof of love and of faith, and that we ought to adore God alone; and there is a distinction between Jesus Christ and his Holy Mother, for as she was subject to death, she cannot be the Divinity; and therefore, Señor Doctor, this accusation cannot be maintained."

XXXIX.—FATALITY.

"The accused, talking with the curate mentioned in the antecedent charge, concerning predestination and of the great number who are lost eternally for not having had a knowledge of the Messiah, said, It is a very hard case that so many should be condemned, for not having ever heard of the son of a carpenter.

"They said they were agreed: that this scandalous proposition was offensive *piarum aurium*, impious, temerarious, erroneous, formally heretical, and approaching to Judaism, which constituted the accused a formal heretic, and suspected of Judaism."

ANSWER.

We have given the verse of Voltaire made use of by Moyen, at page 64, and in which the phrase, "son of the carpenter," is used in a figurative sense, and as a poetical license.*

---

* It was the expressions in a figurative sense, which the inquisitors denounced with the greatest hatred; their literary capacities may be

XL.—The Mule.

"The before mentioned curate was informed that because a muleteer had ill-treated a mule which had fallen with its burden, the accused attacked him furiously, with the intention of doing him serious injury, and asking who had given authority or power to him or any other man to ill-treat or endeavour to kill that mule, or any other animal, when all estimated and judged by the compilation and orthography of the documents of this process of Moyen.† As a proof of the fury of the qualifiers of the Holy Office against all that was symbolical in literature or even in conversation, we give the following account of one of the most celebrated propositions of Antonio Perez, Secretary to Philip II., condemned to the stake by the Inquisition, in virtue, no doubt, of this Tribunal never having been, as Señor Saavedra assures us, an auxiliary of the tyranny and despotism of kings. Here it is with its qualification :—

"A person saying to the said Antonio Perez, that he ought not to speak ill of the Señor Don Juan de Austria, he answered, It is all very well : after that the king has accused me of disfiguring the sense of the letters I have written, and of having sold the secret of the Council, should I consider the honour of any one to refute such a charge ? If God the Father himself should come between us I would pull his nose, that all might see how little of a loyal cavalier the king has shown himself towards me."

Qualification.

"This proposition, in regard to where he says, that if God the Father himself should come between us, I would pull his nose, is blasphemous, scandalous, offensive *piarum aurium, et ut jacet, est suspecta de hæresi vadianorum, dicentium Deum esse corporeum et habere membra humana.* Nor can it be excused by saying that Christ had a body and a nose when he became a man, because it is proved that the accused spoke of the first person in the Trinity, who is the Father."

For this Castilian blasphemy, and others of a similar kind, but much in vogue at that period, the inquisitors applied to the great man the torture of the cord, and afterwards burnt him in effigy, as he luckily for himself had escaped to France.

---

† Of course which cannot be shown in a translation.—*Note by Translator.*

were creatures of God? Afterwards he spoke again of the same thing; and in the presence of the before mentioned curate, and also to another ecclesiastic, the said Frenchman repeated the same words, and added that he would not eat if it were necessary for him to kill any animal to do so; and being reproached for being so tender-hearted for a mule, when he himself in a certain place had thrust through a man with a sword, he replied that he was provoked by the man to do so, but that the mule could not help falling with its cargo, and therefore gave no provocation to ill-treat or kill it.

"They said they were agreed: that this charge contained a superstitious doctrine by excess in the worship of God, erroneous, hypocritical, with a hurtful and pernicious subterfuge, contrary to the truths expressed in the sacred Scriptures, full of error, and of the Manichean heresy, which constituted the accused vehemently suspected in the faith and a Manichean heretic."

Answer.

This is copied from the second relation of Moyen to his advocate and the allegation for the defence.

"Another flattering thing, Señor Doctor, was to have accused me to the Holy Tribunal of Pythagorism, because I said without reflection that a mule was one of God's creatures. It was not because I was ignorant of the generation of a mule. I knew very well that a mule was not according to the order of God, as all other animals were, and that it is a monster of nature.* . . . . . .

. . I had thought that we might without any offence, also call the mule a creature of God, because generally God is considered the Creator of all that is created. And also they might have known that it was thoughtlessness on my part when I said that I would remain without eating, rather than kill a fowl, when in this country I have killed a large

* I have thought proper to omit the physiology of Moyen.

number of irrational animals, and if I have said that I would rather kill a man who provoked me than I would a mule, that cannot offend the Holy Tribunal. I suppose that it would not be a very charitable or Christian act, to consider foolishness as a crime, and which I have since confessed, and where is the reason to accuse me to the Holy Tribunal? Besides as they have related the story as it happened between a muleteer who ill-treated his mule with a stick, and me with my tongue, why did they interfere and afterwards make me talk so, that they might accuse me to the Señor Commissary, Moreover in this accusation there is nothing against the faith, and besides this conversation was at night when one cannot see what he is doing, and the whole of them had drank plenty of brandy, and did not know what they were talking about, and none of them less than myself."

Up to this part we have given the annotations of Moyen himself, those which follow belong to his advocate the Doctor Valdivieso.

"In the 40th charge, he is accused, that upon a certain occasion, a muleteer ill-treating a mule because it had laid down under its burden, he became furiously indignant, and asked the muleteer who gave him authority to ill-treat or attempt to kill the mule, when all were the creatures of God; and speaking of this in presence of another, added that he would not eat if it were necessary for him to kill any animal to do so, and for all that he is accused of hypocrisy, *sapit hæresian Manicheorum*, and of being suspected of the faith and of being a hypocrite."

"Don Francisco in his audience of accusation, in answer to this difficult charge of having said that he would not kill any animals if it were necessary to do so to eat them, says that in France he went out very often to shoot all kinds of game, and in the voyage from the East Indies he killed two sheep, and on the road from Cuzco to this city two or three fowls, and many times he killed game along the road from Buenos Ayres to Potosi. In the last audience, he remembered that, to a muleteer who ill-treated his mule, and called it a brute without the mule understanding him, he had said, do not ill-treat your fellow creature. If the witness who deposed to this, is the same muleteer, it is natural that he might understand *fellow creature* as meaning *creature of God*.

"And even if it was not so, it appears to me from the observation I have made of similar occurrences, that Don Francisco is very far from Manicheism; the action of the beast laying down with his burden and being ill-treated by the muleteer to make it rise, is very often repeated in this city with the asses destined to carry the grass for sale, and when they fall in the streets of this city the occurrence of Don Francisco is seen repeated, for then the drivers begin to beat them with a piece of hide, and then with sticks, and at last they beat them with stones, until the animals lose all feeling, and their backs are reduced to large sores in the raw flesh. Every one who beholds this operation, considers it very cruel. Those of the mob who are the same kind of people as the drivers, mock them and tell them to be careful of their *fellow creatures,* by which they intend to signify that the men are as incapable as the asses to do as they are ordered. The women who have their hearts docile and mortify themselves, try to persuade them, and say, mind they are creatures of God. This argument is very powerful, because God likewise feels an injury by which his creatures are abused. It is lawful to kill animals to eat them because it is to this use they are intended to be put. It is also lawful to kill them in the chase, because also in this they serve their purpose, which is *diversion.*

"But he who destroys any animal from dislike to it, does not do what is lawful, because it is an abuse of the works of the Creator, and in the same manner as they bless God in esteeming his works, so they do offend him in hating them. We have a right to kill them for our use, but he who has a heart so sensible as to feel a repugnance to shed blood, would be justified in not doing it; and it is a fact that the greater part of the illustrious females of this city not only do not kill the fowls themselves, but when they order their servants to do it, they turn away their eyes so that they may not see the operation, and no one suspects them of error!"

After perusing the foregoing, the reader will be inclined to think that the merit of the defence is upon a par with that of the accusation.

Nevertheless we will not express our opinion of the propositions of Moyen however absurd, puerile, and incredible the most of them may appear, and our motive for not doing so is, that under no plea or pretext are we willing, on our part, to allow this present narrative, which is purely one of simple facts divested of all ornament and colouring (as we declared in the preface) to be made a question of dogma. As we have always considered this to be forbidden ground, in whose mute and solemn abodes the only sovereign is the human conscience, with its sublime attributes of free will and faith indestructible, joined to Christian tolerance which is the eternal equilibrium, maintaining those attributes suspended over the moral universe preventing their exuberance from degenerating into perverse fanaticism on the one hand, and into dry and sterile incredulity on the other.

But for the satisfaction of our own humble conscience, concerning the heinousness of the faults or errors of Moyen, supported as he was, entirely by his imperturbable and heroic good faith, in presence of the torture and the stake, we will only make an appeal to the conscience of the illustrious eulogist of the judges which condemned Moyen, and ask him in his character of an Apostle of men's consciences, which it is but natural he exercises amongst the members of our society, what punishment or penitence at the present day would he give to a man, an involuntary victim of doubt, who should kneel at his feet and confess, that he did not believe in the temporal power of the Pope! (one of the most serious charges made against Moyen); or who would submit to him as points to be consulted, the questions of astronomy and

and of natural history concerning whether or no there were a superfluity of orbs in the immensity of space, or whether a mule was a natural object or an unnatural monster?

Would the maximum of priestly severity in a case like the present amount to anything more than the repetition of a few prayers or to the reading of some pious books, or a course of exercises, lasting nine days, in which he could enjoy the coolness of the shade, the sight of beautiful flowers, the perfumed incense of the temple, with the rich and savory delicacies of the table?

The prayers, which the Holy Office imposed upon Moyen to learn, were his chains, the obscurity of his dungeon and the gradual maceration of his body, until it was converted into a species of cadaverous ulcer. The reading of mystical books consisted in the Sambenito, and the marching through the streets mounted upon the back of a beast of burden, exposed to the derision of the mob, his course of exercise was a horrid imprisonment of *twelve years*, and after his repentance and abjuration of his errors which ought to have been a just motive for mercy and pardon, they gave him *absolution* in the form of a horrible sentence to receive *two hundred lashes*, to be held up to public contempt, and other *ten years* of his life, that is to say an imprisonment for that period under the burning sun of Africa!

All this, an entire life of one continued martyrdom, a man had to suffer, a man in the image of God, and only for an opinion, an error, a word; and this too at a time when the horror and execration of the world had reduced to its last stage that scandalous tribunal, to which in our own time, at the present day, a most fearful zeal has erected arches of triumph, and perhaps in secret is praying for its infamous resurrection.

CHAPTER VII.

WHAT remains to be related of Moyen's process is still more horrible than anything we have yet stated.

The discussion of his errors, or according to the forensic language of the Holy Office, the inquisitorial charges lasted an entire year, from the 4th of May, 1752, to the 18th of the same month the following year. The first of these long and darkened debates was the compendious summary of some of the propositions and answers which we have just given.

We have given an account of the implacable fury with which the fiscal Grillo had demanded the *relaxation*, that is to say the death of Moyen, and as his writ or act of accusation had been presented to the Holy Office before the unprotected accused had been heard, but who clamoured for mercy, alleging that that executioner had condemned him without taking into account his refutations of the charges, and the same day in which they closed the audiences of the *propositions*, (18th of May, 1753) he implored them to treat him with clemency, "for his fault of excess, (says literally the *auto* or document of that day,) which resulted in speaking of matters of religion, and for doing which he had *greatly repented* and now asked their pardon and mercy."

Mercy! What? why this was nothing less than a sanguinary sarcasm thrown in the face of those nefarious usurpers of the Divine power, who expected to receive themselves eternal mercy in the name of their sacrilegious impostures.

There was no mercy, then, nor later, nor ever, for the unfortunates condemned by the holy executioners. It was only many months afterwards, when death by the gaugrene apparently was going prematurely to snatch from their hands the victim who entertained their leisure hours and gave pretence for their salaries, for their cruelties and confiscations, that the inquisitors consented to allow *one* of his chains to be removed. "The 15th of November, 1753, (says the respective act, and placed in the process by the notary Orúe), the señors inquisitors Amuzquibar and Rodriguez gave order to the head jailor, Don Francisco Ximenez, to remove from Don Francisco Moyen the shackle from one foot, leaving it upon the other, taking into consideration the epilepsy with which he is attacked, but principally for malignant sores having broken out on the leg and about the ancles, and which there is fear may result in gangrene; and for that let this order be attended to.—*Orúe.*"

And that was the holy and merciful tribunal whose prisoner, says its apologist, (citing, we do not know upon what grounds the opinion of Llorente who has related so many horrors of the Inquisition) never groaned under the weight of chains, *shackles*, stocks, handcuffs, or any other kinds of mortification which were used in all other European prisons. And in this philanthropic 19th century, he himself adds, do they, or not, use shackles and chains in prisons? Ah! still yet those vaunting *humanitarians* of our epoch consider it charitable to decorate their prisoners with those ornaments.*

However, let us continue with a description of the places themselves, in which the Inquisition so lately exercised its mild penal system, and that penitential plan of which its champion makes it the author, thus depriving the Quakers of their right to the invention, which up to the present time has not been disputed.†

---

* "Rapid Sketch," page 64.

† No one is ignorant that the system known under the name of *penitentiary* was invented by the religious set called Quakers, and put in practice near the end of the last century (1786). But the author of the "Rapid Sketch," and his critic of the *Independent*, have confounded the application of the principle, which is the true

CHAPTER VII.

The prisons of the Inquisition were situated upon the same site, which is now occupied by those called *carceletas*, or little prisons, in the square of the same name, in front of the statue erected to the liberator Bolivar, the *quemadero*, or place of burning, was in front of this, but the Rimac flowed between, and about half the distance from one part to the other in going up to the bridge stood, and in the same place where it now stands, the Church of the *Desamparados*,* because it was there that the inquisitors abandoned their victims, under the legal fiction, that is to say hypocritical, of delivering them to the secular power, that it, and not themselves who condemned them, might conduct them to the flames.

It was in one of the cells of the dark vaults of the Holy Office, that Moyen was confined,—a wilderness of brick, a species of cemetery, in which the prisoners were as it were buried alive, without light, without air, suffering from damp, and covered with filthy vermin. And here, caused by the rack, by the scourge, by the wheel, by the lighted brasiers for the feet, the screws for the hands, and all those diabolical inventions congregated in the hall of torture, † occurred so frequently the deaths of the accused,

penitentiary system, with the principle itself, which might have belonged to the Inquisition, as M. Guizot says in his " Course of Modern History." We ourselves, in conformity with his opinion, have said, in a work published eleven years ago on the penitentiary system, these words, " The Inquisition, in its essence, was nothing more than this same principle (viz. to punish in correcting) carried to the most horrible extremes by fanaticism and political passions."— (" Memoir on the General Penitentiary System," 1857.)

* Forsaken.

† The English traveller, Mr. Stevenson, already alluded to,—and who was present at the sackage of the Inquisition, on the 3rd of September, 1813, and to which edifice he gained access on that day, with the permission of the Viceroy Abascal, through the influence of the lady of General Gainza,—mentions curious details of that act of popular indignation, and truly the reader is horrified with what he relates of his visit (although he declared that it was his intention to dissipate the exaggerations made of the Inquisition). In the hall of torture

and their subsequent burning in effigy, or else sad procession of their remains to be thrown into the burning pile.*

was still the rack, with its wheels and thongs to stretch the joints of the penitentials, and which, according to Stevenson, was a table eight feet long and seven wide. There was likewise the pillory, or vertical excavation in the wall, in which the sufferer was introduced for the purpose of being flogged, and as all the parts of the body except the posterior were let into the wall, he could not make the slightest movement. As for the smaller instruments of torture, such as collars of iron for the neck, human bones used as gags, the thongs of the whips still covered with clotted blood, the screws to compress the fingers, and which had the form of a half moon, the pasteboard caps, the *sambenitos*, or tunics, painted with devils and reptiles, all were found there as in a horrible museum.

Of the docments already mentioned, which we saw in Lima, 1860, relating to the inventory of the articles which belonged to the Holy Office, and which were delivered up in 1814, in consequence of the abolition of the decree of the Cortes which had suppressed it, the result was that among the objects plundered in September, 1813, and not returned, in spite of the excommunication major, fulminated by the Archbishop Las Heras, were the following articles:—Five pair of *shackles*, two pair of *breeches*, a worm-eaten wooden *rack*, eleven *St. Andrew's crosses*, and half ditto, sixteen *paste board caps*, three pair of *gags*, sixteen candles of green wax, and *thirty-four boxes to embark money*. . . . . The rich and beautiful urn, which served to hold the sentences in the solemn acts of faith, never made its appearance, and they only recovered one of the silver rings which had adorned it. Likewise were wanting some books from the archives, such as the "Laws of the Indies;" "The Politics of Bovadilla, &c." Stevenson says, that he carried to his house fifteen despatches of processes of little importance, and adds that two of them

---

* According to Rodriguez Buron, of the 6860 Spaniards burnt in effigy by Torquemada, from 1481 to 1487, four thousand at least had died in the dungeons of the Inquisition, in consequence of their horrible treatment, and 2000 were exhumed many years after their death. Generally their effigies represented the victims of the dungeons as tall, dry, and meagre, and no doubt they were pretty fair personifications of the subjects of the mild penal system of the Inquisition, and as nothing was more difficult than to escape from its vaults, consequently, they had to represent in effigy very few absent or fugitives, one of the last, however, was the famous Antonio Perez.

The actual edifice, notwithstanding its horrible aspect, scarcely gives an idea of the old one, which was destroyed had, in the first act of the process, the denunciation of the accused by their own confessors. . . .

We must bear in mind that this frightful list was of the objects wanting in the inventory of 1814, having been plundered in 1813. The existence of things deposited belonging to the mild Inquisition before that period must have been consequently much more considerable.

And before these authentic data, what can be said by the champion of the glory, of the justice, and of the mildness of the Inquisition? Will he still persist in his enthusiasm for it, in his tender feeling, in his adoration? God forbid, for his own honour and that of our clergy! But we fear that his ideas are too far advanced to afford us any hope. "Behold, then," he exclaims, in a fragment we have already given (page 117), "ye stubborn enemies of the Spanish Inquisition, in what manner it made use of the torture which the practice of the European tribunals and the national laws had formed to its hands. See how it surrounded its application with charitable precautions that the accused should not suffer too much; and how it was rendering more difficult its use and preparing for its entire abolition. Is this cruelty?"

"If ignorance or passion," he adds, "did not blind them, they would clearly see that the torture made use of by the Spanish Inquisition was the most moderate and humane of all that was practised at that time in the civil tribunals, and that manner of using it presented itself in the horizon of jurisprudence as the beautiful aurora of a splendid day!"

"At the sight of those instruments," (beautiful aurora of a splendid day) exclaims the traveller Stevenson, relating their destruction by the instantaneous and irresistible fury of the populace, "who could excuse the monsters who made use of them to consolidate the faith of Jesus Christ, as He taught it by His example, and propagated it by mildness and kindness? Immediately the rack and pillory were broken into fragments: and such was the fury of more than a hundred persons, that if the instruments had been of iron they could not have resisted the violence of the assailants."

"A subterraneous vault," says Rodriguez Buron in his *Compendium of the Critical History of Llorente* (vol. i. p. 121), "the descent to which is by winding steps, was the place destined for the torture. The profound silence which reigned in this room of torment, and the frightful apparatus of the instruments of torture that was dimly seen by the

by the earthquake of the 28th of October, 1647, and in which would have perished the greater part of those con-

pale and tremulous light of two candles, would necessarily fill the soul of the sufferer with mortal anguish. Scarcely had the unfortunate wretch presented himself before the inquisitors, when the executioners, clothed in a tunic of black linen, with their heads covered by hoods of the same material, having holes for the eyes, nose, and mouth, seized him and stripped him of everything but his shirt."

Afterwards, describing the different kinds of torture which the Holy Office made use of in preference, the same author expresses himself in the following terms: "There were three kinds of torture, that of the cord, the water, and the fire. In the first of these they tied the hands of the sufferer behind his back, and by means of a pulley fixed in the roof, the executioners raised him as high as they could, and allowed him to remain suspended in this manner for some time, and then let him suddenly drop, when he would fall to within half a foot of the ground. The terrible shock thus produced would dislocate his joints, and as the cord was made fast to his wrists, it cut the flesh to the bone, laying bare all the tendons. This punishment, which was repeated for more than an hour, at most times left the sufferer without power and without motion; and it was not until the surgeon of the Inquisition declared that he could not suffer any more without perishing that the inquisitor gave orders to bear him to his prison, where they left him, abandoned to the most cruel pains and his own despair, until the moment in which the Holy Office had prepared for him another torture still more horrible, and which they inflicted by means of water."

This consisted in placing the victim upon a kind of wooden horse in the shape of a trough, adapted to receive the body of a man. It had no other bottom than a stick placed across it. Over this stick they bent the body by means of mechanism attached to the trough, placing it in such a position that the feet were higher than the head. This posture caused the respiration to be performed with difficulty, and the victim suffered the most excruciating pains in all his members in consequence of the pressure of the cords which bound him, the turns of which entered his flesh, causing the blood to start even before they applied the garotte. When the victim was bound in this cruel manner, the executioners introduced into his throat a piece of fine linen, wet, and with a piece of the same they covered his nostrils; they then poured water into his mouth and nose, which filtered through the linen rag, but so slowly that it required an hour at least for him to be

fined within its walls had it not been for the exertions of the visitor Arenaza, who, notwithstanding he was an

able to swallow a quart, notwithstanding the liquid kept falling without interruption; and for this reason the victim had not an interval left to breathe; and although at each moment he made efforts to swallow, hoping by this means to admit a portion of air to the lungs, the wet linen prevented him; and as the water kept entering the nostrils at the same time, we may easily conceive with how great difficulty was performed one of the most important functions of life. And it happened frequently that when the torture was concluded, and they drew from the throat the linen rag, it was found to be covered with blood, in consequence of the rupture of some vessel of the lungs by the desperate efforts made to breathe by the miserable victim. Nor was this all, for at each instant a strong arm tightened the fatal garrote to such an extent that the cords which bound the arms and legs of the unfortunate sufferer penetrated sometimes to the bone!

If the inquisitors did not succeed in making the accused confess by the second kind of torture, they then tried the effects of fire; and for that purpose the executioners commenced by tying his hands and feet in such a manner that there was no possibility for them to become loose; they then rubbed the feet with some penetrating substance, such as fat, oil, or lard, and placed them over a pan of burning charcoal until the flesh was scorched and shrivelled up in such a manner that the nerves and bones everywhere protruded.

The Señor Saavedra does not appear to be willing to admit any description of torture, except what he himself has given in a note at page 70 of his book, and according to which the Inquisition employed three kinds of torture: 1st. They passed a rope over a pulley and made it fast to the wrists of the criminal, whose hands were tied behind his back, his feet were fastened with fetters to which was attached a hundred weight of iron, and in this manner he was drawn up and suspended in the air; 2nd. The criminal was stripped naked and stretched upon a wooden frame, to which he was made fast by his hands, feet, and head, and in this position they dealt him eight blows, viz. two on the fleshy part of the arms, two below the elbows, and the other four on the legs, and made him swallow one quart of water; 3rd. The feet were placed naked in the stocks, and the soles were rubbed with lard, and then a brazier full of burning coals was placed close to them. This was considered the most cruel of all.

The Señor Saavedra, however, has made this recapitulation to contrast it favourably with the more severe tortures made use of by Pro-

inquisitor, gave proofs of a compassionate disposition; for which reason very likely it was that he was recalled to Spain. He died in Carthagena of the Indies, but whether from the fever or from grief we do not know.*

testants; and they might have been, for aught we know, as brutal, as savage, and as infernal as those made use of by the Inquisition.† But if so, both the one and the other were the fruit of the same barbarous and atrocious religious intolerance, and which is now represented to be of such a sublime nature by its partizans.

Nevertheless we must in our conscience confess, that for us this system of comparisons, and applying them for the purpose of palliating and excusing the lesser of two crimes by the enormity or magnitude of the greater, is not worthy of an argument, and we consider those by whom it is so applied to be wanting in common sense. Suppose, for example, that one of those terrible descendants of Luther of whom Señor Saavedra makes mention, should, in his eagerness to kill all the Catholics, apply a lighted brand to the chapel of the *Sagrario* (in Santiago), when perhaps it contained some 500 persons, setting it on fire and consuming them all, would it lessen, we ask, the enormity of his crime, would it palliate his barbarity by alleging in his defence that others who were not descendants of Luther but of Eratostratus or Torquemada had burnt 2000 persons in the church of the Compania?

* Arenaza was, it appears, a pretty tolerable man for an inquisitor. Fuentes declares that in the earthquake of 1647 those who were confined in the Inquisition owed their lives to the efforts which he made to disinter them from the ruins. "His good qualities," says the viceroy Manso, who supported him in the suit that he instituted against the robbers Unda and Calderon, "gained him the estimation of all right-thinking men." Nevertheless a very different account was given of him by the accused inquisitors, and the Inquisitor-General in Spain, Perez del Prado, ordered him to return in disgrace.

† It cannot be denied but that Protestants on many occasions made use of tortures and have been guilty of great barbarities; but I scarcely believe that among all the denominations of Protestants *one* individual could be found at the present day who, with a heart dead to all feelings of humanity, would be bold enough to hold himself up to the execration of the civilized world by publishing a book (as Señor Saavedra has done) for the express purpose of defending such barbarities, no matter by whom committed, and still less to commend and praise the infernal monsters who perpetrated such cruelties in the name of a God of goodness and mercy.—*Note by Translator.*

A modern writer, in referring to the present state of the prisons, says: "To give a description of this locality, worthy of the institution to which it owes its origin, and to represent the disorder and want of cleanliness in which it is, would be a task beyond my powers to perform."*

* M. A. Fuentes, Statistics of Lima, page 202. On various occasions in the year 1860 we visited that horrible place, and we certainly had sufficient opportunities to see confirmed the opinion of Fuentes; and if Señor Saavedra would like to convince himself of the penitentiary system, the invention of which he attributes with so much laudation to the Holy Office, he could not do better than take a trip to Lima, and there he would have the gratification of seeing the rooms, *lofty*, *dry*, and *ventilated*, and which, in quoting Llorente, drew forth such commendation from him and his critic of the *Independent*. With respect to the prison of the Inquisition in Spain and the treatment of its prisoners, we would beg of him to read the Memoirs of General Van Halen, who was one of its guests in Seville in the year 1820.

"The prisons of the Holy Office," says Rodriguez Buron, in his work, vol. i. p. 118, "were, in the greater part of the cities, generally speaking, stinking rooms or cells 12 feet long by 10 wide, and dimly lighted by a small hole in the roof, but in such a manner that the prisoners could not distinguish any object without great difficulty. Half the space was occupied by a few boards for them to sleep upon; but as there was only access for three persons, while at times there were as many as six shut up together, the most robust were compelled to sleep upon the bare ground, and where they had less space than is allotted to the dead in their graves!"

Another author (Torres de Castilla, vol. 1, page 727) demonstrating the *mild* penal system of the Inquisition of Lisbon, (the horrors of which no doubt Moyen had been acquainted with, as he spoke of them during his journey to Potosi) expresses himself in these terms: " The criminals are there confounded together, not only are there those condemned for cases of conscience, but also malefactors judged by the ordinary tribunals, and it is not a rare thing to see bound to the same chain, an honourable man condemned for suspicion of Judaism, because he has never been seen to eat pork, and a brigand or a robber on the public roads."

"The condemned are made fast two and two by the same chain, which is not less than eight feet long."

"Once a month they have the chin and head shaved, and their clothing consists of nothing more than a tunic, and a rug of coarse

And if this was written ten years ago of a prison, improved in accordance to our modern ideas and advancement, in what state must it have been when the unfortunate frieze, the latter of which serves them in the day for a cloak, and at night as a coverlid."

"Should any one commit a fault he is flogged in a most cruel manner, they strip him naked and lay him on the ground with his face downwards, and in this position he is held by several men while others flog him most unmercifully with cords stiffened by being dipped in melted pitch, and which bring away the flesh at every stroke until the back is nothing less than one large ulcer, and which prevents the poor wretch from doing anything for a long time."

The same author, speaking afterwards of the dungeons of the Portuguese Inquisition of Goa, says: "The prison of the Inquisition at Goa is the dirtiest, darkest, and most horrible that possibly can be. It is a species of cavern, to which light is with difficulty admitted through a small embrasure, but through which the rays of the sun never penetrate. The kind of noxious air that must be there respired, may be imagined, when it is known that a dry well in the middle of the space where the prisoners are confined, and which is always uncovered, is used as a privy, the emanations from which have no other outlet for escape, than the small opening above mentioned. And truly it may be said without exaggeration that the prisoners live in a common privy!"

Are these the prisons which Señor Saavedra and his commentators so much delight in?

We have no doubt that Llorente speaks of some Inquisitions which may have had lofty dungeons, dry and ventilated, &c., and even the edifices may have been sumptuously built, as was the burning place at Seville, which was made of hewn stone; but it must be understood, that though having these qualities they were not the less horrible! "Because (as according to Rodriguez Buron, vol. 1, page 120, Llorente himself says) besides the stain of vulgar infamy attached to it, which did to no other prison, civil or ecclesiastical, it produced in the prisoner a feeling of profound sadness, by the continued solitude, his utter ignorance of the state of his case, the impossibility of receiving any relief by communication with his advocate, the many hours of darkness in the winter time, as he was not allowed to have light from nine in the evening until seven the following morning, long enough to produce a mortal hypochondria, besides suffering from the cold, as he was denied the use of fire."

Moyen entered its walls, only four years after it had been reduced to a heap of ruins, and had suffered by an inundation? "Consider your Reverence, what I suffer," said Moyen himself to his judge, the grand inquisitor Amuzquibar, in a letter capable of exciting in the most callous mind sentiments of compassion, "in a room dark and full of fleas, in irons and my feet filled with chigoes* and subject to this complaint,† and what is the most dreadful of all to be deprived of my exercises, how can I bear every day of my life to suffer such terrible afflictions?"

But not even this was sufficient to inspire pity in the heart of those infamous wretches, those demons of casuistry and theology. It was the most dreadful thing of all to the agonized spirit of their victim, as he himself said, to be deprived of his exercises, that is to say, of his beloved connection with the arts, for they had even confiscated his violin, his last friend, whose sympathetic sounds had cheered his saddened soul in those gloomy dungeons, the sombre silence of which was only broken by the harsh creaking of the machinery with which they applied the torture, the shrieks of the victims and the groans of the dying. Even the inoffensive and silent occupation of painting, the head jailor, Don Francisco Ximenez, had prohibited, by the express order of the inquisitor Amuzquibar. In the same letter just referred to, the martyred artist tells his executioners, "Here, within this place, I have occupied myself in painting a representation of madness,' as the cause, and which it was, without any other intention than to please

---

* The Chigoe is a minute insect, abundant in the West Indies, which penetrates the skin of the feet and forms a little cyst beneath it, in which it deposits its eggs. It produces a violent itching. The negroes dexterously extract the cyst with the point of a needle, and fill the cavity which is left with tobacco ashes. If the bag is broken in the extraction so that the young chigoes escape, violent inflammation is the result. *Surgeon's Vade Mecum, by Robert Dunitt.*

† The attacks of epilepsy.

your reverence, but because Señor Don Francisco has told me that you do not like such kind of paintings, I have rubbed it out."

Poor Moyen, painting within those gloomy walls in which his life was consumed, the desperation, the frenzy and the madness of his captive soul; and when he was ordered to efface his own likeness, to avoid an addition to his punishment, found himself obliged to pretend that the sublime inspiration of his art, prompted by his anguish, was nothing more than the ordinary madness feigned by criminals for the purpose of extenuating their faults! From this we may comprehend his bitter and unintelligible phrase, "as the cause, and which it was," that is to say, that madness was the cause of his errors. *

By this time the sufferings of the miserable victim had reached their utmost height; for at the beginning of the winter of 1754, when he had been now five years confined, driven to despair, he made a vain attempt to escape by the desperate method of setting fire to the door of his cell with the candle he was allowed to have while eating his supper. From that time he was deprived of all light, and, like the wild beasts, he had to take his meals in darkness. On another occasion, as we learn from the process, he meditated flight by some other method, but he was denounced by a

---

* Neverthless, when the inquisitor Amuzquibar, at a later period required the pencil of Moyen, he made him paint some pictures for himself and the Archbishop of Lima, as we are informed by the process itself.

It would seem that this priest was an amateur in paintings, for when he died in 1763, he left sixty-nine paintings and engravings, the merits of which must have been considerable, for even at that time, when an artist was only paid the wages of a day labourer, they were valued at £1,076 dollars 3 reals. How many of these were the work of the unfortunate Frenchman? If he had nothing tangible for the greedy vultures of the Inquisition to confiscate, they nevertheless confiscated his talents, and the inspirations of his genius.

perfidious negro called Domingo de Arcaya, who was confined in a neighbouring cell, he having been accused of heresy.*

Meanwhile the process dragged itself along with most tantalizing slowness, they had named for the advocate of Moyen a certain doctor called Don José Miguel Valdivieso in the same week in which were terminated the audiences of the charges, (25th of May, 1753), and they had also at the same time sent the declarations of the process to the commissary at Potosi, for their legal ratification, notwithstanding that all the witnesses, at the time they had given them, had ratified them *ad perpetuam.*

This tedious affair must have been done with the utmost prolixity, according to the instructions of the apostolical inquisitor Amuzquibar, who himself compiled a formulary expressly for that effect, writing upon the margin of each declaration in a clear character, and as cutting as the edge of a knife, the points or principal heresies to be attended to in the ratification. †

In consequence of these injunctions, this transaction occu-

* It appears, however, that some years later Moyen went out to the house of his old friend and protector, the Conde de las Torres, who, when he returned, sent him shut up in his own coach, that the inquisitors should not have any knowledge of that poor concession. They did know it nevertheless, and expressed their displeasure, as may be seen by a letter from Moyen to Amuzquibar, in which "he beseeches his pardon." In relating this occurrence we afford an argument to our antagonists in favour of the mild penal system of the Inquisition, but we concede it to them with pleasure, because we consider that in works of discussion everything must give way to truth!

† Amuzquibar, like Arenaza, was not the worst of the inquisitors, although sufficiently cruel to merit the name of the executioner of Moyen, and which in truth he was. The Viceroy Amat, who was no friend to the priests, praised him in his vice-regal memoir, saying that in the war with the English, in 1762, he had conducted himself with great zeal for the crown, offering to form a company of his familiars. Truly an excellent idea in a war with heretics!

pied two years! For the writings of the process state that the commissary of Potosi only returned the documents to Lima, in April, 1755. Most certainly all this delay was intended to protect the innocency of the accused, and to prevent him from becoming the victim of calumny! For the same reasons, the confessions forced by the torture from the accused were of no value, as we are told, unless they were ratified voluntarily twenty-four hours after having the joints dislocated upon the rack! The infernal brutes, what right had they to arrogate to themselves the power of representing the Divinity?*

The next proceeding was the publication of proofs, and this was only done on the 3rd of September, 1755, when Moyen had suffered six years of his harsh captivity, and in a manner, says the corresponding document, "to conceal the names and surnames, and other circumstances which might lead to a recognition of the persons of the witnesses according to the instruction and use of the Holy Office." And this was called by those atrocious tribunals, *publication of proofs*, as if in the testimonial proof, the only one acknowledged in the proceedings of the Holy Office, the witnesses were not the essence of the proof, or legally speaking, the proof itself!

To this followed the audiences to examine the ratifica-

* Throughout the whole of the process of Moyen, we do not find that upon any occasion the torture was ever applied, although it may be said that he suffered a continual torture by the permanency of his fetters, his ulcers, and his epilepsy! With respect to the precautions taken to protect the criminals against the torture, as we are informed by the Señor Saavedra, one was the required presence at that punishment of the diocesan of the accused. In the appendix will be seen the copy of a singular document, already mentioned, in which the Ecclesiastical Synod of Santiago in 1806, gives full powers to the inquisitors themselves to apply at their own free will, and in their (the members of the chapter) name, the tortures which they may think proper!

tions, occupying 400 pages in folio, exactly double the number employed in the writings of the previous declarations of the denunciation.

Six of these audiences were celebrated with some slight activity, yet nevertheless they occupied the best part of a year; for the first was held, as we have said, on the 3rd of September, 1755, and the sixth on the 3rd of June of the year following.

The principal cause however of this dilatoriness was the miserable condition of the accused, each day more prostrated by his sufferings, his chains, and the gangrene of his wounds, but principally on account of his old complaint, the epilepsy, the attacks of which had become more aggravated every day. In the second audience of ratification, which was held on the 11th of September, 1755, when the proceedings must have occupied something less than an hour, they appear to have terminated abruptly, for we find that the secretary had written one sheet of the act of that day, and at the end of which are the following words: "Being seized with an attack of *gota-coral* (epilepsy), to which he is subject, with all the symptoms denoting that complaint, the audience was postponed, and he was ordered to be removed to his cell."

For the same reason, the third session had also to be postponed to the month of February of the year following. This took place on the 12th of that month, and it appears they were going to hold the fourth two days later, but we find that the act of the process of that date, 14th of February, only contains the following note upon its margin: "This audience did not take place, because the jailor had notified that the accused was indisposed in consequence of an attack of epilepsy, to which he is subject."

And thus this dreadful complaint of the unfortunate Moyen, which formerly was an accident of his nervous system, had now become converted into a disease of terror. Every time that the presence of his judges was announced to him was more than the flesh and the spirit could bear, and they succumbed to the dreaded name!

At length the sixth audience took place on the 3rd of June, 1756, but was suspended, so says the respective act, "on account of urgent official impediments, as also for the indisposition of the señor inquisitor (Amuzquibar), and likewise for the sickness of the accused."

Did the contagion of that continued agony of the accused influence and act upon, as a punishment, the body and mind of his executioner?

After that audience, in which both prisoner and judge, stricken by sickness, had to retire from that gloomy hall, the place of so many abominations, there was a pause of nearly *twenty-one months*.

The seventh audience was held on the 18th of February, 1758!

Moyen had entered on the ninth year of his martyrdom, thanks to the mild penal system of the Inquisition!

Unhappy man! If the first three years of his captivity had transformed his sprightly youth into a premature and sickly old age, what must have been his frightful condition in the others, through which he passed?

Finally, on the 14th of March, 1758, was concluded the so-called publication of proofs, and a convenient term was allowed him for his defence.

This in a great measure was composed by the accused himself, with a power of logic and a conviction decided and calm, which may be seen to reveal itself in the extracts already given of his defence,* and shows how great must have been the vivacity and the intelligence of that truly

---

* The defence of Moyen was in fact written by himself in a character extremely clear and distinct, occupying altogether 100 pages in folio, and although they seemed to be only notes for his advocate, they showed proofs of extraordinary erudition, and his language, though incorrect and even barbarous, was considerably improved from the French-Portuguese jargon of his earlier writings.

singular man, martyred by a crowd of cruel and ignorant pettifoggers!

Notwithstanding that the ceremony of the publication of proofs was concluded, as we have said, on the 14th of March, 1758, and from which time Moyen hastened to prepare the notes he had taken, his advocate, the Doctor Valdivieso, was not ready to present his defence until *twenty months* later, the 8th of November, 1759!

The defence was a most lengthy allegation, in the same style as was then used, as well as at the present time, and its forensic and literary merit may be estimated by the specimen we have given at page 143, where he treats concerning the heresy of the mule.

Its principal, perhaps its only merit, is its conclusion, because, besides being clear and laconic, under the veil of compassion for the victim, it throws into the face of the executioners their cool and persistent iniquity. "And finally, in effect," says that document, "taking into consideration that his confessed crime precisely consists in a garrulity in the manner of expressing himself against the supreme dignitaries of the Church, in consequence of having read certain books, and also in part the liberty of the French. For all this, and calling the attention of this Holy Tribunal to the imprisonment, which in justice may from its length be considered as a capital punishment,—the imprisonment being greater than the punishment corresponding to this crime, because it is a great part of a life within a narrow prison, which necessarily exceeds the inconveniences of a long banishment,—and therefore in consideration of all this I demand that he may be absolved from his crime," &c.

What remained now was the production of the last piece of that process which had lasted ten years and a half, viz. the definitive sentence; but the year 1759, in which the defence had been given in, passed away, the entire year of 1760 followed, and also part of the year 1761, and yet neither the inquisitors nor their council had been able to meet to pronounce the definitive act.

And why not? What were those solemn and sanguinary idlers doing all this time? Did the urgent official impediments occupy them so much that they could not find time to finish the cause of an unfortunate foreigner, who had been the last *twelve years* dying of misery and disease in their abominable dungeons?

Silvio Pellico, victim of the political Inquisition of Austria, filled the present age with lamentations of his *carcere dura* in Spielberg; and the histories of Baron Trenck, and of the man with the iron mask, have become the popular stories of our time: and yet nevertheless, in the present case of Francisco Moyen, the minute incidents of which are verified by the writings of the process which was carried on against the victim, hitherto obscure and unknown,—we find a sad and gloomy history, far surpassing in horror and cruelty those of the persons we have just mentioned.*

---

* The process of Moyen is in itself (certainly not because we have been the means of bringing it to light) a truly American curiosity, and without doubt would also be so considered in Europe, should it ever become known there. It is, perhaps, the only American process which does not treat of witches, devilries, blasphemies, and other vulgar and ridiculous absurdities. On the contrary, it is a contest between a rational and instructed man, and the nefarious ignorance of those who impiously call themselves the great apostles of the faith. It has, moreover, another circumstance not a little remarkable, and that is, that it takes its origin in the ideas of the 18th century, which also occasioned in a great measure the emancipation of our continent.

As a proof of what we have just said, we need only recall to mind the deep impression produced by the appearance of the book of the Frenchman Delon, persecuted and condemned by the obscure and remote Portuguese Inquisition at Goa, in 1674; and the no less famous case of another Frenchman, (the French, for being such great *talkers*, have been in every epoch an easy prey to the Holy Office,) mentioned by Llorente, and whose history is related in the following

Francisco Moyen, the lighthearted and merry musician and painter of Potosi, had now become a decrepit and sickly

lines, taken from the Compendium of Rodriguez Buron, vol. 1, page 136:—

"Among the numerous processes which were formed in that epoch (the end of the last century,) there are some particularly worthy of attention; that of the Marseillais, Miguel de Rieux, known in Spain by the name of the *man of nature*, presents a frightful catastrophe, enough to fill the mind with bitterness and indignation against the horrible secret of the Holy Office. Miguel de Rieux was apprehended as a heretic in the year 1791, and conducted to the prisons of the Inquisition. He was a well informed man, and confessed in good faith to the inquisitors that by reading the works of Voltaire, Rousseau, and other philosophers, he had formed the opinion that the only true religion was that of nature, and that all the rest were nothing more than human inventions; that in his studies all he sought for was to find the truth, and consequently he was always disposed to give up the natural religion, and adopt the Catholic, provided that any one was willing and able to convince him that he had been deceived.

A bishop who was very eloquent undertook to convert him, and succeeded in persuading him to acknowledge the utility and even the necessity of a revelation, and in consequence the man of nature showed himself disposed to be reconciled to the Church. The Holy Office secretly consented to this, inasmuch as Rieux was not an obstinate heretic, but he had to be present at a particular *auto de fé*, there to receive the penance awarded to him; but he being ignorant of the result of his case, was highly astonished one morning to see enter his dungeon several familiars of the Holy Office, who desired him to put on the sambenito, a rope around his neck, and carry a wax candle in his hand, and go and receive his sentence. Upon hearing this, the unfortunate man trembled violently, became irritated, and would not submit except by force; scarcely had he presented himself at the door of the hall of audience, when, seeing the numbers who were assembled to witness the *auto de fé*, he lost all control over himself, and getting highly excited by his anger, he broke forth into a thousand execrations against the barbarity of the inquisitors; and amongst other things said: "Truly, if this is ordered by the Catholic religion, I will detest it; for nothing can be good that dishonours a simple man." Immediately he was taken back to his dungeon, where he never ceased calling upon them to take him to the pile. Until tired with waiting for his executioners, he hung himself,

old man. His *mask of iron*, was the complete transformation of his countenance, furrowed with deep wrinkles, haggard and dark, contrasting strongly with the premature gray hairs, as we are told by the process, which appeared in abundance in the first quarter of his prolonged agonizing imprisonment.

At length, on the 18th of February, 1761, the Council of Qualifiers of the Inquisition, being assembled in audience of consultation, upon causes relating to the faith, they, after occupying sixteen days in the reading of the acts, pronounced the following decision as a definitive and final sentence, the hypocrisy and barbarity of which is only equalled by the vain pomposity displayed in the titles and honours of those worthy Bœotian blockheads :—

"In the Holy Office of the Inquisition, in the city of the Kings, on the eighteenth day of the month of February, one thousand seven hunderd and sixty-one. The Señor Inquisitor Doctor Don Matheo Amuzquibar, (who assisted only for his colleague, the Señor Inquisitor Fiscal, he being prevented attending by an impediment,) being in his morning audience in consultation, and in examining causes of faith. And for Ordinary of this Archbishopric and that of Chuquizaca, the Reverend Father Fray Thomas Santiago Concha, ex-Lecturer, ex-Councillor, ex-Provincial of this holy province, Doctor in Theology, and Professor of the primary lectures of subtle Scotus in this Royal University of St. Mark, Synodal Examiner, Qualifier and Councillor of this Inquisition, who holds power as such, of which I certify; and for Councillors the Reverend Fathers, Master Fray Antonio de la Cueba, of the order of Preachers, Doctor in Theology and Professor of Morals in the said Royal University, and Qualifier of this Inquisition; Fray Agustin Diego de Aragon, of the order of Hermits of our great Father St. Augustin,

first stuffing a handkerchief into his mouth, that he might die the sooner. Such was the mild penal system of the Inquisition, that converted the scaffold into absolution! Will Señor Saavedra say likewise that the Inquisition converted suicide into absolution?

Doctor in Theology in the said Royal University, and Regent of Studies of the College of San Idelphonso, of this city; Juan Sanchez Sargado, of the Company of Jesus, ex-Professor of Philosophy, and of Sacred Theology in the Maximus College of St. Paul of this city, Synodal Examiner of this Archbishopric, Qualifier of this Holy Office; the Doctor Don Francisco Tamayo, Collegiate of the Major and Royal Philip, of this city, Advocate of this Royal Audience, ex-Professor of Ancient Civil Law, in the said University; and the Doctor Don Fernando Roman de Aulestia, Collegiate of the same College, Advocate of the said Royal Audience, and of Presas* of this Holy Office, and Head Chaplain of this Holy Office, ex-Regius Professor of Elementary Laws in the said Royal University, Councillors of this Holy Office. Having seen the process and criminal cause of faith which has been carried on in this Holy Office—against Don Francisco Moyen, a native of the city of Paris, in the kingdom of France, for heretical propositions of which a relation has been made in the days 15th, 19th, 21st, 24th, 26th, 27th, 28th, and 30th of January; the 5th, 6th, 7th, 9th, 11th, 12th, 13th, and 14th of February, of this present year. And in consideration that it is not possible to condemn him to the torture on account of the disease which he suffers, and in which we all agree."

Up to this part is the definitive vote or decision, and it terminates with the formula of the sentence in all its details. But as the composing of the real sentence shows the exact style of the inquisitors, we have thought proper to give it just as it was pronounced in the first days in April, suppressing

* Presas, *Anglice*, captures, prizes, spoils, booty. We do not know if these words refer to human prizes or to goods, because the Inquisition had to do with both; although we are inclined to think that the last is intended, for it is well known that Philip II. established an Inquisition for the fleet, to burn heretical seamen; and another Inquisition for the custom-houses, to confiscate heresies in the shape of money, books, paintings, &c.

the rest of the definitive vote, it being entirely the same as the sentence. It proceeds thus:—

"And having agreed in our deliberation with learned persons and of right consciences—

"*Christi nomine invocato.* We find, taking into consideration the acts and merits of the said process, that the said Promoter-Fiscal *has not proved his intention,* according and as it ought to be proved for the said Don Francisco Moyen to be declared a heretic, but for the fault which results against the said Don Francisco Moyen, and we desiring to act favourably and mercifully towards him, and not with the rigour of justice, being moved thereto by certain reasons and motives, in penalty and punishment for what he has done, said and committed, we order and command that he present himself in a public *auto de fé,* if there is shortly one to be celebrated, and if not, in a particular *auto* in a church, or in the hall of this tribunal, in the form of a penitential, with a sambenito, on which is half a cross, a cap on his head, a rope round his neck, a gag in his mouth, and a taper of green wax in his hand, and thus our sentence is to be read; and for the vehement suspicion resulting against this criminal of the said process, we command him to abjure, and that he abjure publicly and vehemently the errors of which by the said process he has been accused and witnessed against, and from which, and being gravely suspected, *he is absolved ad cautelem,* and also gravely advised, censured and threatened, and we condemn him to the confiscation and loss of half his goods, and which we adjudge to the Royal Fiscal of his Majesty, and in his royal name to the Receiver-General of this Holy Office, and we banish him perpetually from both the Americas and Islands adjacent, subject to the crown of Spain,* and from the city of Madrid, the court of

---

* The banishment of Moyen was not a discretionary power in the Inquisitors, it was thus ordained by Philip II. and Philip III. for all foreigners, in the royal orders of the 23rd of December, 1595, and the 12th of December, 1619. These ordinances are included in the Code

his Majesty, for the term of *ten years*, which time must be passed in one of the garrisons of Africa, Oran, Ceuta or Melilla, or else in the penitentiary-house of the tribunal of the Holy Office of the Inquisition at Seville, at the discretion of the illustrious Señor Inquisitor-General, and of the Señors of the Supreme Council of the Holy General Inquisition, to whose disposal he be remitted, duly registered, and for the space of the said ten years he must confess and receive the sacrament at Easter, on Whit Sunday, and Christmas day, and also repeat a part of the rosary to the most Holy Mary. And the day following the said *auto*, he must go out to be disgraced in the public streets, placed upon a beast of burden, and with the same marks of infamy as in the said *auto*, and the voice of the crier is to make public his crime, and although we have condemned him to receive two hundred lashes, we command that they be not given, in consideration of the complaint he suffers, and that this sentence be executed *notwithstanding any supplication*, and for this it is our definitive sentence, and so we pronounce it, and command it in these writings and by them.

"DOCTOR DON MATHEO DE AMUZQUIBAR.
"FRAY THOMAS DE SANTIAGO CONCHA."

Holy God! And all this is done in thy name! Thy name, the symbol of supreme and infinite goodness, and to a man, one of thy creatures, and whom they have declared *innocent;* this they have done to one, whose heresy, that is to say, whose delinquency has not been proved even by his own accusers. This they have done to a penitential declared *absolved* by the very sentence which decrees his dishonour, and his martyrdom!

And when?

of the Indies, and are as follows: "*Idem.* We command that no foreigners of whatever nation they may be, be permitted to reside in the provinces of the Indies, nor the natives of those kingdoms who may have been condemned by the Holy Office, but must depart, and in no case can they remain in those parts, or return until the time in which are concluded the punishments imposed by the Holy Office."

When he had been *twelve years* locked up in these dungeons, the third part of an average life of man—*twelve years* which had been only one horrible agony of chains and of sickness, of solitude and of misery!

And in what manner?

Declaring the *accused innocent* of the crime for which he was persecuted, and condemning him for suspicion! (Behold ye adorers of the mild penal system of the Holy Office, for suspicions!)—to all the punishments above detailed, which was equivalent to a death more horrible, although slower, than that of the burning pile itself!

"And do ye not blush yet?" exclaims triumphantly the apologist of the Inquisition, whom we have combatted with his own weapons; "do they not blush yet, the many ignorant who keep repeating *ad nauseam* the chorus of iniquitous proceedings of the Inquisition? Will they still persist in saying that a mere information was enough to cause a man to be chained in their frightful dungeons and to be led to the stake?"*

No, Señor Prebendary, we do not blush—nor do we, as Christians, or as writers, or as being ignorant as you have declared, require of you to blush in your turn, but as this work will go forth to the world, we shall leave to an intelligent, a humane, and an enlightened public to decide who has most reason, in this age of civilization, to feel the blush of shame tingling in their cheek for the part they have taken in this polemic.

The horrible sentence of the *innocent* but *suspected* accused was carried into effect with all its barbarous details, on the 6th of April, 1761; and Francisco Moyen, that man endowed with intelligence and full of vigour, inspired by the love of science and of art; that Christian who had made a pilgrimage to the tombs of the Apostles; that Catholic who in Buenos Ayres had submitted to practise the exercises of St. Ignacio, and gave a portion of the produce of his

* "Rapid Sketch," page 62.

labour to assist in maintaining the ceremonies of public worship in Potosi; that man, convicted of suspicion, but who had declared his repentance, and had humbly begged pardon for his ignorance; that martyr, in short, that innocent man, even according to the process itself of his executioners, came out of those dungeons, in which he had groaned the third part of his life, and arrayed in the tunic of infamy, with a rope around his neck, a St. Andrew's cross of wood upon his shoulders, and mounted upon a beast of burden, was led about as an idiot amidst the derision of an ignorant and brutal mob, whilst his Satanic persecutors, the cause of all his pains and misery, proudly seated in their superb coaches, followed, enjoying with delight the bitter fruit of their own handiwork!

And all this to one they had absolved, and desired "to act favourably and mercifully towards him, and not with the rigour of justice, being moved thereto by certain reasons and motives."

But we have not yet concluded.

The cruelty of his judges had been carried into effect; but something still was wanting to complete their work of infamy!

The ceremony of his public abjuration being terminated on the 6th of April, Moyen was brought for the last time before his jailors, and in their presence received an ulterior mandate, obliging him immediately and under the penalty of excommunication major, *late sentenciæ*, to the performance of an act of baseness and villany,—which was, to denounce all that he knew concerning the heresies that he might have heard uttered by any of his companions in captivity, or even by those employed in the service of the Inquisition! So that this horrible process, which had begun by a vile and treacherous denunciation, finished by the obligation of another still greater! And in this manner was forged link upon link in the chain of the abominable and frightful crimes of those wretches, who had the blasphemy to represent as their accomplice, a God of eternal justice and of mercy inexhaustible! . . . .

The day following that infamous scene, the 11th of April, 1761, one of those clumsy looking ships known as galleons, and called the 'San Juan Bautista,' spread her sails in the port of Callao. It was in these vessels they were accustomed to send to the king, with a registered invoice, his fifth part of the gold and silver extracted from the mines in South America, as well as the offenders against their liege Majesty.

On board, in irons, and bearing himself an extract of his suit,* Francisco Moyen took his departure to undergo another process before the Supreme of Madrid, and to submit himself to the merciful sentence of his persecutors of Lima, which would be equivalent to nearly half his life, (*twenty-two years,*) delivered up to solitude, to shame, and to the eternal agonies of a dungeon!

What was afterwards the destiny of that martyr, of that innocent man, declared to be so by the tribunal itself that judged him?

We know not, and in our ignorance we feel a consolation!

Nevertheless there is a tradition preserved in Lima, but which however we were not able to verify, that the ship 'San Juan Bautista' was overtaken by a dreadful hurricane off Cape Horn, and sank with all on board.

And if it was so, we can say, without incurring the sin of heresy, that Francisco Moyen was absolved, and that Nature,—whose sublime disorders he had witnessed on that day when he and his party had encamped in the pass of Jujui, and where to the confusion of the elements he joined the sweet melody of his violin and his innate devotion and love for all creation, congenial to the Christian and believer,—had by this fatality shown more mercy to the victim than did his holy judges the self-styled ministers of God!

* This was composed of 187 leaves in folio.

CHAPTER VIII.

Such was the process of Francisco Moyen, in which we believe that we have answered all and each of the arguments evidently erroneous or sophistical of the learned, but in our humble opinion infatuated eulogist, whose inexhaustible store of citations is equal to the accumulation of his false conceptions, whether they refer to the ecclesiastical or Spanish Inquisition, which he distinguishes and confounds together alternately, although in reality they are one and the same; that is, the expression of religious intolerance and fanaticism more or less ardent, more or less ferocious, according to the race, the climate and the country where it is exercised. At any rate the Inquisition has answered the Inquisition; and now, having performed our promise, we abide the decision of every well informed and sensible person, both in our own country or in any other where this work may be seen.

But if, as an element of polemics, the process of Moyen has been a terrible weapon in this argumentative controversy, it becomes necessary to show the evidence of its historical merit, inasmuch as it was a document entirely unknown,* and more than this, that, considering it in this point of view, it puts us in the way better to understand its inquisitorial character.

Even as the processes of Froilan Dias, confessor to

---

* Really it appears strange that a document so curious and interesting should have existed in a public library so long without having been before consulted by previous writers, so fond of these investigations, such as Cordova, Urrutra, Fuentes, Palma and Lavalle, who have published curious episodes of the Inquisition of Lima.

Charles II., and that of Don Pablo Olavide, agent of Charles III., marked, in the opinion of a distinguished Spanish writer, the maximum of the height and the point of descent of the Inquisition in the Peninsula, so it may be said that those of the judaizing Manuel Bautista Perez (1630), and of Francisco Moyen, almost contemporaneous with the latter (1778), indicated one and the other of those periods in Spanish America.

Almost at the same time in fact that Moyen was consigned to the vaults of the Inquisition at Lima (March (1752), was received in that capital the famous royal letters patent of the 28th of June, 1751, in which was given the first death-blow to that institution, causing it to lose its moral prestige, and preparing the way for its final abolition amidst the applauses of avenged humanity. That sovereign mandate was the fruit of the oppressions, of the insolence, of the frauds, and of the excesses of all kinds, to which the American Holy Office had given itself up in the frenzy of its predominance and utter irresponsibility. And at last, not finding in the illustrious Manso a wicked accomplice like Toledo, a fanatic like Henriquez, or a covetous man like Chinchon, but an upright functionary and jealous of his prerogatives, it had to succumb before the Court, notwithstanding all its powerful intrigues.*

Nevertheless ten years had the Viceroy to contend hand to hand with those terrible rivals, and although they raised a thousand difficulties of frivolity and vexation,—for example that one already mentioned concerning the kind of dress which the judge should wear, who formed with them the *sala refleja*, †—he kept them within due bounds. But as

---

* To such an extent had they been carried that, according to Manso, no one was willing to accept the title of visitor of the Inquisition, for which the Viceroy held dispatches, "for fear, says that functionary, of drawing upon himself such powerful enemies as the inquisitors had the power to be."

† *Sala refleja* is a mixed court, composed of civil and ecclesiastical judges, to decide upon questions in which both powers are concerned. —*Note by Translator.*

the Court had resolutely determined to support their representative, who now commenced to be distinct from that of Rome, so that when the inquisitors were notified of the second royal letter patent of the 29th of February, 1760, in which it was ordered that the first of 1751 was to be complied with, and which deprived them of their most cherished prerogatives, being those most fruitful to them of power and doubloons, they were compelled to humble themselves and say to the Viceroy, "That with all due submission they would obey his commands."

What a change had taken place in the course of a century, since the inquisitor Juan de Mañosca, ordered the Dean Santiago, his commissary in Chile, not to recede one step before the Royal Audience, and when the faithful in Santiago and the Serena (Coquimbo), divided into two turbulent and highly excited parties, went about the streets shouting vociferously, "*Here the King—here the Inquisition.*"

To Manso succeeded the irritable, stubborn and grasping Catalonian Amat, the scourge of the Jesuits during his government in Chile, who manifested to the Inquisition, as he himself boasted, "how little respect he felt for them." He humbled their arrogance to such a degree as to enroll their familiars, whom before none dared to touch (not even their servants), under the penalty of being excommunicated,—in the militia of the country in consequence of the war with the English (1767).[7]

The illustrious Charles III. the destroyer of the colossus of Saint Ignatius, had just prostrated with his other hand the head of Torquemada, (both of which institutions were contemporaneous in their birth and in the proximity of their end, from thence their bond of alliance), and had banished one no less than the grand inquisitor Quintana, for having prohibited a Christian catechism which the King himself had ordered to be compiled. " Charles III. was religious and devout," says the most reputed and voluminous of the

Spanish historians,* but an ardent admirer and protector of instruction and progress, a zealous defender of the rights and royal prerogatives, and surrounded by wise ministers and councillors, supporters of royalty and animated, one and all of them, by the spirit of reform which had been initiated and developed in the last two reigns; all this rendered incompatible the ancient rigidity and also unnecessary the existence of an institution which created by religious zeal, fostered by fanaticism and strengthened by the usurpation of power, both regal and civil, had been for ages enslaving the understanding and preventing the expansion of enlightened ideas.† We speak of the tribunal of the Holy Office. Already in the reign of Ferdinand VI. the inquisitorial power had lost its ancient omnipotence, and thought had commenced to achieve its liberty and shake off the tyranny under which it had so long groaned, and the more that knowledge grew and developed itself, so much the more decreased the rigour, authority and influence of that antiquated and sombre institution!"

* La Fuentes, History of Spain.

By royal letters patent, later than 18th of August, 1763, Charles III. deprived the Holy Brotherhood of all privileges, in consequence of the insolence of its familiars, amongst whom was one Diego de Mesa, familiar of the Inquisition in the Canary Islands, who said to a ranger of woods belonging to the King, when he was told that he must not cut down the trees, that his licence to do so was in his axe.

† Although we have answered the incredible assertion of Señor Saavedra, when speaking of the Inquisition (expressly created to prevent all progress, the free exercise of thought and especially the use of books), he says that when it was established the *Belles lettres* began to *flourish*, but he must allow us to remind him of the *autos de fé* ordered by Torquemada for the express purpose of burning Bibles,— and also of the indexes (besides those of Rome existing at the present day), which the grand inquisitor Tapata ordered to be made, in which were included among the books prohibited, the works of the jurisconsults Talgado and Salcedo. Rodriguez Buron, speaking of the destruction of books by the first grand inquisitor, says, " there were

During the long reign of his successor Charles IV., 1788 to 1808, the preponderance of the Holy Office had become so weakened, that not one *auto de fé* was celebrated in the whole of that period; and such was its fallen condition, that in spite of all the efforts made by the famous curate of Esco, Don Miguel Solano, to get himself burned alive, by going about preaching in the streets and public squares against the simony of the bishops and others of the clergy, he could not succeed, so out of use had become the stake and the faggot.

It may truly be said that the Inquisition expired at the commencement of the age in which we live, and therefore we must keep ourselves alive to the end of it, should we wish to witness the celebration according to the modern ritual of its respective *centenary*.

We have seen how the heretic Stevenson was treated in

burnt more than six thousand volumes, which the qualifiers of the council of the Inquisition had declared dangerous, and nevertheless among them were many works of merit, whose only defect was, that they were not understood by their ignorant destroyers. The insolence of Torquemada rose to such an extreme that he gave orders for the whole of the library belonging to Don Enrique of Aragon, a prince of the royal blood, to be destroyed; thus involving in his vandalic proscription literature, science, and the arts, with theology and the superstitious practices of witchcraft." "Those who have the patience," exclaims Michelet, speaking of the obscurity in the Peninsula caused by the Inquisition, "to examine the annals of the Spanish press of the 15th and 16th centuries, will find only two kinds of books, the *Amadis*, mundane literature, and the *Rosaries*, and other books of the Virgin, conventual literature, not less gallant and sometimes bolder in expression!"

It is well known that Philip II. decreed the penalty of death to all importers and sellers of prohibited books. He also established the Inquisition of custom-houses; "the object of which was to prevent the introduction of prohibited books. Commissaries of the Holy Office were established at every port; and their vexatious annoyances greatly contributed to paralyze the maritime commerce of Spain!"

1806, in consequence of the denouncement of father Bustamante, relating to the affair of the Virgin of the Rosary. The condescension of the inquisitors by that time had arrived to such a degree of amiability, that after having admonished the English heretic, the fiscal invited him to breakfast at his house, and there enjoying the exquisite dishes on the table and sipping their chocolate they became perfectly reconciled.

The same Stevenson informs us that shortly after he was witness to a private *auto* in the chapel of the Inquisition: the penitentials being a priest overwhelmed with remorse, and a wizard, the latter of whom upon hearing the ridiculous absurdities imputed to him,* could not contain himself from laughing, in which the whole of the auditory joined. Comedy had succeeded to the horrible tragedies of past ages!

Notwithstanding all this there were little *autos* and private *autos de fé* until the year 1812, in one of which was condemned the celebrated seaman Urdaneja, for heretical propositions and for reading the works of the French philosophers, (the great heresy of the age, from Moyen to the fabulist Tomas de Iriarte, and the politico-literary Martinez de la Rosa),—to fastings and prayers, and to be confined in the Descalzos of Lima; but the first night of his expiation, he made such a sudden attack upon the friars and created such a disturbance that they were almost frightened out

* That some idea may be formed of these absurdities, it will be sufficient to mention a few of those attributed to the celebrated witch Angela Carranza, condemned by the Inquisition of Lima in 1674, the most notorious of their female victims, after the famous Ana or Inés de Castro.

According to the confession of that impostor, (a species of maniac) Jesus Christ one day asked her if she knew the number of the size of the shoes his mother (the Virgin) wore, as he had quite forgot? Upon another occasion she had lent her own shoes to the Queen of heaven; another time she saw the devils in hell, dancing, and all of them dressed in the habit of Dominican monks; and lastly, that she herself had been brought to bed of a litter of puppies, and when any one seemed to doubt her word, she always flew into a violent passion!

of their senses; and the inquisitors had to send him to be confined in the castle called Boca Chica, in the bay of Cathagena; but from whence, nevertheless, *the last of the heretics* made his escape, and went and joined the patriots of Mexico, in which country he died.*

* Stevenson mentions this case, but without naming Urdaneja, whom he designates only as a seaman of Andalusia. The Señor Don Francisco Mariategni, who was present at the *auto*, gave us the account which we have related.

The French traveller, Julian Mellet, who visited Lima in 1815, also mentions a curious case of a poor fellow who, in 1812, tried to gain a living in the streets of Lima, by showing some cats and dogs which he had taught to dance, but being accused as a wizard he was immediately shut up in the dungeons of the Inquisition. "It would be impossible," says the same Mellet, referring to the case (Voyage dans l'Amerique meridionale,) "to form an idea of the pitiable state to which the unfortunate man was reduced, when he was set at liberty after an imprisonment of six months, caused by the tortures he had suffered. He would never relate them to anyone; only saying to those who asked him, that he had been absolved; but any one who saw him would have supposed he was a skeleton just come out of the grave." If this was the case in six months, what could have been the state of Moyen after *twelve years* of that *mild* penitentiary system! Of this very same thing we have omitted to say that in the prisons at Lima, (which truly were not the worst,) they punished in the *auto de fé* of 1639, (according to Rodriguez Buron,) three jailors of the Holy Office convicted of having permitted some of the prisoners to hold communication with each other.

With respect to the futility of many of the inquisitorial persecutions some idea may be formed. According to the *Directory of Eymerico* it was considered as heresy to export horses to France, and truly this was more serious than to cause dogs to dance, or to make cats talk like the devotee Argomedo. †

---

† A very devout old woman in Santiago, who pretends to make cats talk, to effect which she wraps the animal in a cloth, and while with one hand she pinches its tail, with the other she grasps the nose and mouth, and with a little manœuvering she forces it to utter sounds which are said to resemble the human voice.—*Note by Translator.*

When the Spanish Cortes, in 1813, promulgated their celebrated decree for the abolition of the Holy Office, it was consequently only as a *de profundis* over its fetid and loathsome corpse. And here we ought to remind the Señor Prebendary of Santiago, of one of his arguments, the most original, viz. that the Inquisition was not cruel or persecuting, because that when the army of Napoleon entered Spain his heretical soldiers did not find a single prisoner in its dungeons, a fact, which although to us it appears doubtful, might nevertheless be true, for the reason that the Holy Office at that time did not exist except in name; but granting that what he asserts was so in 1808, let him demand of history how many illustrious prisoners were shut up by the Holy Brotherhood in their dungeons during the dark period of absolutism of 1814 to 1828, when the perjured King endeavoured to give it new life, and this, when the Inquisi-

<blockquote>
According to Llorente, a member of the town council of Seville was persecuted for having said " that the immense sum expended in fitting up the altar in the street for the procession on Holy Thursday, would have relieved many families which had not bread to eat, and to have employed it thus, would have been more acceptable to God."

Dominguez, in his Spanish Dictionary, mentions the case of a Frenchman who was burned at Marseilles for having maintained (before Harvey) the theory of the circulation of the blood. We are not certain if the Inquisition did not persecute Juan Fernandez as a wizard, for having made in a month the passage from Valparaiso to Callao, but which usually occupied six. (It was the same voyage in which he discovered the islands which bear his name, 1574.) But it is notorious that excommunication major was denounced against all masters of vessels who, in defiance of storms, sailed from Valparaiso between the months of July and October. The same traveller Mellet, above mentioned, gives an account of a curious affair connected with the Inquisition, which occurred to him in Lambayeque in 1816. He having wished to compel a curate to return him the change of an ounce in gold which he had given to pay for a supper for himself and his companion, had to suffer the inconvenience of fetters and imprisonment until he managed to free himself by a few more ounces without asking for change, assisted by the influence of the bishop of Trujillo.
</blockquote>

tion (as the Señor Prebendary asserts with a candour truly astonishing) never lent its unsoiled hand to favour either the despotism or the avarice of Kings!

"The denunciations of hatred," says a Spanish writer, referring to this abominable epoch in the history of Spain, "by which the clergy made themselves the vile instruments of a vile policy, joined to the envy, revenge, and the spirit of party, produced effects so disastrous at this moment as never before had been equalled. Fortunately the Pope Pius VII. had just abolished the use of the torture, but the secret prisons and dungeons were filled with new victims of the Inquisition, and the islands were peopled by illustrious exiles." (Rodriguez Buron.)

Be this question as it may, it is now decided by the whole world.* With respect to ourselves, Chilians, we were unwilling to know the Holy Office, according to the expressive language of the Dean of Santiago, who wished to make us acquainted with it. We claim for our country, as one of its highest and most legitimate glories, as being the first, and perhaps the only one in Spanish America which resisted from its foundation that diabolical invention, which had subdued the most vigorous nations by terror: and in

* The Inquisition was abolished in Tuscany by the illustrious Leopold I. in the year 1787; in Milan it had been before that by Joseph II., and by the Duke of Parma in his estates in 1769. Napoleon abolished it in Spain by a decree dated in Chamartin, the 4th of December, 1808.

The liberal Cortes, in 1820, definitely abolished the Spanish Holy Office, and "then," says Rodriguez Buron, "in every place where there was a tribunal of the Holy Office, the people rushed to the prisons, broke open the doors, took out the victims who had been groaning in them, demolished the palaces of the inquisitors and their horrible dungeons, shattered to pieces the cruel instruments of torture, and erected trophies to the constitution upon the same places which had been so long polluted by those odious edifices."

How is it then, if in 1808 Napoleon found no prisoner in the Inquisition—that Rafael Riego found so many? And if the people loved so much the Inquisition, why did they treat it at its extinction just as they did at its establishment?

advance of all, and even of Spain itself, abolished it, de facto, in the days of our revolution. Our first congress (1811)*

* In the Congress of 1811, it was decreed to suspend for the future the sending to Lima of the funds, arising from the two suppressed canonships, and to apply the amount which before had been invested in supporting the Tribunal of the Inquisition, to purposes equally useful and pious.

More about this particular affair will be seen in the Appendix, where the reader may consult the curious documents relating to the reclamations made in favour of the inquisitorial quota in 1812 by the last treasurer, Don Judas Tadeo de Reyes, and the official letter which the last representative in Lima of that ominous vampire, now insatiable of gold as before it was of blood, sent to the general, who had by force of arms conquered us in Rancagua, to plunder us in the name of the Holy Brotherhood newly called to life.

With respect to its last and definitive extinction in Peru, coeval with the invasion by our bands of liberators in 1820, we here give the words of the illustrious national writer, Garcia Calderon, whom we have several times quoted,—" The liberal ideas which spread among the natives of Spain at the beginning of this century, and the disrepute into which the Inquisition had fallen, in consequence of the opinion formed of it and of Spain by the other nations of Europe, gave occasion for the issuing of a royal decree, dated the 9th of March, 1820, by which were suppressed the Tribunals of the Holy Office. The news of this suppression, according as we have been informed, was received in Lima with frantic outbursts of enthusiasm, the crowds expressed by their excitement the transition from a state of continued alarm and insecurity to one in which they could repose without fear in the bosom of their domestic homes."

As in 1821 the independence of Peru was declared in Lima, the suppression of the Holy Office remained confirmed. The property it possessed was transferred to the State, and it was destined for the purpose of public instruction, with the object no doubt of employing in intellectual progress the same resources which before had been applied to restrain it.

With that which relates to Chile, and as a specimen of the different ideas held by our fathers, and even our grandfathers forty years ago, about the education of their children, it affords us great pleasure to be able to quote the following words from the text of the *Moral Philosophy*, dictated by the professor, Don José Miguel Varas, to the students of the National Institute, in 1828, and which was printed in

thus displaying, if we may be permitted this plagiarism of that elegant phrase of the Señor Prebendary applied to the torture, "The beautiful aurora of a splendid day."

the same year at the cost of the students themselves. It may be seen in the 31st vol. 4to. of national printed books in the public library at Santiago.

"There is another class of tolerance which is called religious (says the author in the chapter ' on Tolerance,') and all that I ought to tell you on this point is, that the religion we profess is the only true one; it is celestial, sublime, and at the same time simple. . . . . And although others may profess whatsoever they please; they are always men, and as such we ought to tolerate their defects, so that we may have the right to exact the same from them. Far be it from us to hate a man for his opinions, and the *barbarous* zeal with which many persist in instilling into the minds of others their own mode of thinking by the force of rigour. *What right have we over the conscience?* The Inquisition alone might believe it had."

How much have we advanced in forty years!

CHAPTER IX.

Our intention to present in one authentic and faithful view the whole of whatever was horrible and infamous connected with the Holy Office, being terminated with the process of the unfortunate Moyen, and the preceding historical considerations, it only now remains for us to investigate the personal charges which the Señor Prebendary Saavedra has thought proper to bring against us in his book, in which he defends and justifies that ominous tribunal whose ministers we have repeatedly called in our work which he impugned, as also in this, executioners and impious plunderers.

These charges are reduced in substance to two: the first is the avarice *falsely* imputed to the inquisitors of America, and especially to those of Lima; and the second, their *supposed* cruelty.

Whether we have or not fully proved in this work the correctness and justice of both appellations, is a question that neither Señor Saavedra or ourselves are competent to decide. That belongs exclusively to public opinion, to whose judgment we shall leave it consigned.

But for many reasons we consider it our duty to remove the imputations cast upon us by Señor Saavedra, representing us as a voluntary falsifier of history, in the small work upon the Inquisition which we published in 1862, exactly a century after the cruel events we have related.

We will discuss the charges in the same order in which they are made.

In that historical memoir we said, that the principal income of the Inquisition was especially composed of the emoluments produced by a fund assigned to it by Philip II. at the time of its installation in 1569, whose proceeds amounted annually to 32,817 dollars, $3\frac{1}{2}$ reals, and from an income, which sixty years later Philip IV. granted to it; suppressing for that purpose eight canonships in the principal capitals of America, and applying the revenues of these when they became vacant to the use of the Inquisition, which alteration was truly the cause of the disturbances in Chile, provoked by the greediness of the agents empowered by the Inquisition.

Well, the Señor Prebendary Saavedra, attributing to us that for the authority of these data we have followed the text of the historiographer of the Inquisition of Lima, Don Manuel Antonio Fuentes in his " Statistics of Lima," declares categorically that we have employed a most 'notable equivocation.'

"With respect to the rents of the Inquisition," says the author of the 'Rapid Sketch,' (page 85,) "the Señor Vicuña has used a most notable equivocation. Fuentes in his 'Statistics of Lima,' from whom it appears that Señor Vicuña has taken his data, *says entirely the contrary;* these are his words, 'The tribunal possessed an annual rent of 32,817 dollars, 3¼ reals, arising from a fund destined for that purpose by Philip II. and from the suppression of eight canonships decreed by the Pope Urban III. in the cathedrals of Lima, Quito, Trujillo, Arequipa, Cuzco, Paz, Chuquisaca, and Santiago, in Chile.' By which manner the income of the tribunal of Lima is derived," says Señor Saavedra, "copulatively from two different funds; and the Señor Vicuña, *probably blinded by his hate of the avarice of the Inquisition,* has given a disjunctive sense to the words of Fuentes, to criminate the Inquisition."

Here many questions might be started by those taught in theology had we been casuists; because, in the first place, what reason has Señor Saavedra to attribute to us that we have exclusively followed Fuentes? And in the second place, why should the words of this writer, which the eulogist of the Inquisition interprets copulatively, because thus it suits him, not be understood in a contrary sense, as its manner of expression, as given by our impugner himself, would lead us to suppose? But this is merely a question of grammar, and as such we will leave it, and go into the ground of the error, and see if it is ours, or that of our adversary's.

Immediately it is evident that we have not followed the writer Fuentes so implicitly as Señor Saavedra has imagined, and truly this he ought to have known had he paid proper attention, before accusing us of falsehood, to what we have distinctly said, viz. that a rent was assigned by Philip II. and another by Philip IV., showing between the two concessions a period of sixty years. "Sixty years later," we textually said at page 7 of our work, "Pope Urban III. at the petition of Philip IV. ordered the suppression of eight canonships, &c."

And as Fuentes says nothing of this in his "Statistica," it was natural that for our data we must have had some other authority.

And this was the truth, for we had taken from other sources the origin of those two *disjunctive* rents, and to convince the Señor Prebendary of his error, without giving room to a subterfuge of logic, we will cite them. These sources are the correspondence of Don Thomas de Santiago, Commissary of the Inquisition in Chile, with the Grand Inquisitor of Lima, Juan de Mañosca (1635 to 1640), the originals of which we have preserved, and from which in each page of our University discourse we cited numerous fragments. If Señor Saavedra had fixed his attention sufficiently on these, he would have been convinced that the rent of 32,000 dollars of Philip II. was one, and that it was different from the other of the suppressed canonships sixty years later, for which reason the passage of Señor Fuentes ought to be understood *disjunctively*, as we have understood it, and not *copulatively*, as the Señor Prebendary has thought proper to do.

But if the Señor Prebendary, corrector of the erudite calculations of Llorente, and the simple ones of ours, should still doubt that unfortunately it is himself and not us that has "employed a most notable equivocation," let him read the laws 4th, 24th, and 25th, title 19, book the 1st, of the Code of the Indies, and the Apostolic Brief of the Pope Urban VIII. of the 10th of March, 1627; both of which documents are alluded to in a representation of the last treasure of the Inquisition in Chile, which may be seen in the Appendix, and he will be convinced that it was not our " blind hatred" to the Inquisition, but our love of truth and our never impugned scrupulosity in our historical investigations which induced us to state the facts as they really were. Let him read also the royal letter patent of the 14th of April, 1633, which we cited expressly in 1862, and by which it was commanded to carry into effect the bull of Urban VIII. and he will then fully convince himself of our veracity and of his own error.

Now with respect to the deductions which may be drawn by the Señor Prebendary from this notable equivocation, we shall make no account, considering as we do that it is entirely destroyed in its very foundation. But we must observe, that it is not just in our impugner, and much less true for him to say, that we have applied the total of the rents above-mentioned only to the inquisitors, and not to those employed by them, for we have most distinctly said, " that the rescript of Philip II. ordered to be founded three principal tribunals, endowing them with a fund, &c." from which it may be seen that we spoke altogether of the rents of the Holy Office and· its tribunals, without particularising how they made the distribution of them. Moreover, speaking of inquisitors it was not to be understood exclusively of their individual persons, but naturally of all their dependents, from the fiscal to the executioner. As for the error, which afforded so much rejoicing to Señor Saavedra, where Urban III. stands in our text instead of Urban VIII. he can attribute it to an error in printing, or that we have followed

Fuentes, whose error was the occasion of ours, or if it is more agreeable to him, he can attribute it to our supine ignorance in the chronology of the Popes, and which we are not ashamed to confess to a learned priest, because it is a truth of conscience. It remains then an evident triumph of our impugner, and deserves the infantile applauses of the refectory of the Fathers of San Ignatius! In his work he actually says, speaking of our error, "Are there no more equivocations in that short piece? Yes, indeed. To attribute an occurrence of the 18th century to Urban III. who lived in the 12th." Wonderful novelty!*

---

* One of the chief and earnest endeavours of the learned defender of the Inquisition has been to disprove the most serious of the charges made against it, viz. cruelty and avarice. If he has succeeded or not in his object, all those will be able to declare who have calmly and dispassionately read our work of 1862, in which it was proved that the spoliations by the inquisitors were nearly on the point of causing an insurrection; and in the present work we have proved their shameful fraud by the unexceptionable testimony of the Viceroys of Lima. Should any still doubt, they may read those memoirs, in which they will find new data to confirm this truth, as that famous trial of competence in the *sala refleja* of which the Viceroy Manso gives an account, and from which it appeared that, "for the interest of one of its secretaries," the honourable Inquisition had interfered in civil lawsuits, and those merely commercial, no doubt with the intention of making use of their excommunications *late sentenciæ*, and other spiritual weapons, in those times very efficacious indeed.

To prove the poverty of the Inquisition of Lima the Señor Saavedra uses a strange argument. At page 86 of his work he says: "That tribunal could not be rich, because the Viceroy Toledo ordered that the town council should be at the expense of the extravagant preparations of the *autos de fé*, and also because the Inquisition solicited the same again in 1736." That this was done by Toledo, who was no other than a ferocious inquisitor of the sword, so cruel and such a villain that he disgusted his proper master, Philip II., may easily be understood; and also because at that time the Inquisition was recently founded, and probably had no money before its first *autos de fé*, as it was just these which were the fruitful sources of its income. But that the Holy Office should allege poverty in 1736 as an excuse for not construct-

We will now go to the other charge, that of the cruelty inflicted upon the Chile *witches* by the Inquisition of Lima;

ing the scaffold, was it not only another proof of its refined avarice? Was it not at this same time when the inquisitors Unda and Calderon were gorging themselves with gold to such an extent as to render it necessary that a high official should be sent from Spain to inquire into their proceedings? What had become of the confiscated millions of the Judaizing merchants, Manuel Bautista Perez, and his companions? What of the 200,000 ducats for which the Conde de Chinchon sold the permission of residence to the 6000 Portuguese (also Judaizing because they were rich), and whom, for the purpose of robbing them, he threatened with expulsion? And, lastly, what of the annual produce of the 32,000 dollars of Philip II., and of the suppressed canonships of Santiago, Lima, and all the capitals of Spanish America south of the Equator?

The quotation by Señor Saavedra of the hypocritical mendicity of the Holy Office in 1736 is exact, and as a curiosity we will here give the official letter, in which they solicited assistance from the town council,—those honourable beggars, who could give security for 50,000 dollars, who retired to their estates, and could disgorge their extortions to the sum of 30,000 dollars, &c. &c. It runs thus:—

" Most noble and loyal Council of this City of the Kings.

" By our secretary of the Secret, Don Joseph Toribio Roman de Aulestia, we make known to your honourable Council, the sixteenth of the present month, that we have resolved to celebrate a public *auto de fé* in the principal square of this city, on the 23rd of December (provided that nothing should impede or prevent), and because we infer that your honourable Council is acquainted with the decree of the Señor Don Francisco de Toledo, remitted to this Council in the year 1518, by which it is declared that it is at the charge of your honourable Council the construction and erecting of the scaffolding necessary for the said function, and which is to be seen in one of the coloured books of the archives, we bring it to the consideration of your honourable Council, that in your ability to contribute on your part to such a commendable act; and although for reasons we cannot explain, for those which were celebrated in the past years of 1595 and 1600, the city was relieved from this obligation by contributing only 700 dollars, this we bring to the notice of your honourable Council, that being advised of one and the other, proper steps may be taken to have the scaffolding erected, taking into consideration the necessity of this royal fiscal, who has wished to relieve entirely your honourable Council from this burden, but

that is, if such a subject ought to be taken notice of in a serious work.

Here, in short, is the case. In page 11 of our pamphlet the state and poverty of the times has placed us in the necessity to solicit by every means the aid and favour which we expect from your honourable Council. May God guard your honourable Council in his keeping many years.

"Inquisition of the Kings, 12th November, 1736.
"Doctor Don GASPAR IDANEZ.
" Doctor Don CHRISTOVAL SANCHEZ CALDERON.
" Licentiate Don DIEGO DE UNDA.
" By the mandate of the Holy Office of the Inquisition,
" Don JOSEPH TORIBIO ROMAN AULESTIA, *Secretary*."

We have already seen in another place of this work, that at the reestablishment of the Inquisition in 1814 there were missing no less than thirty-four boxes for embarking money of the stock which the *poor* inquisitors had in their warehouses to make their remittances to Spain—or to their own houses!

With very good reason says the illustrious Peruvian, Garcia Calderon: " The Inquisition had the same power to impose penances and punishments, that is to say, to inflict fines upon heretics, and to confiscate their goods. The sums obtained by either of these methods were destined to pay the salaries of all those employed by the Inquisition. This, in our opinion, was the most serious defect of the Holy Office; and as we are convinced that interest is the cause of the greater part of the crimes committed in the world, who can assure us that the Holy Inquisition did not forge accusations of heresy to fill their chests with the large fortune of the heretic? Who can deny the truth of history, which affords so many examples of this fact?"

Who can deny? We have seen who can!

The truth is that Señor Saavedra, in his fondness for making comparisons, has gone a little beyond himself in the following : " It is hard certainly (he says in his *Rapid Sketch*) to deprive a man of his goods, and also a painful thing to deprive him of his life, but however painful it may be, society is obliged to have recourse to these measures to repress the perverse, as they would have recourse to the amputation of a cancerous or gangrenous limb."

According to this theory, each one of the rich of our earth has an occult cancer, and the banks are nothing more than an active gangrene. What a great pity it is that the Inquisition cannot be restored to cure them! But patience, its centenary will arrive!

of 1862 we said as follows : " Although we have read, we do not remember where, that a woman called the Chilian Flea (Pulga) was burnt for a witch in the square of Acho in Lima, and also the bones of a bachelor called Obando, a native of Chile, the ashes of which were scattered to the winds, nevertheless neither of these facts has been mentioned by the timorous Peruvian writer, Cordova Urrutia, who has related so many cases of the Inquisition in his work entitled, ' The Three Epochs of Peru,' nor yet the learned Fuentes, in his prolix ' Statistics of Lima.' "

Now, the Señor Saavedra, in referring to those authors we have named, denies the fact, and have we affirmed it? Did we not simply say, and as a vague allusion, or rather as a thing to be doubted, that we had read, we did not know where ? On the contrary did we not affirm that those authors did not give an account of it, notwithstanding that one of them gave many cases of the Inquisition, and that the other was prolix in his investigations ? Could we give a proof more honourable, or more indisputable of modesty, and of historical scrupulosity ? But Señor Saavedra has discovered that neither the Chilian Flea nor the bachelor Obando, (who was not a bachelor, but a miner), were burnt, but received milder punishments. Well and good ! The learned prebendary has cleared up and explained our doubt, and from to-day henceforth we know that the parchment entitled " Triumphs of the Peruvian Holy Office," (which we had not had the good fortune previously to have met with), gives an account of the case of the Flea, and the little Flea her daughter.

But even of the expression ' we did not know where,' and which we wrote for the sake of our veracity, we wish to give an explanation, because it is certain there was some confusion in our memory of names and things as the expressions we made use of would show. No doubt we had read in some book that there had been witches and bachelors burnt by the Inquisition of Lima, and the fact is that such was the case with the celebrated Madam Castro, the *flyer*, who was a

Spanish woman, and the *bachelor* Francisco Maldonado, who was not a Chilian, but a native of what is now known as the Argentine Republic. Nevertheless there were two natives of Santiago, Don Juan Francisco de Ulloa, and Don Juan Francisco de Velasco, who having died in their prisons, were burnt in effigy.*

And thus it appears there were more Chilians burned than we were aware of, and by some means we had confused their names in our memory. A sad and serious error, of which we confess ourselves guilty, although fortunately our victim was only a flea.

With respect to errors in detail without intention of falsehood, or induced by the fault of others, we are willing not to treat this question inquisitorily, but on the contrary to propose to our adversary that we willingly consent to an indefinitive truce, we granting that our slight blunders of grammar and arithmetic are fully proved, unless that the Señor Prebendary in his terrible enthusiasm for the Holy Office, should do the same as those who absolved Moyen from the crime of heresy, and condemned him to die for suspicion! In which case we shall consider our proposal of no effect, and placing ourselves upon our defence await with fortitude and resignation the fiery storm with which we are threatened.

But before concluding this *Contra Rapid Sketch*, which we

* In the Appendix will be found an extensive account of the *auto de fé* of the 23rd of December, 1736, in which these punishments were inflicted.

As for the other Chilian victims of the Holy Office, the terror which imposed silence on the living has also rendered dumb the voice of tradition. A case is given of a Frenchman, a guest in the house of the ex-judge Don Alonso de Guzman (somewhere about the year 1770), who was taken away in a mysterious manner in the green coach without ever having been heard of afterwards, and of another European, who having married into the family of Irigoyen, went to mass on the morning following the celebration of his nuptials, and never returned to see his bride, nor his house, nor 6000 dollars he had given her for a dower. . . .

were discourteous enough to declare at the beginning we had undertaken against our own inclination, let us be permitted to direct to the intelligent public who may compare this present work with the *Rapid Sketch* of Señor Saavedra, and with the article of his reviewer in the *Independent*, these two last questions of polemic.*

With respect of the *Rapid Sketch* of the Señor Saavedra:—

Firstly. Is it certain that the Señor Saavedra has "rendered evident (his own words) throughout his work, that the enemies of the Inquisition have calumniated it in all they have said about it?" Is it certain that our testimony ought not to be received for being, as he qualifies us, "barefaced slanderers?" (literal) and finally, is it certain that "those calumniators have in general been declared enemies of catholicism, and highly interested that their theories should not be qualified as criminal, and the penalty of death be applied to them and their co-religionists?"†

With respect to the reviewer of the *Independent*.

Secondly. Is it certain that there could not have been

---

* The principal arguments for the defence of the Inquisition used by Señor Saavedra in his pamphlet, entitled "The Inquisition—A Rapid Sketch of that ancient Institution,"—are embodied in the present work, and although the English reader may not have seen the original, yet he will have from the many quotations made from it by our author a sufficient knowledge of its contents to be enabled to answer the above questions.—*Note by Translator.*

† On this most singular conception, the benevolent Señor Saavedra, who pauses little in his words (and less in his comparisons), in the same paragraph treats us to the following beautiful specimen, truly not very christian-like, in reference to those who calumniate the Inquisition for the fear they have of it, he says, "If assassins and robbers had well founded expectations that by lying and calumniating without reserve, they could obtain the abolition of all the tribunals of justice which condemn them to death, and could with impunity deliver up themselves without restraint to their instincts of blood and pillage, can we believe that they would have the least scruple in making use of such means?" (Rapid Sketch, page 121.)

rendered a more signal service to the friends of the Church, than what has been done by the Señor Saavedra in dissipating errors and combatting prejudices which discredit and illtreat it?"*

Let the public answer!

* It would appear that these clerical writers are determined that the Inquisition shall be identified with the Catholic religion, as part and parcel of it, one and indivisible, and as a man who associates with thieves must expect to bear the stigma of dishonesty, are they then willing that their church should go down to posterity, branded with the crimes of bloodshed and hypocrisy, condemned and execrated by all true and honest men, whether Catholic or Protestant? . . . *Quem deus vult perdere, prius dementat.—Note by Translator.*

CHAPTER X.

But let us conclude, and among the accumulation of important truths taught by history, let us leave at least one deposited, as the fruit of this discussion, which otherwise would be contracted in its personality and sterile in its actual result.

This truth is, that Chile, whether for the energy of its illustrious and ancient clergy, or for its remoteness and poverty, offered no harvests as a temptation to the ministers of imposture; in short, whether by the rude ignorance of its sons which kept it apart from the dangerous theological controversies of past ages, certain it is that it afforded no shelter within its unstained limits, nor offered any soil for the horrible seed which the Holy Office had sown broadcast over the whole of the Catholic world. And for this supreme good we are indebted to the dignity and firmness of our fathers, who by the hand of a monk, president of our first Congress, levelled to the ground the fragile structure with which they had endeavoured in vain during the course of two ages to consolidate among us.

And may this same sentiment of national dignity and firmness again declare itself, lofty and inflexible, against all attempts to resuscitate the dark and gloomy past, for ever condemned; and may our sons say of the country we bequeath them, that never were we a party to permit to be enthroned in its laws that atrocious intolerance of which in the present day we are witnessing so many indications ; and of whose fruits, speaks an historian (Torres de Castilla), in the following words, applied originally to the country which served as a cradle and the nurse to the Holy Office, and at the same time as a tutor and step-mother to our populations.

"How different would have been the fate of Spain, how brilliant its industry, its arts, its commerce; how populous and well cultivated its fields; how immense had been its power, how solid its strength, how enviable its prosperity,—if the just principle of toleration, in a condition more or less vast, had governed the states of the Catholic kings, and instead of being violently suppressed, had enlarged itself, drawing together all Spaniards in the bonds of peace and harmony, and vivifying the country with the sacred fire of fraternity, instead of ruining and degrading it, converting it into a heap of blackened ruins by the sinister splendour of the inquisitorial fires!

"Dearly Spain paid for its fanaticism! Let us felicitate our fathers, who for ever decided against the Inquisition, and let us hope that the progress of enlightenment by them initiated, may advance in its path through the course of ages."

Yes; let us hope so!

APPENDIX.

I.

EXTRACTS FROM THE MANUAL OF INQUISITORS, FOR THE USE OF THE INQUISITIONS OF SPAIN AND PORTUGAL.

As the Señor Saavedra has given himself the laborious but useless trouble to study all the constitutions and principal laws of the Holy Office for the purpose of extolling its excellency, it appeared to us that it would be opportune and also useful to reproduce here some of the precepts of the fundamental code of the inquisitors, the most famous and lasting institute of its nefarious office; for it was compiled by one of its most celebrated oracles (the Grand Inquisitor of Aragon, Nicolas Eymerico), and was adopted, strengthened, and even exaggerated by his worthy followers, Torquemada, Deza, Valdes, and others, introducing, during the last century, some slight modifications, until it became of no further use.

This short extract is based upon the compendium, which from the "Directory of Inquisitors," Don J. Machena made and published in 1821 at Montpellier, with some additions of his own, which edition (a small volume in 8vo.)* has been very common in our libraries, for which reason we greatly marvel that it has not fallen into the hands of the learned and indefatigable investigator, Señor Saavedra, or if, having found it, he has not cited it.

EXTRACT.

CHAPTER I.—*Of the Summary.*

1st. When the delation made has no appearance of being true, not for this should the inquisitor cancel the process, for what is not discovered in one day may be made manifest in another. (*Directory of Eymerico*, part iii. p. 288.)

2nd. In every parish must be named two clergymen, with two or three laymen, who, after having been sworn, shall make continued and rigorous investigations in every house, in all rooms,

---

* We think it necessary to make known, for the better understanding of its origin, that the compendium by Marchena is a translation made from the Latin edition of the *Directory of Eymerico*, published by Doctor Peña, with annotations and explanatory observations, in Rome, 1558.

The compendium is divided into 14 chapters, and contains 150 pages. The words which we use are the same as in the extract by Marchena, only we have put in italics the most notable passages, the most impious and scandalous.

For the better understanding we have divided the matter of each chapter into numbered paragraphs.

garrets, lofts and cellars, to ascertain if there are any heretics concealed.*—(*Directory*, part iii. p. 284.)

3rd. It is sufficient the delation of two witnesses agreeing, that they have heard say that So-and-so is a heretic; this declaration being valid, even when the two witnesses have not heard anything bad from the mouth of the said accused.—(*Annotation by Peña, 3rd Book of the Directory.*)

CHAPTER II.—*Of the Witnesses.*

1st. In causes of heresy with respect to the faith the testimony of the excommunicated is received, as also that of the accomplices of the accused, of the *infamous*, of the criminals accused of any crime whatever, in short, also that of heretics; always provided that these testimonies are against the accused but never in their favour.

2nd. The testimony of *false witnesses* against the accused is also admitted; so that should a false witness retract his first declaration favourable to the accused, the judges must attend to the second. This law is peculiar to the process against heretics, because in the ordinary tribunals it is the first declaration that is valid. It is to be understood that the second declaration is only of value when it is to the prejudice of the accused; should it be in their favour, the judge must only admit the first. Let us suppose, for example, that So-and-so has said that the priests were the inventors of purgatory, and afterwards denies his accusation, the first declaration will remain good, notwithstanding the posterior retractation, if in case that the second declaration weakens the force of the first; and he that retracts must be punished for being a false witness. The judge must be careful not to give too much credit to such retractations, because in that might result the impunity of heresy.—(*Directory and Annotations*, book iii. note 122.)

3rd. Against the accused is also admitted the declaration of domestic witnesses, that is, of his wife, of his children, of his relations and servants, but *never in his favour;* and thus it has been ordered because these declarations are of much weight.—(*Directory*, part iii. question 70,)

4th. It is an opinion agreed to by all moralists that in causes of heresy a brother can declare against a brother, and a son against his father. Father Simancas wished to exempt from this law the father and the children, but his opinion is not admissible, because it would render erroneous the most convincing reasons, which are, that we ought to obey God in preference to our

---

* In the directions sent by the Roman Emperor Trajan to the celebrated Pliny with regard to his manner of dealing with the Christians (the heretics of those days), he prohibited the magistrates from making any search after them. He orders them also to reject anonymous charges, and to require for their conviction the positive evidence of a fair and *open* accuser. It is true that Trajan was not a Christian inquisitor; he was nothing more than a benighted Pagan.— *Note by Translator.*

fathers, and that if it is lawful for one to take away the life of his father when he becomes an enemy to his country, how much more ought he to denounce him when he becomes guilty of the crime of heresy? A son, accuser of his father, does not incur the penalties fulminated by the law against the children of heretics, and this is the premium for his delation.* (*In premium delationis, Annot.* Book ii. Note 12.)

5th. We have said that the declaration of domestic witnesses is admitted, that is of the relations, friends and servants of the accused against him, but not in his favour. The declarations of these witnesses for another reason are very necessary, because most generally the sin of heresy is committed within the domestic walls.—(*Annot. of Peña on 3rd book of the Directory.*)

6th. In strictness *two witnesses* are enough to give a definitive sentence against the heretic.—(*Direct. part 3rd, question* 71.)

7th. When a copy of the accusation is given to the prisoner it is when the most care should be taken that he may not be able to divine who are the witnesses that have declared against him. The means to prevent this are the following:—1st. To invert the order in which their names are in the process, attributing to one the declaration of another. 2nd. To communicate the accusation without the names of the witnesses, and to separate the names of those, mixing with them the names of others who have not declared against the accused. (Nevertheless both these methods are dangerous for the delators, and for this reason should be seldom resorted to.)

In this part, the practice of the Spanish Inquisition may serve as a model, in it the accusation is communicated, but all the circumstances of time, place and persons are suppressed, and also anything which might afford a clue to the accused to divine who are his accusers.†—(*Annot. of Peña on 3rd book, cited from the Directory.*)

* According to the Constitutions of Frederic II. quoted by Gallois in his "History of the Inquisition," the children of heretics were disinherited, except when they denounced their parents. This high domestic morality introduced by the Inquisition is confirmed by the following edifying case, which we copy from the Compendium of Rodriguez de Buron (vol. i. p. 99): "Among the accused who were fortunate enough to take refuge in France, there was a member of a distinguished family, called Gaspar de Santa Cruz. He died at Toulon, while they burnt him in effigy at Zaragosa. A son of his was arrested for having favoured his escape. The inquisitors condemned him to be present at a public *auto de fé*, and afterwards to go to Toulon and ask the Dominicans of that city to disinter the body of his father and burn it; and moreover to return to Zaragosa and deliver to the inquisitors a certificate of having done so. The terror with which the inquisitors inspired the son of Santa Cruz was so great that he submitted without complaint to the barbarous commands they gave him, and he had the baseness to comply with such an execrable penance. This sentence, enough to make the most inhuman shudder with horror, ought to be sufficient to characterize the inquisitors who pronounced it, and to give a just idea of the state of degradation to which they had reduced the people."

† By the documents we have published of the process of Moyen, it is seen how strictly they have observed these rules in the practice. They designate no person, or place, or object; it is always a certain subject, a certain day, in a certain place, &c.

Chapter III.—*The Interrogation of the Accused.*

1st. Of the *ten stratagems* which commonly occur to heretics to elude the suspicions of the inquisitors, the most notable which Eymerico mentions are the three last, to wit.

The eighth stratagem of the heretics is to feign giddiness when they find themselves hard pressed with questions, they pretend that their head goes round and that they cannot stand, and begging that their declaration may be suspended, they lay down in their bed to think what they ought to answer. They avail themselves of this stratagem especially when they see that they are going to be put to the torture, and say that they are very weak and will lose their lives, and the women pretend to have complaints peculiar to their sex, so that they may delay the torture and deceive the inquisitors.

The ninth is to pretend to be insane.

The tenth is to affect modesty in their clothing, in their face, and in all their actions.—(*Direct. part 3rd, page* 289, 290 *and* 291.)

2nd. Against the ten subterfuges of which the *Directory* makes mention, it teaches as many expedients to impede or discover them, and the most notable and characteristic of these is the following, which is the third in the order of the *Directory*.

When the declarations of the witnesses against the heretic are not sufficient proof, but afford vehement indications, and he persists in his denial, he should be made to appear before the inquisitor, who ought to ask him trifling questions, and when he denies anything (*cuando neyat hoc vel illud*) the judge should turn over the leaves of the acts which contain the former interrogations, and say, it is certain that you do not declare the truth; do not deceive any more. In this manner the accused will believe himself convicted, and think that in the acts there are proofs against him, (*Sic ut ille credat se convictum esse et sic apparece in processu.*) Likewise the inquisitor may turn over the leaves of any law papers whatever, and when the accused denies anything, pretend that he is astonished, saying, "How can you deny such a thing when it is true," and reading immediately the papers, turning them over again add, "Did I not say so? confess the truth." (*Teneat in mnaum suam cedulam* . . . . *et quasi admirans dicat ei: comodo hæc potes negare? nonne clarum est mihi? et tunc legat in cedula sua, et pervertat eam, et legat, et post dicat, &c.*) But in all this the Inquisition should take care not to explain any circumstance by which the accused might suspect that he knew nothing, and only to make use of general terms.—(*Direct. part* 3, *page* 292.)

Chapter IV.—*The Defence of the Accused.*

In this chapter the *Directory* only treats of the impediments placed in the way of the defence of the accused, such as the naming of the advocate, which is done by the inquisitor himself;

the conferences between him and his client which must always take place in the presence of the inquisitor; the refusing of an advocate which cannot be admitted except in case of mortal enmity, &c.

Chapter V.—*Of the Torture.*

1st. The torture is not an infallible method to obtain the truth, there are men so pusilanimous that at the first feeling of pain confess crimes they never committed, others there are so valiant and robust that they bear the most cruel torments. Those who have been once placed upon the rack, suffer it with great courage, because their limbs accommodate themselves to it with great facility and resist with force, others with charms render themselves insensible and will die before they will confess anything. These impiously use for their enchantments passages of the Scriptures which they write in an extravagant manner upon virgin parchment, mixing them with the names of unknown angels, with circles and strange letters, these they have in some occult parts of their body. I do not know if there are any remedies against these enchantments, but always it is well to strip and carefully examine the accused before putting them on the rack.—(*Annotations of Peña on book 3rd.*)

2nd. When sentence of torture has been given and while the executioner is preparing to apply it, the inquisitor and the grave persons who assist him should make fresh attempts to persuade the accused to confess the truth; the executioners and their assistants while stripping him should affect uneasiness, haste and sadness, endeavouring thus to instil fear into his mind, and when he is stripped naked, the inquisitors should take him aside, exhorting him to confess, and promising him his life upon condition of doing so, provided that he is not a *relapsed*, because in such case they cannot promise him that.

3rd. When all this is useless, and they apply the question of torture, they proceed to the interrogatories, beginning with the points less serious for which he is judged, because he will confess the lighter crimes before the ones of more importance. If he still persists in denying, he should be shown the instruments of other punishments, telling him that he will have to suffer all those if he does not confess the truth. In short, if he will not yet confess, the torture may be continued the second and third day; this may be *continued* but not *repeated*, because it cannot be repeated without fresh indications being shown in the cause, but it is lawful to continue it. (*An continuandum non ad iterandum, quia iterari uon debent, misi novis supervenientibus indiciis sed continuari non prohibentur.*)

Chapters VI. VII. VIII. and IX.

These chapters treat respectively of default and flight of the accused, of absolution, of penalties inflicted, and of abjuration; they offer nothing very particular.

Chapter X.—*Of Fines and Confiscations.*

1st. Besides penances, the Inquisition imposes fines for the same causes that it commands pilgrimages, fastings, and repeating prayers. These fines are to be invested in performing pious works, such as the maintenance and decorum of the Holy Office, which effectively is quite conformable to justice, that those who are condemned by the Holy Tribunal should pay for its subsistence, because St. Paul says, 1 Cor. chap. ix. "No one has an obligation to make war at his own cost:" *Nemo cogitur stipendiis suis militare.**

2nd. Among all the works of piety the most advantageous being the existence and permanence of the Inquisition, it does not admit of a doubt that they should apply the fines to the necessities and maintenance of the inquisitors and familiars, without a case of urgent necessity being requisite for their application, because it is above all things useful and advantageous to the faith of Christ for the inquisitors to have plenty of money, so that they can maintain and pay well the familiars who search out and apprehend heretics; and also defray the other expenses of their ministry, and this is the more indispensable that they should thus apply the amount of the fines, because as Guido Fulcodio says, who afterwards became Pope by the name of Clement IV., "the hands of the prelates are tenacious, and their pockets closely tied up:" *Quia prælatorum tenaces sunt manus, et marsupia constipata*—that is to say, they do not assist with pleasure to defray the expenses caused by the searching out and punishing of heretics. (*Annot. book 3rd.*)

3rd. If the property of those who repent before sentence has been given, is not confiscated, it is because of that same *benignity* which consents that they should live, they being unworthy to enjoy either life or property, because from the mere fact of incurring the guilt of heresy, the goods they possessed are no longer theirs. (*Direct. part* 3, *quest.* 109. *Annot. book* 3, *note* 151.)

4th. Compassion for the children of the delinquent, compelled to beg charity, cannot ameliorate the severity, because by divine and human law the *children ought to be punished* for the sins of the fathers. (*Direct. part* 1, *page* 58.) From this law the children of heretics are not exempt, although they be Catholics, and neither for this are they to be given their lawful portion, which would appear they should inherit by natural right.

5th. After the death of the heretic, they can confiscate the property he held, depriving his heirs of it, although his condemnation was posterior to his decease. (*Direct. part* 3, *page* 303.) And though it be an incontrovertible rule in civil law, that with death ends all criminal action, that law is not valid in causes for heresy, it being so serious a crime, and thus proceedings may be

---

* This is an exemplification of the proverb, *the devil quoting Scripture.* A pirate or a highwayman could justify his robberies with quite as much reason as the Inquisition, by quoting in his favour the above passage from the Bible!—*Note by Translator.*

carried on against heretics after they are dead, declaring them as such, to confiscate their property, (*ad finem confiscandi,*) and taking it from its owners, although it may have passed through many hands, applying it for the benefit of the Holy Office.

6th. It is a question much controverted to know, whether the heretic is not obliged in his conscience, although he has not been prosecuted or even denounced, to deliver up all his goods to the fiscal or to the Inquisition, and if he is not in mortal sin while he has not done so. Panormitano, Felyn, Maguerio, Tiraquelo, Alfonso Castro, and others, held that the occult heretic is obliged to make the said restitution; but other doctors no less learned, as Corrado, Sylvestre, Gomez, Simancas, Vasquez, Gabriel, &c. say that he has no such obligation. And effectively if the heretic is obliged to deliver up his goods to the inquisitors, he is also obliged to denounce himself, which is a very hard thing. The Rev. Father Simancas has victoriously refuted the arguments for the first opinion alleged by Alfonso Castro. (*Institut. Cathol. title 9.*)

CHAPTER XI.—*The punishment of Heretics in their Children.*

It is limited in establishing the right in which that chapter is founded, confirming it by various canonists. The principal part is the following:—

The children of heretics are incapable of holding possession or of acquiring any kinds of office and rights, a very just thing because they retain the stigna of infamy of their parents, and these are stained with the crime by the paternal love. Some authors think that in this penalty are not included the children born before that the father incurred the crime of heresy; but there is no solid foundation for such distinction, because this punishment was ordained for the purpose of restraining the parents by the bonds of paternal love, it ought to embrace all, because the parents love with equal affection those children who were born before as after the commission of the crime.

CHAPTER XII.—*Of Perpetual Imprisonment.*

1st. Generally speaking the repentant heretic ought to be sentenced to perpetual imprisonment. Nevertheless there are exceptions to this rule, and its rigour is mitigated for those who reconcile themselves with the Church before being accused or denounced, for those who confess their crime (although they are in prison,) and discover their accomplices in the heresy, and for those who though they delay in confessing nevertheless do so before they are notified of the declarations of the witnesses, but in the two last cases it is better and more conformable to justice to condemn the heretic to perpetual imprisonment, and afterwards to pardon him, as is the practice of the Inquisition of Rome.— (*Annot. book 3, note 142.*)

2nd. Nevertheless it is necessary that the dungeons should not be horrible nor too much unhealthy, because if they should occasion the death of the prisoners, the inquisitors would incur an irregularity, and this is the reason that Tabarella, Locato and other learned doctors (*Annot. idem.*) hold that the inquisitors and those commissioned by them have the faculties to absolve one another from these irregularities which they have incurred involuntarily, and which faculties were given by Urban IV.—(*Direct. part 9, page* 358.)

3rd. Secondly. The insalubrity and obscurity of the dungeons are to be proportioned to the gravity of the offence and circumstances of the culprits. Thirdly. The men are to be separated from the women. Fourthly. The husband and wife cannot be in the same prison when both have been condemned; but if one of them, the wife for example, is innocent, she may be permitted to communicate with her husband. Fifthly. Two prisoners cannot be in the same dungeon, unless when the inquisitors order it for some especial motive, and this is because that the common misfortune of two condemned, causes them to form a strict friendship, and contrive together plans to escape, to hide the truth, &c. &c.

Chapter XIII.—*Of the Relaxation.**

As we have in the body of this work treated extensively in this matter, we shall only here give a few of the precepts relating to it.

1st. A few days having passed in which the condemned have had time to prepare themselves to die, the inquisitors will give notice to the civil judges, that on such a day, at such an hour, and in such a place will be delivered to them so many heretics, and they will invite the people to the ceremony, in which a sermon concerning the faith will be preached, and all those who assist will gain the customary indulgences. (*Direct.* part iii. p. 331.)

2nd. Sometimes the heretics, before the execution of the sentence, become insane, and some authors have said that advantage should be taken during their lucid intervals to carry them to execution; but the most sure thing in such a case would be to consult the Sovereign Pontiff. (*Annotation on Book 3 of the Directory.*)

3rd. The obstinate and relapsed heretic (that is to say, one that has fallen back into his error) is to be delivered to the civil judges as the forementioned, but observing what we here say, he is to be put into a very dark and damp dungeon, in fetters, and chained, and placed in the stocks, so that he cannot escape and infect the faithful. The inquisitors should call him frequently, and try to convert him; and if, by the grace of God, they should succeed, they must give him to understand, making use for that purpose of God-fearing persons, that he cannot escape his punishment, but must think seriously for his soul. When a sufficient time has passed for him to prepare to die, whether or not he may

---

* Delivering the condemned up to the civil power.

have repented, he must be delivered to the civil justice in conformity to his sentence.

4th. This ought to be done in the following form:—

"Forasmuch as the Church, not being able to do anything with you, and having in vain used all the means it possesses to convert sinners, we declare you a relapsed and obstinate heretic, and we relax you to the civil power, but whom nevertheless we *beseech with earnestness* not to punish you with the penalty of death, nor shed your blood, &c."

CHAPTER XIV.—*Of the Crimes of which the Holy Office is cognizant.*

1st. Blasphemers, who blaspheming say anything against the faith of Christ, ought to be considered as heretics, and punished as such by the inquisitors with the legal penalties; as, for example, any one who says, "The weather is so bad that God Himself cannot make it better," sins in the faith against the first article of the Creed. (*Direct.* Part ii. Question 41.)

2nd. Some authors hold that drunkards who utter blasphemies ought to be punished as heretics when they have become sober, because we may *presume* that they say when they are drunk what they feel when they are in their senses.*

3rd. Those ought to be considered as blasphemers who say concerning the faith, God and the Saints, as though any one should say, "If I am not married in this world, I shall be in the other," and sustain this nonsense, which ought to be reputed in the category of heresy.

4th. In the third place, the Holy Office takes cognizance of those who invoke the devil, and which are divided into three classes. Of the first are those who render him worship by idolatry, sacrificing to him, kneeling to him, singing hymns to him, observing chastity or fasting to his glory, illuminating his images, and offering him incense, &c. The second confine themselves to the worship of *dulia* or *hyperdulia*, mixing the names of the devils with those of the saints in the litanies, and praying them to be their intercessors with God, &c. The last are those who invoke the demon, by drawing magical figures, placing a child in the middle of a circle, making use of a sword, a looking-glass, a bed, &c.; and generally those who invoke the demon may be known with great facility by their horrible look and frightful face, which are caused by their continual intercourse with the devil.

* In this same opinion coincides the author of an act of accusation of our tribunals about the end of the last century, and which we found among the papers of Don Judas Tadeo Reyes. In it, speaking of drunkards, he expresses himself in the following terms:—

"The theologians say that if a drunkard talks heresy, the Holy Tribunal of the Inquisition can punish him, not perhaps as a heretic, if there is no other collateral evidence, but for suspicion that when he is sober he holds some error about which he talks when he is inebriated."

All those who invoke the devil, by whichever of these three methods, are subject to the jurisdiction of the Holy Office as heretics, and to be punished as such. And effectively any invocation of the devil by one of the three species which we have just indicated is an act of heresy, in whichever way it is practised. (*Directory*, Part ii. Question 33.)

Notwithstanding, if any one should ask of the devil things properly belonging to him, as, for example, that he may tempt a woman to commit a carnal sin, provided he does not use words of adoration or prayer, but only imperative expressions, it is believed by some learned authors that the crime of heresy is not incurred. (*Idem.*)

5th. Infidels and Jews are subject to the Inquisition, the last when they sin against the articles of their faith, which are the same in both religions, as sacrificing to the devil, this being against the unity of God, an article admitted by Jews and Christians.

6th. Likewise is reputed for a heretic, his property confiscated, and himself condemned to perpetual imprisonment, he who, when the inquisitors are pursuing a heretic, pretends to be him, and allows himself to be taken, to prevent the apprehending of the criminal, he being a true Catholic. The same punishment is applied to those who do not denounce heretics when they know them for such; nevertheless the wife is exempted from the rigour of this penalty, although she should not denounce her husband for eating meat on a Friday, when she does not do so for fear that he would kill her by beating her should he come to know that she had denounced him. (*Annot.* Book ii. p. 59.)

7th. According to the commentator Marchena, in his additions to the Compendium of Eymerico, the following are indications of Judaism: To put on a clean shirt or clothes on the Saturdays; to remove the fat from the meat which they are going to eat; to examine if the knife is notched with which they are going to kill a fowl or other animal; to repeat the Psalms without the *Gloria Patri*. Of Mohammedanism: To get up and eat before daylight, wash directly the mouth, and go to bed again; to wash the arms up to the elbows, the face, the nostrils, the ears, and the private parts; not to eat pork nor drink wine; to sing Moorish songs and make zambras.* Of the heresy of the *illuminati*: To shut the eyes at the lifting of the Host. Of the suspected in the faith: To be a year or more without having received the sacrament; to tell fortunes by the lines of the hands; to remove the *sambenito* from where it was placed by the Inquisition.

8th. The contraband in saltpetre, sulphur and gunpowder is also a crime of the Inquisition; because it might so happen that these articles may be applied to the service of infidels or heretics to make war against the Catholics. (*Edicts of the Supreme Inquisition of the 23rd December,* 1572, *and* 20*th February,* 1616.)

9th. The exportation of horses from Spain is also a crime of

---

* Zambra, a Moorish festival, attended with dancing and music.

the Inquisition since 1569. In 1574 it was qualified as a crime of heresy by the tribunal; so that, according to the symbol of faith of our inquisitors, it is a heresy to believe that one could be a Christian who should say, I think, or I presume, that "the hack born in Spain can lawfully live north of the Pyrenees." The suspected of this contraband are suspected of heresy, and treated as such (*Edicts of the Holy Office, of 26th March and 21st August*, 1590), and those who assist, protect and conceal them are abettors of heresy. (*Edicts of the Holy Office of 21st March and 6th May*, 1592.)

II.

A Description of the Auto de Fé celebrated in Lima the 23rd of December, 1736.

(An extract from the book which contains it entire, the title of which is, "Triumphs of the Peruvian Holy Office; a Panegyrical, Historical, and Political Relation of the public *auto de fé* celebrated the 23rd of December, 1736, by Doctor Don Pedro José Bermudez de la Torre y Solar.)*

* This curious book, forming a volume in 4to, containing more than 300 pages, was printed in Lima in 1737, and is a most wonderful production of pedantry and stupidity, of gross adulation and barbarous fanaticism, as will be seen by the extracts we shall have to make from it. For the present it will be sufficient to comprehend its capacity, its philosophy, and its style, by the reading of the following lines which serve as the heading of its introduction :—
"From the æthereal, sublime, and luminous region, in whose placid, clear and tranquil sphere, the least movement is order, and the slightest sound is harmony, is resigned to the subordinate elements and sublunary materials the efficacious influence with which the care of heaven directs with proper and just proportion the government of the world."
In the first pages of this work we said that this same author gave as his own the strange idea that "God was the first inquisitor;" but in this part we must declare that the good Doctor Bermudez was nothing more than a poor plagiarist.
In fact, Luis de Paramo, cited by Bermudez, in his work entitled, "*De Origine et Progressu Officii Sanctæ Inquisitionis*," describes the first *auto de fé* in the following manner, which for its curiosity we cannot do less than present to our readers.
First, he says, Adam was cited—*Adam ubi es?*—teaching thus to all future tribunals of the Holy Inquisition that where the summons is wanting the process is null and void. Adam presented himself, and God began His interrogations, judging the criminal by himself and in secret. Exactly in the same form follow the inquisitors, having taken it from God Himself!
The dresses of skins which God made for Adam and Eve is notoriously the pattern of the *sambenito* which they put upon the condemned heretics. The crosses which were figured upon it at the beginning were straight; but immediately they became inclined, taking the form of that of St. Andrew, to indicate that those who bear them have wandered from the rectitude of the faith in Christ.
God having clothed Adam in this dress of infamy, figuring that man by his sin has made himself like the beasts, He expelled him from the terrestrial Paradise; and from this is derived the style of the Inquisition in confiscating the property of the heretics. There is no doubt but that this law is very proper,

The *auto de fé* of which the book of the Doctor Bermudez gives a description was without doubt the most famous after that which a century earlier (1639) was celebrated by the inquisitor Mañosca to burn the Judaizing millionaire, Manuel Bautista Perez and his wealthy companions.

Its principal attraction was the burning of Madame Castro and the punishment of ten other women, amongst whom were the Chilian Flea, and the Little Flea, her daughter, all of them for being witches!

The circumstance of having preceded only by a few years the imprisonment of Moyen, and having some of the judges connected with his process to assist in it, gives it sufficient interest for us to make from the endless absurdities of Doctor Bermudez the following slight extract, adapting ourselves as much as possible to the peculiar forms of the original.

It also appears proper and logical to observe in the practice the application of the theory of which we have given a sketch in the former article.

At that season (1736) were members of "the resplendent heaven of the sublime sacred tribunal of the Holy Office of the Inquisition,"* Don Gaspar Ibañez de Peralta, Don Cristobal Sanchez Calderon (he that was accused and convicted of being a thief), and Don Diego de Unda y Mallea (the same who for robbery had his jewels confiscated, although he retained them so long that it was nearly a century afterwards), of whose three illustrious names are heard to be those which in these spacious circuits of the earth give a clear testimony of the faith, being all three the same sun, which sheds from its refulgent sphere the vital splendour with benefit to him who desires by the prayers and tears of penitence and sorrow to imitate the Phœnix in newness of life."†

---

because, as Plato says (*Liber* 4, *De Legibus*), and Aristotle (*Liber* 2, *Magn. Moralium*), without virtue the goods of the earth are pernicious for their possessors, being an incitement to their passions and instruments of their crimes.

"Adam was likewise deprived of the command he had over the brutes. From this is deduced that the heretic loses all natural rights, civil and political, that his children cease to be under his dominion, his slaves become free, and his vassals released from the obedience which before was his due."

Now in the face of these theories of the origin of the Inquisition, ought the Senor Saavedra to take it ill that we compare his modern theory of the torture of witches, exhumation, &c., with those of Luis de Paramo, or with that of the Doctor Bermudez, whom he himself cites?

We have yet to add that another venerable writer, the Father Macedo, who published a panegyric of the Inquisition two centuries before Senor Saavedra (Padua, 1676), traces the divine origin of the Holy Office still higher; for, according to him, the expulsion of Lucifer was the first *auto de fé* we have on record.

* Bermudez, page 4.
† Bermudez, page 5. The definition which the author gives of the Phœnix is the following (page 2): "Heat, which distributed in atoms kindles, according to poetical ideas, the light which animates with new life the wonderful bird of Arabia." The *honourable* Unda, the bird Phœnix (and of prey) of Doctor Bermudez, he also styles, "shining, springing, lustrous Onda (wave) of the pure, sparkling, and pellucid fountains of the faith."

APPENDIX.

As the Inquisition, according to Capefigue and the Prebendary Saavedra, was a national institution of the Spaniards, and it has been seen that in this we have scarcely contradicted either one or the other, the people and also the upper classes were invited to the entertainment, in the same manner, neither more nor less, than they would have been in those days to a bull fight, or in the present one to a philharmonic or other social diversion.

Forty days before the time fixed for the ceremony, the inquisitor Unda, in his capacity as fiscal, repaired to the palace, the 13th November, 1736, for the purpose of inviting in person the Viceroy Villagarcia; " and withdrawing himself from this sphere of political splendour, he passed to the heaven of holy veneration,"* inviting the archbishop Don Francisco Antonio Escandon.

At the same time the Secretary of the *Secret*, Auslestia, invited the judges of the Royal Audience, whom he encountered in the temple of Astræa, under the canopy of Minerva, seated on the throne of Jupiter, surrounded by the divinities, and covered with the veil of Arachne; after which the seraphims and cherubims, who were nothing more than the sluggish canons of the chapter, and lastly, all of the university, that " envy of Memphis, Heliopolis, Rhodes and Alexandria, Throne of Learning, Garden of the Graces, and Mount of the Muses, whose virtues are reverently kissed by the foam of the Rimac."†

These invitations of etiquette having been made, the inquisitors, mounted on horseback, and with loud din and noise of flutes and kettle-drums, paraded the streets, publishing the proclamation of the festival, inviting the populace to the entertainment by placards, which were read aloud, and were literally as follows:—

" The Holy Office of the Inquisition makes known to all the faithful Christians, inhabitants of the city of the kings, and others, that on the 23rd of December of this present year, 1736, an *auto da fé* will be celebrated for the exaltation of our holy Catholic Faith in the principal square of this city, so that all the faithful assisting by their presence may gain the privileges and indulgences granted by the Sovereign Pontiffs to all who assist, accompany, and aid the said *auto*, which is ordered to be published and proclaimed that it may be known to all."‡

The next thing was the ornaments for the amphitheatre, the preparations for which must have greatly outshined the running cornice with curious mouldings, the marvellous seats, and the half pyramid, which appeared so majestic to the friar Torquemada in the great square of Mexico.

---

* Bermudez (page 12). The "heaven of holy veneration" of which Bermudez speaks would not be much to the taste of the inquisitors, because, in honour of the Archbishops of Lima, some of them had been their most severe censors. Frezier, who visited Lima forty years before Moyen (1713), says that at that time they feared less the holy executioners, because the viceroy and the archbishop with a vigorous hand confined them to their duties.—*Frezier Voyages dans la Amerique meridionale*, 1712, 1713, and 1714.

† The name of the river which runs past Lima.   ‡ Bermudez.

P

The place which they had chosen this time was also the great square of Lima.

In consequence, on the 11th December, that is to say, two weeks before the *auto da fe*, the inquisitors demanded of the Consulate and other public offices the use of their balconies to place seats in them for the wives of the judges, members of the town-council, and other functionaries of the colonial staff. As for the viceroy and the archbishop with their families, the ecclesiastical chapter, the jesuits, the communities of regulars, the members of which at that time were counted by hundreds, all had their especial seats, formed in gradation, and according to the same order of honour observed by Spanish etiquette in the equestrian exercises of throwing canes, or other festivities in the great square. The University and town council gave 600 dollars towards defraying the expenses of the ceremony. The Consulate gave 400. The Inquisition, which, according to a document of this same *auto de fe*, given at page 155 of this work, purposely complained of extreme poverty, when the functionaries were filling bags with the gold of the heretics for their own use, must have contributed but very little to the splendour of the day.

In the centre of the square was erected the vast amphitheatre of the inquisitors, in the middle of which was the tumulus of the penitentials, surmounted by a green cross, the theological symbol of the Inquisition, the wood of which had been first used a centuay before by Juan de Mañosca, in the *auto* of 1639, and which is seen on the days of punishment shrouded in a dense black veil, in sign of the church's mourning for the boisterous festival which the same church offered for the entertainment of the faithful; on one side of the tumulus was placed a pulpit from which was to be preached a sermon, on the other a cage, within which the condemned would hear their sentences read, and in front of this was the seat of the Viceroy placed between two inquisitors, whom (although it may be a sin of heresy, is not of lying, to say) might be called the good and bad thieves. "In front of the gate which looks towards the south," says Doctor Bermudez, "was erected a lofty throne, on which illumined the elevated shadow of the sublime canopy, the most excellent Señor, Marquis of Villa Garcia, Viceroy of these kingdoms, seated in the midst, between the two Señors inquisitors, Don Gaspar Ibañez de Peralta, and Don Cristobal Sanchez Calderon, a more brilliant place than that which the presumptuous Chosroes, monarch of the Persians, aspired to retain in that artificial machine which his pride caused to be fabricated for astonishment and admiration, being in its form an imitation of the heavens, in whose luminous space sparkled the celestial figures and glittering constellations, deceiving the eyes and confounding the ears with lightnings and thunders, and in the midst of light and of angels the same respectful prince showed himself attentive to all with the sight and splendour of human Deity." The secretaries, reporters, constables, familiars, and other militia of the executioners, and the godfathers of the condemned, had their respective seats and chairs in places preferable to those assigned to the laity.

The day fixed for the *auto* was, as we said, the 23rd of December, in commemoration of the foundation of Jerusalem by Judas Maccabeus. In the evening before, a solemn procession was made, in which was carried the green wood of Juan de Mañosca, and collocated with great pomp in the place it was to occupy on the following day.

The night which preceded the execution was one of great anxiety, although fictitious. They were only going to burn an old woman, and flog ten or twelve negro women and mulattos, and yet, nevertheless, the whole of that night the garrison of the city was under arms, part was stationary, under the Portal de Escribanos on one side of the great square, the commercial battalion was distributed in companies in the houses of their respective captains, and the cavalry in the square of the Inquisition. General don José de Ilamas marched up and down the streets at the head of numerous patrols. Nothing in short was wanting in the preparations for the sanguinary battle!

Thus it was, that as soon as the light began to dawn of the appointed day, "was heard saluting the wished for aurora to the tender compass of the melodious voices of the birds, the warlike sound of military instruments, in whose noble idiom was expressed to the companies in their quarters, the order to form in battalion."

It was on a Sunday, because it was ordered, as we have said,* to choose the feast days to give more sumptuousness to the burning pile. The people began to accumulate from daybreak, because those feasts sometimes lasted from sunrise to sunset, and at times even to midnight, when (as it happened in Zaragoza, in the time of Antonio Perez) some hundreds of heretics had to be carbonized at a slow fire.

No sooner had the day begun to dawn than the condemned were marched out of their prison, in the same order and with the same dress as described by Torquemada, skilled in this art. Every one wore sambenitos,† a kind of yellow shroud, girding the

---

* Doctor Pena, the commentator of Eymerico, says, in one of his glosses, "that he thinks it better to celebrate the *autos de fé* on feast days, it being advantageous that much people should be present to witness the punishment and atonement of the criminals, that fear may keep them from crime. For this motive without doubt the tribunals of Spain determined to celebrate the *autos de fé* on feast days, and to solemnize them with the attendance of the town councils, audiences and other persons in authority. This spectacle will infuse terror into the hearts of the beholders, presenting to them the tremendous image of the final judgment, will leave in their minds a salutary effect, and produce portentous results.

† Richard Palmer, in his curious episodes about the Inquisition at Lima, published in the "South American Review" (1861) erroneously attributes the name of *sambenito* to the intervention in the first *autos de fé* of certain monks of the Order of San Benito (St. Bennett.) But the name is derived from *saco bendito* (blessed sack). It had a form like to the aprons worn by the friars over their cassock as the scapulary of their order, and was a very essential part in the inquisitorial celebrations, as we have seen that it was a direct crime of

body and painted with devils and reptiles, a *coroza*,* or cap of derision, the same as the sugar loaf conical caps still used by the brotherhood of the Holy Sepulchre. On their backs were crosses of St. Andrew, and in their hands they carried tapers of green wax, which corresponded to the three theological virtues, the *wick* in the middle being the *faith*, the *wax* which enveloped it being *hope*, and the flame *charity*, which burns and shines with splendour. †

This time the effigies of the dead and their bones were carried in advance of the condemned in the procession, "Preceding these," says Doctor Bermudez, "were the effigies of those who could come in person, having been prevented by their anticipated death or violent flight. But they carried for a device the *sambenito*, and the other penitential vestments. And upon all the effigies could be read the names of those they represented, written in large and easily distinguishable letters on labels upon their breasts, and also a certificate accompanied the boxes of bones, wretched spoil of the narrow sepulchre, from whose sad and awful bosom, before they were reduced to dust, they were taken to become unprofitable ashes by the violence of the impetuous flames, caused by the conflagration of the burning pile." And this, although Señor Saavedra maintains that it was false to say that they burnt the bones of the condemned!

The procession of the condemned having arrived at the 'marvellous' scaffolding, the Viceroy took his seat, but before doing so standing with his head uncovered and his hands placed upon the Gospels, as the King would do in the same case, he swore, with a loud voice, the following oath, which was proposed to him by the Grand Inquisitor, and which acknowledges the terrible omnipotence of the Inquisition created by kings and blessed by popes.

"Your Excellency swears and promises by your faith and word, which, as a true and Catholic Viceroy, appointed by his Catholic Majesty Don Philip V., that you will defend with all your power the Catholic faith, held and believed by the Holy Mother Church Apostolic of Rome, the preservation and increase of it, that you will persecute and cause to be persecuted all heretics and apostates, enemies of the Church, and that you will give and order to be given the favour and aid necessary to the Holy Office of the Inquisition and its ministers, so that heretics,

---

heresy to remove the *sambenites* from where they had been placed by the inquisitors. In the Directory of Eymerico it says, "Sometimes it is possible to dispense with imprisonment, with fasting on bread and water, but never can there be the least indulgence in regard to the dress and the sambenito, because they are a penance very salutary to those who wear them, and a thing of great edification to all the faithful."—(*Direct*. part 3.)

* The *corozas* or caps were generally made of pasteboard, and on them were painted figures of devils and reptiles, those of the judaizing had tails twisted around them, and from this very likely came the vulgar idea (and which we in our childhood believed as an article of faith) that the Jews had tails like monkeys.

† Bermudez (page 8).

disturbers of our Christian religion, be apprehended and punished in conformity to justice and the sacred canons, without any omission on the part of Your Excellency, nor exception of any person, whatever may be their rank or quality." And His Excellency answered: "All this I swear and promise by my faith and word."

In consequence of which the same señor inquisitor replied to His Excellency: "Thus doing, your Excellency, as from your earnest religion and great christianity we expect, may our Lord exalt your Excellency, and all your actions in his holy service, and bestow upon your Excellency good health, and as long a life as this kingdom and the service of His Majesty may require." *

After which the royal audience took the oath of respect for the supreme jurisdiction of the Holy Office, and then a reporter called the *reader* arose, and addressing himself to the immense concourse of people who were crowding in all directions, cried out with all the force of his voice—

"All lift up your hands and say, every one—

"I swear by God and Holy Mary, and by the sign of the cross, and the words of the Holy Gospels, that I will favour and defend and assist the Holy Catholic Faith and the Holy Inquisition, its officers and ministers, and that I will declare and discover all heretics whatsoever, abettors, defenders and concealers of them, disturbers and obstructers of the said Holy Office, and that I will not give them favour nor help, nor concealment, but that immediately that I know them I will reveal and declare them to the señors inquisitors, and should I act differently may God so punish me as he or those deserve who knowingly and wilfully perjure themselves."

The reporter then cried, "All of you say *Amen*." †

After all this, then followed the sermon, which was the great honour of the day, and this time it was the fortune of the Franciscan Father Juan de Gacitua to preach it. It must have occupied the monk some hours in delivering such an accumulation of gross absurdities. The patient and orthodox Don Mariano Egaña himself, on examining the fifty pages in which it is contained with its innumerable barbarous and mongrel Latin phrases, could not restrain himself from writing upon the margin, these words of natural but not very Christian-like exasperation, "How much more did this great rogue merit the fire!"

---

* Bermudez (page 91).

† Idem (page 132). It may be seen by this horrible oath, taken *en masse*, that delation was consecrated almost as a dogma, and such in fact it was; because, as the first question the modern confessor asks his penitent is, "if he has bought the bull of the crusade,"—so in those times the first inquiry of conscience was, if he had had intercourse with a heretic, and who he was?

We have already mentioned that Stevenson had declared that he took from the secret archives of the Inquisition at Lima various denunciations of heretics made by their own confessors, but apart from this there exists at the present time a respectable gentleman in Santiago, who, having confessed himself in Lima, in 1817, when he was only seventeen years old, found himself obliged to hold a profound theological discussion with his confessor, who was a Father

After the word which they called *divine* followed the benignant operation of burning the witch of Toledo, Ana de Castro, *alias* The Flyer, round about whom, carrying her from the square to the burning place by the bridge of the Rimac, after having, at the gate of the Desamparados, delivered her to the civil power, " they all formed a perfect circle," says, not without a certain air of coquetry, the complacent historian whom we follow, " and arriving at the appointed place in whose spacious circumference was executed the arranged punishment, delivering up the criminal to the tightened rope and then to the blazing pile, which by the fury of its active flames reduced her to pallid ashes, and to which the effigies were equally resolved."*

Porras, of St. Domingo, respecting whether he ought to denounce or not the ill-fated and clever Chilian Don Joaquin Eyana, † at that time banished to Lima, and a great admirer of Voltaire and the French philosophers ; the Father nevertheless was not like the founder of his order, nor like the famous prior Torquemada, nor even like the Father Bustamante, who in 1806 accused Stevenson, and he advised the young sinner not to attend to the precept of delation of the Holy Office, abolished in 1812, and agonizing again in that year (1817.)

* We will occupy ourselves once more for a moment about the question of witchcraft, because we have been assured that belief in it is one of the principal grounds on which Señor Saavedra rests for his remarkable defence of the Inquisition.

With regard to the witches burnt by the Inquisition we refer Señor Saavedra in preference to Llorente, to Torres de Castilla, and others, who give innumerable cases of this nature.

Merely as a specimen we copy the following fragment of the official relation of the famous *auto de fé* at Leghorn, 1610, in which they burnt six witches, known as such because, looking at them sideways, a little *shoe* could be discovered in their left eye. " The devil," says the relation, " to propagate this abominable sect, takes advantage of the oldest wizards, who occupy themselves as masters in teaching it ; and those whom they persuade to become witches cannot be taken to the place of meeting without having first consented to be witches and promised to deny their religion. And having consented and given their promise to such effect, on the night when there is to be a meeting the master goes in person to their bedside or where else they are sleeping, about two hours before midnight, and awakening them, he anoints with a dark greenish water, very foetid and nasty, the head, temples, breasts, private parts, and soles of the feet, and immediately he carries them with him through the air, the devil taking them through the doors or windows, or any other little hole or crack, and with great velocity they arrive at the place of meeting, which has already been agreed upon, when the master wizard presents the novitiate to the devil, who is seated upon a chair which sometimes looks like gold, and at other times it appears to be only made of black wood, with great solemnity, majesty, and gravity, but with a visage sad, ugly and angry."

As for the advantages gained by the persecutions of the Inquisition against witches, they were something like those against heretics (the other great category of the accused by the Holy Office) : " The burnings by the Inquisition," says the author of the 'Persecutions,' vol. i. page 431, " so far from extirpating those who did not believe in the Catholic dogmas, they converted them into worshippers of the devil. The mania of witchcraft developed itself in a degree

---

† Don Joaquin Egaña, brother of Don Mariano, both sons of Don Juan Egaña, a lawyer of eminence belonging to Lima, but who established himself in Chile towards the end of the century. Don Joaquin was liberal in his ideas, as much so as his brother was conservative ; unfortunately for his country he died very young.—*Note by Translator.*

On this occasion, likewise, they cast into the burning pile the bones of the Santiago merchant of whom we have given an account at page 191, and who had died in the power of the Inquisition,* no doubt by the influence of that mild penitentiary system invented by the institution, by the benignity of its torture, or by the daily gratification of the five reals which they gave to the prisoners, and for which they could have for their table whatsoever they chose to ask for, and the salubrious condition of the dry, lofty and well-ventilated rooms in which they lived! It is true they were dead to this world, but not to their executioners. " Venerable tribunal!" exclaimed Father Gacitua in his sermon, transported by his holy fervour, " not alone ought the living to bend the knee before thee, but also from thence, from that land of forgetfulness, ought to be terrified by thy parallel with the Inquisition, and they both decayed and expired about the same time."

* We have said that his companion the ecclesiastic (who had died years before in his cloister in Santiago) was the jesuit, Juan Francisco de Ulloa, whom they accused of following the theological doctrines concerning grace which, then so much in vogue, had been promulgated by a member of his own confraternity, the Spanish jesuit, Miguel Molinos, in his work, the " Spiritual Guide," so much applauded at first by the inquisitors themselves. His sentence declared that he was condemned " as a heretic, an apostate, an abettor and concealer of other sectaries, and excommunicated by the excommunication major ; and that after reading the said cause and publishing his sentence, his effigy was to be relaxed, and his bones to be disinterred from the place where they had been buried among the faithful, delivering them to the justice of the civil power for the purpose of burning them publicly."

As for the notable sentence of the unfortunate Velasco we transcribe it entire, to show the burning rancour it exhibits, notwithstanding it is poured upon a corpse :—

"This criminal was Juan Francisco de Velasco, a native of the city of Santiago, in the kingdom of Chile, married, and by profession a merchant. He appeared at the *auto* in effigy; because, having begun a cause against him, he died a prisoner in the secret dungeons of the Holy Tribunal, and afterwards the cause was continued until concluded, with an advocate to defend his memory and character. His effigy was carried, dressed in a short cloak, with St. Andrew's crosses, a cap painted with flames, a rope round its neck, and a label containing his name. His sentence being read, the said criminal was declared publicly to have committed the crimes of formal heresy and apostasy, being a stigmatizer and a follower of the sects of the Illuminati, Molinos, and other heretics, and died in his errors of heresy, apostate, abettor and concealer of other heretics, and excommunicated with excommunication major, and he is declared and pronounced as such, his memory and character defamed, and all his goods confiscated and delivered to the fiscal of his majesty, and, in his name, to the treasurer of the Holy Office, and that after the reading of his sentence, his effigy is to be relaxed and delivered, and also the box in which are the bones of this criminal, to the justice of the secular power, that they may be publicly burned, in detestation of such grave crimes and errors, so that his memory may not remain on the face of the earth, except the *Sambenito* placed over the inscription of his name in the accustomed public place, and for this purpose it is ordered to be in this holy cathedral church."

It was also in this *auto de fé,* in which it was ordered to burn the ashes and defame the memory of two of our countrymen for questions purely theological, that is to say, for ideas, that they condemned to one year's seclusion in the church of St. Peter, a clergyman, native of Santiago, Francisco Javier de Neira, whom they accused of enormous crimes, such as having solicited at confession for leave to say two masses in one day, &c.

severities, even the pallid dead and rigid bodies."* And the Prebendary Saavedra has read in the same book as ourselves these horrid blasphemies, uttered in the seat from which nothing should proceed but the promptings of the Holy Spirit, and has not protested against them!

The people, highly diverted, returned to the square in a tumultuous and confused manner, whilst the inquisitors, the Viceroy and the other bodies, civil and ecclesiastical, entered the palace, perhaps even while the flesh of the witch of Toledo was hissing in the fire, to refresh themselves with the ices and cooling drinks of Lima, as it must not be forgotten that all this took place in the middle of summer only two days before Christmas day.

What took place afterwards in that divine *auto de fe*, as it is styled by its historian, was of no great interest. It was the farce after the tragedy. The burning pile of the *voladora* (flyer) being quenched, then were read the sentences of various witches, and negroes who were delivered to their godfathers (all of them persons of high rank, who considered it an honour to have this title) and immediately by them to the executioner to receive their floggings, the public infamy and other punishments; one of the last of these was our countrywoman, Maria Hernandez (the *flea*), an old witch, "who, stimulated by her natural turbulency, rendered herself worthy of her acquired name;" for which, and because she was a native of Penco, says her biographer, when they gave her the 200 lashes which she was condemned to receive, "the executioner compressed the Penca and the Pulgar." † What a genius! exclaimed Doctor Egaña, upon reading this beautiful figure of the Doctor of St. Mark!

The historian has not told us at what hour terminated the festival in honour of the Maccabees, but taking into consideration that the description alone occupied more than 300 pages, it is not too much to believe that the spectacle and its mysteries lasted to a late hour of the night. ‡

---

* Bermudez.

† It is not very easy to show or explain in English the point of the doctor's joke. *Penca* is a leather strap, with which the hangman flogs criminals. *Pulgar* signifies the thumb, and as the woman was called *Pulga* (flea), and came from a place named *Penco*, Doctor Bermudez, to show his wit by a miserable pun, said that the executioner compressed or squeezed the *penca* (strap), and the woman from Penco, and also his thumb (*pulgar*) and the woman *Pulga* (flea). Well might Doctor Egana exclaim, " What a genius!"—*Note by Translator*.

‡ We have never pretended to contradict. either Capefigue or the Senor Saavedra, who say that the *autos de fé* were for the Spaniards truly national festivals. In fact to read an account of *autos de fé* is the same as to read a description of a bull fight. The difference was only in the brute and the man, between the torch and the sword, the sambenito and the cloak. But the truth is, that the populace assisted with the same tumultuous rejoicings at the one as the other. We have already seen with what *gusto* the monk Torquemada speaks of those of Mexico. "In Laval," says another monk (the inquisitor Eymerico of the Directory) "were burnt at one time and together 400 Albigenses, and I must confess that in all the histories I have read of the Inquisition, I have seen no other *auto de fé* so solemn, nor so festive a spectacle!"

So was described, with a gross but peculiar ingenuousness, the *auto de fe*, the most remarkable which preceded the trial of Moyen, and which, as may be seen, is entirely different, in respect to ceremony and ostentation. Things are omitted in the process of the latter, whose indisputable historical merit constitutes it perhaps the only one in America in which does not figure witchcraft, or other fabulous nonsense; but this is a serious difference, placing in a remarkable contrast the light of modern civilization with the unfathomable obscurity of past ages.

III.

The Power of the Chapter of Santiago, the Bishopric being vacant, given to the Inquisitors of Lima to represent it in the application of Torture, and in all other Inquisitorial Judicial Proceedings.

In the city of Santiago, of Chile, 3rd of the month of July, 1809, before the present notary of his Majesty and witnesses. The most Illustrious Venerable Dean and Chapter, the Bishopric being vacant, as ordinary diocesan Prelate declares that, forasmuch as it belongs, according to right, to have and to hold a vote in the Holy Office of the Inquisition of the kingdoms of Peru, in the sentences pronounced against persons belonging to the district of the said bishopric. And not being able to be present, because of the obligations to assist in the said bishopric, it is necessary to name some person for him, according as it has been requested. And therefore full powers are given, and all that according to right may be necessary or required to the Most Illustrious Señors apostolical inquisitors of the tribunal of the Holy Inquisition of the kingdoms of Peru, who now at present reside in the city of the kings, and who may, in future, *simul insolidum*, especially to represent him in name and person in assisting at the causes of criminals belonging to the said bishopric, that in the said tribunal of the Holy Office they may treat in whatever state the cause may be, and in the same may give their vote and opinion, so as to determine and sentence definitely, as also in whatever act of imprisonment or application of the torture. And that the said señors, inquisitors, or any of them may delegate the said power to the person or persons they may think proper, so that acting according to their conscience in the said causes they may vote in them what may appear to them conformable to right, and what is dictated by their conscience and learning. And they may revoke the said power of

"Such were," indignantly exclaimed the author of the compendium of Llorente (vol. 1, page 135), "the formalities and ceremonies employed in these barbarous executions, which they have dared to call *autos de fé* (acts of faith), and at which the King and his court assisted, as though it were a grand entertainment. Spain owes to them the loss of half her population, and the disgrace and shame of having tolerated them in cold blood during so many ages!"

the said substitutes, and name other or others for absence or for death, always when it seems to them convenient, this said power remaining in force and vigour. Whatever may be required sufficient and ample for the said power, the same is given and granted to the said inquisitors, and substitutes, in its forms and dependencies, its annexes and rights, without exception of anything, and with free and general administration and the usual in form, and thus we authorize and sign, being present as witnesses, Don Rafael Barreda y and Don Alejandro Avendaño; DOCTOR ESTANISLAO DE RECABARREN; JERONIMO JOSE DE HERRERA; DOCTOR D. PEDRO VIVAR; DOCTOR JOSE SANTIAGO RODRIGUEZ; DOCTOR JUAN PABLO FRETES; DOCTOR VICENTE LARRAIN; DOCTOR MIGUEL DE PALACIOS; PEDRO MONTT; —Before me, NICOLAS DE HERRERA, notary of his Majesty.

IV.

THE OFFICIAL LETTER FROM THE CHILIAN CONGRESS OF 1811 TO THE ADMINISTRATIVE JUNTA TO STOP THE SENDING TO LIMA THE INQUISITORIAL QUOTA WHICH THE CHURCH IN CHILE PAID TO THE HOLY OEFICE.

In the two cathedrals of this kingdom are two canonships suppressed, for the purpose of remitting to Lima the part which corresponds to them, and destined to assist and maintain in that city the tribunal of the Inquisition. For the same design, or some other pious one equivalent, it is necessary to withhold these sums, and your Excellency is requested to give the corresponding order for that purpose. May God preserve your Excellency many years,—Hall of Congress, 25th September, 1811—JOAQUIN LARRAIN, President; MANUEL A. RECABARREN, Vice-President; MANUEL DE SALAS, Secretary; Most Excellent Señor, president and voters of the junta of the government.

Santiago, *26th September*, 1811—Make it known immediately to the ministers of State and Finance, and write to Conception. ROSALES—ARGOMEDO.

V.

REPRESENTATION OF THE LAST TREASURER OF THE INQUISITION IN CHILE, DON JUDAS TADEO DE REYES, PROTESTING AGAINST THE ANTERIOR RESOLUTION.

Most Excellent Señor,
Don Judas Tadeo de Reyes, treasurer of the Holy Office of the Inquisition of the bishopric of Santiago, in the best form of law, and in the exercise of my privilege, I appear before your Excellency, and say, That Señor Don Joaquin de Larrain,

presbyter, being president of the upper Congress of this kingdom now dissolved, he passed an order of the 25th of September of the last year, 1811, to the most excellent executive junta, which passed it over to the ministers of the general treasury, for them to retain the rents of the suppressed canonships of the two cathedrals of this kingdom assigned to the Holy Inquisition of Peru, with the intention of diverting them to other uses equally pious. For this spoliation no indication of cause was given, nor audience of the respresentatives of the fiscal of the Holy Office, nor even afterwards was any judicial notice given us as is customary, to govern our conduct in the recovery of the rents of this property, which has always been exempt from the jurisdiction of the minister of finance, from all which it results, that this decree, notoriously violent, rapacious, against all justice, and offensive to the rights and privileges of the Holy Office, and to the ecclesiastical community in general, is consequently *null* and *void*, and of no value or effect, and your Excellency ought to order such retention to be removed, restoring to the Holy Inquisition the possession of its rents in this bishopric of Santiago, the only one it enjoys in this kingdom, having no part whatever in that of the city of Conception as the said order supposes, and which is a proof of the equivocations with which it has been issued.

It is necessary to observe that the Sovereign Pontiffs, visible heads of the Holy Church, with the power given to them by Jesus Christ as his vicars, and guided by His Divine Spirit, to regulate according to the times the discipline most convenient to the holiness, decorum and propagation of the Catholic religion, instituted the Holy Office of the Inquisition as useful and necessary to maintain the purity of our holy faith against heretical depravity and apostasy. It had its beginning in the 13th century, in which the Albigenses combatted the principal dogmas and usurped by force of arms the jurisdiction and property of the Church, and having seen by experience its good effects, manifested by the visible protection of heaven, in Toulon and other parts of France, it was extended to various kingdoms of Europe, not without great consolation to the Catholic populations.

"It was a divine ordination to erect a tribunal so supreme," says the most excellent Señor Villarroel, " and as such could not be less than gratefully received in our Spain, as the nation most distinguished in the profession of Catholicism. And thus, at the petition of the Señors the Catholic kings, the Pope Sixtus IV. conceded to them the faculties of naming in their kingdoms delegates and apostolical inquisitors; and America being discovered care was taken to establish these tribunals in their principal cities of Lima and Mexico, that the holy faith might be expanded and propagated, and also to extirpate the errors and false and suspicious doctrines with which the heretics and libertines always endeavour to pervert and separate from the true religion its devout believers, according as advises the law, 1st title 19, book 1st, of these dominions."

It would now be superfluous to make an apology for the Inquisition, so worthily performed by many writers both natives and foreigners, and the veneration for it which we have inherited from our forefathers. It is sufficient to reflect that the Catholic countries which have refused to receive it, sooner or later have departed from the dogmas or evangelical law. France, the ancient centre of impiety and now of secret lodges, disquieting herself by her insidious, impolitical and irreligious designs upon our peninsula, has always endeavoured to destroy the devotion of the Spaniards, that watchful guardian of the Church, and now more than ever should make us the more alert against its domestic opponents. And how can it be sustained if the stipend be taken from those who protect and guard it?

So distant from these ideas were our pious Legislators, that, acknowledging their essential obligation to maintain the ministers of religion, they endowed the inquisitors from their royal estate, obtaining from Pope Urban VIII. the brief of the 10th March, 1627, in which he assigned for their salaries the rent of a canonship which he permitted to be suppressed in each of the metropolitan churches and cathedrals of the Indies, as it is indicated in the laws, 4th, 24th and 25th of the cited title and book of our municipalities. And here we see titles the most sacred and imperturbable that are possible to be found in the founts of civil and canonical jurisprudence; because, of a truth, if the donations of princes to any particular persons ought by the rules of justice to be permanent and perpetual, how much more so that which has been suppressed, and which is preceptive with the force of law, of the supreme power of the Church and of the empire, and also embraces the sacred cause of religion, in whose favour it was constituted?

Moreover, reasons of justice also intervene in it, because the Inquisition of Lima extends its power to all the dioceses suffragan of its archbishopric, comprehending this of Santiago, where it provides subalterns for the functions of its institution, who consequently partake of the benefit it receives; and it is just that that tribunal should be maintained and assisted to defray its expenses of *autos de fe* of its ecclesiastical court, the keep of prisoners, and many other things, for all of which its principal funds consist in what has been suppressed; for although it is said to possess other endowments, it is not taken into consideration that they are merely of patronage or of administration, nor of the conditions annexed to them by their founders; it being notorious that in their fulfilment the tribunal expends continually, in giving dowers to young women for the state of matrimony or the church, and in other works of piety and mercy. Nor could these particular revenues, even in case of having them, consisting as they do of contingent capitals, substitute that of the suppressed canonships, which ought to be sure in the patrimony of the Church to its ministers perpetually.

To these imposts are naturally subject the tithes which the faithful pay with this object; and if in the Indies, by the concession of the most holy pope Alexander VI., they belong to the King, it is with the fixed and perpetual condition to contribute all that is necessary for the propagation of the faith, and the maintenance of public worship and its ministers, whose institutions and provision for its ministers must be regulated by the ecclesiastical jurisdiction, which is competent to distinguish the functions and necessities corresponding to the title and spiritual ministry of each, and which gives them legitimate power by divine right to exact the wages of the labourer as authorised by the apostle and evangelist.

For these reasons the distributions of the tithes are employed in the erection of churches and other establishments by the authority of the Holy See, the compliance with which is ordered by the law, 9th title, 2nd and 23rd, title 16 to Book I. of the Indies; and although it receives likewise the approbation of the King, yet not for that do they lose the condition and ecclesiastical privilege of the revenues derived from them and enjoyed by their partakers annexed to its benefices and ministries by a perpetual title, reserving to the sovereign in possession the two ninth reals as a mark of superiority and as a right of patronage, and also for the acquisition of the ground, according as it is expressed for the erection of this cathedral, as likewise the extraordinary ninth, annual rents, corporation fees, subsidies, and other things, for the exaction of which it has been necessary to obtain especial pontifical indulgences.

The innovation of the revenue suppressed cannot be rendered legitimate by its application to other pious purposes, as announced in the order for its retention, because the temporal power is not competent to make this commutation, it being peculiar to the prelates of the Church. The knowledge of what, in the dispensation of the property of which they are the guardians, is most convenient to the service of God and the welfare of the Christian community, principally as the assignation of the suppressed to the Holy Office, was sanctioned as preferable for religion by the Sovereign Pontiff, whose testimony does not admit of contradiction, nor is it permitted to doubt the truth professed in his rescripts, according to the opinion of the Canonists, founded on the Clementina *de probationibus*.

Neither can this commutation be arbitrary, even in the case of the revenue of the suppressed ceasing to belong to the Inquisition, for then it ought to augment the residentiary prebends as a part of the table of the chapter, in conformity with the institution, and which it is not lawful to transgress, unless the suppressed should be of the class of temporary vacancies which are caused by death or resignation, the produce of which. is received in the royal exchequer, and has by royal letters patent a different application.

This brings to mind that our Catholic Sovereigns having determined to dispose of certain vacancies, it took more than a century of discussion and consultations concerning the doubts to whom they belonged, and to decide on their application, during which time they formed for this purpose many juntas of theologians, canonists and learned ministers of all the supreme councils of Spain, who gave to the public various learned opinions upon this question, until in conformity with them, Señor Don Philip V. issued the royal letter patent of the 5th October, 1737, by which this branch was destined for the transport, viaticum and synods of evangelical missionaries. And in presence of this religious example of our princes, and also that your Excellency has availed yourself of similar consultations, in other affairs which have occurred in your government, can it be possible to consent to that decree of spoliation, devoid of plan and without an examination of the rights opposed to it, and which interferes with the sacred rights of the jurisdiction and immunity of the Church.

Truly the gravity of this matter requires great circumspection so as not to expose one to thrust his sickle into the harvest of another, or without being initiated into the priesthood, lay hands on the censer, this was what the great Osius impugned in the Emperor Constantine, and it is condemned by the canons, and corroborated by the sacred council of Trent in the decree of the reform. sec. 22, cap. 11, in which the Sovereign Pontiff imposes reserved excommunication on whatever clergyman on layman of whatever dignity, although it may be imperial or royal, who on whatever pretext should usurp the jurisdiction and properties of the Church, or of any pious institution, or should prevent those from receiving them to whom they legitimately belong, and if they have patronage they will also be deprived of this right.

It may be that these reflections do not apply to the intention of this act, but it cannot be denied that at least there are grounds for very great doubt, the decision of which will be always scrupulous and dangerous to the conscience, if not supported by the opinions of those learned in the ecclesiastical sciences, and of an accredited religiousness. When I speak to Your Excellency with this sincerity, I believe I am giving you a proof of my respect to your authority, and that I acknowledge the rectitude of your intentions, holding the opinion that magistrates, the higher their position, the less they are liable to fall into the deception of base flattery, but on the contrary desire the more to be enlightened by all that may conduce to the right attainment of their object, in imitation of the Kings, our Señors, who had no hesitation to declare for law, that their desires in the government of their kingdoms being the conservation of our religion in the most refined purity, and also its increase, the good of their subjects, the right administration of justice, the extirpation of vice and the exaltation of virtue, these being the motives for which God has placed in the hands of monarchs the reins of government, and to be their will, that his ministers not only should represent them in what they judged convenient to these ends with entire Christian liberty, and without any regard whatever for human considerations, but that they would impugn their resolutions, that is, of the kings themselves always when they considered them to have been taken without a proper and just knowledge, according as it is literally expressed in the acts 56 and 70, title 4th, book 2, of Castile.

I will conclude with directing the intention of Your Excellency to the fact that the Inquisition being deprived of this revenue, its commissary in this bishopric is left without any means whatever to defray its expenses either fixed or those eventual, however urgent, which usually occur, for the fault of which this holy institution will suffer a decay, and even abandonment on some occasions. Putting aside my own particular injury which it inflicts, depriving me of the remuneration which is assigned to me as treasurer and administrator of this property, with the responsibility, securities and obligation to render accounts, I am not influenced in this question by any such interest, but only to cover the responsibility of my office and promote the glory and greater service of God and Christianity in which this question is involved. And in proof of this I offer to resign the amount of my assignation referred to, for the actual urgencies of the exchequer of this kingdom if the Inquisition is restored to the enjoyment of the suppressed. And in addition to all, I ask and supplicate of Your Excellency that you will declare and order to be attended to, what has been stated in the exordium of this petition, and which I reproduce at the conclusion, it being an act of justice. JUDAS TADEO DE REYES.*

SEÑOR COMMISSARY OF THE HOLY OFFICE.—The suppressed Congress which governed this kingdom decreed by an order of the 25th of last September to withhold the revenue of the suppressed canonship of this cathedral of Santiago, belonging, by the pontifical constitution and royal law, to the Holy Office of the Inquisition, without any communication being made to me as its treasurer which I am, and I suppose neither to your worship, I considered that we should become responsible to the tribunal which has committed to us its interests in this bishopric, and principally to God for the injuries which would accrue to His holy service, if we consented to this spoliation without taking the

---

* The treasurer Reyes in his official copy of this document forwarded to the Inquisition at Lima, and which is dated 15th June, 1812, expresses himself in the following remarkable terms, which demonstrate the consoling fact, that the ideas which found a protection on our soil in 1640 concerning the Inquisition, had been preserved intact and vigorous until 1810.

" I have enforced, (said the zealous and intelligent treasurer) all that I was able with the imperfect knowledge I possess, the rights of the Inquisition to the revenue derived from the suppressed canonship, and the nullity and incompetence of the decree of detention. Not for that do I hope to obtain a favourable determination, knowing that my application has been looked upon with an evil eye, and I have been threatened with some bad result, because the authorities and doctrines which I lay down, are in opposition to the maxims and political opinions of the day, but I have the satisfaction to have combatted in this the cause of religion, united with that of the Holy Office, against that which is seen already to develop itself in public papers, the seed of civil convulsions of these countries."

legal steps incumbent upon our duties, and which the circumstances permit, I, to comply with my duty, have drawn up the accompanying representation which I forward to your worship, with the object that if by your greater illustration you should find in it something to be corrected, you will make me acquainted that I may rectify it, and if not that you will support and enforce it with whatever reasons may occur to you, in some official communication to the most excellent junta of the government of the King, from the rectitude of which is to be expected the solicited revocation, the same as has been done in the decrees of the said Congress after having been convinced of their injustice. May our Lord preserve your worship many years.

JUDAS TADEO DE REYES,

Señor Commissary of the Holy Office of the Inquisition, Doctor Don José Antonio de Errazuriz.

VI.

MINUTE OF THE OFFICIAL LETTER FROM THE INQUISITORS AT LIMA TO THEIR TREASURER IN SANTIAGO, GIVING HIM THANKS FOR HIS ENDEAVOURS TO RECOVER THE RENT OF THE HOLY OFFICE IN CHILE.

29th August, 1812.

We have received the official letter of Don Judas Tadeo de Reyes, treasurer of this tribunal in the city of Santiago, of Chile, dated 15th of last June, with the adjunct copy of the representation which he directed to the actual government of that kingdom, soliciting it to revoke the decree of the former one, by which it took posession effectively of the fruits of the suppressed canonship of the holy cathedral church of the said city. By favour of this holy official letter we give him the most expressive thanks for the attention and zeal with which he endeavoured to procure the conservation of the interests, the collection of which we had committed to his care and diligence, and we hope he will acquaint us with the results of the process now pending, and which we believe will be favourable, because we cannot persuade ourselves that the Christianity of the individuals who compose the junta will attack the holy religion we profess, as it will do if they try to deprive of the means of subsistence a tribunal whose object is to preserve it safe in its true purity; but should they act contrary, God, whose cause it is, will defend it; and from the present we ought to compassionate *the tragical end* which will come upon the authors of this innovation and as many as engage to sustain it. God help you, &c.

ABARCA ZALDUEGUI GRACEDO, *Secretary.*

VII.

AN OFFICIAL LETTER FROM THE HOLY OFFICE IN LIMA TO GENERAL OSORIO, SOLICITING HIS INTERVENTION IN THE PAYMENT OF THE INQUISITORIAL QUOTA SUPPRESSED BY THE NATIONAL GOVERNMENT IN 1811.

Lima, 19th November, 1814.

The scarcity of the funds with which the salaries should be paid of those employed by the suppressed Inquisition, to satisfy whom I am commissioned, as also for the preservation of the property, has placed me, by the representation of the head treasurer, in a position in which I am compelled to trouble Your Excellency, by calling your attention, so that you may support by your justifiable decrees the claims made by Don Judas Tadeo de Reyes, the treasurer commissioned to recover the interests which belonged to the suppressed canonship of that city enjoyed by the said tribunal; and also to interpose your authority for the removal of the alterations caused by the insurrection, from which Your Excellency has freed this kingdom, as also to restore the said rent to its primitive condition, so that the settlement of the affairs still pending may be obtained, and trusting to your attention and love for what is right, that for your part you will assist in the accomplishment of the intentions here proposed, offering myself to your disposal, and giving you with this motive the most hearty felicitations for the interesting victory obtained under your direction by the arms of the King, and for the new decorations so worthily merited. May God, &c.

JUAN MARIA DE GALVEZ.

Señor Don Mariano Osorio, Brigadier of the Royal Armies, and President of the Royal Audience and Kingdom of Chile.

THE END.

www.ingramcontent.com/pod-product-compliance
Lightning Source LLC
Chambersburg PA
CBHW021818230426
43669CB00008B/794